Introduction

Lead Safety for Renovation, Repair, and Painting

- **Welcome and Introductions**
  - Please tell the class:
    Your name, the company you work for, and what you do.
- **Module Overview:**
  - Course agenda
  - Course manual
  - You will learn...
  - This course...

Feb 09

1

Why Are You Here?

- The traditional renovation work you do now can create significant dust-lead hazards if lead-based paint is disturbed.

- The leaded dust generated by traditional renovation work can cause lead poisoning in children. It can also poison pregnant women, yourself and other workers and even pets. Practical changes in work practices can minimize and contain dust. The use of lead-safe work practices makes the job safer and reduces your liability exposure.

- EPA's Renovation, Repair and Painting Final Rule (40 CFR 745) requires that renovations conducted for compensation, must be performed by Certified Firms using Certified Renovators. Renovation firms that wish to work in pre-1978 homes and child-occupied facilities must apply to EPA and pay a fee in order to become certified. Renovators seeking to become Certified Renovators must successfully complete an EPA-accredited renovator course or a course accredited by an EPA authorized State or Tribe. This course is the EPA model course for Certified Renovators and as such meets all requirements in 40 CFR 745.90.

- This course will teach you how to comply with the EPA Renovation, Repair and Painting Rule and the HUD Lead Safe Housing Rule, and how to perform lead-safe work practices safely and effectively.

- Once you have successfully completed a Certified Renovator Course, delivered by an EPA-accredited training provider, you are an EPA Certified Renovator. EPA Certified Renovator status will allow you to do lead safe renovation, repair, and painting work in pre-1978 housing and in child-occupied facilities where work will disturb lead-based paint. Your certification is valid for five years from the date of completion of the course. To renew certification after five years, you must successfully complete an EPA-accredited Certified Renovator Refresher Course before your initial certification expires. Refresher training must be taken every five years to maintain certification. If the certified renovator training is not refreshed within five years of the previous training, you must retake the initial course to become certified again.

Course Agenda

- **Introduction and welcome**
- **Module 1: Why Should I Be Concerned About Lead Paint?**
- **Module 2: Regulations**
- Break
- **Module 3: Before Beginning Work**
- **Module 4: Contain Dust During Work**
- Lunch
- **Module 5: During the Work**

- Break
- **Module 6: Cleaning Activities and Checking Your Work**
- **Module 7: Recordkeeping**
- Break
- **Module 8: Training Non-Certified Renovation Workers**
- Review
- Test

Feb 09

2

Training Manual Overview

- **Eight modules**
- **Interactive and hands-on exercises, in 11 Skill Sets**
- **Key appendices**
  - Appendix 1 - EPA's Renovation, Repair, and Maintenance Program Final Rule (40 CFR Part 745)
  - Appendix 2 - U.S. Department of Housing and Urban Development (HUD) Requirements
  - Appendix 3 - *Renovate Right: Important Lead Hazard Information for Families, Child Care Providers and Schools*
  - Appendix 4 - *Small Entity Compliance Guide to Renovate Right*
  - Appendix 5 - *Steps to LEAD SAFE Renovation, Repair, and Painting*
  - Appendix 6 - Hands-on Exercises

⊕EPA
United States
Environmental Protection
Agency

Feb 09   3

Modules - In addition to this introduction, there are eight modules in this course:
- Module 1: Why Should I Be Concerned About Lead Paint?
- Module 2: Regulations
- Module 3: Before Beginning Work (includes Skill Set #1)
- Module 4: Contain Dust During Work (includes Skill Sets #2 - #5)
- Module 5: During the Work (includes Skill Set #6)
- Module 6: Cleaning Activities and Checking Your Work (includes Skill Sets #7 - #11)
- Module 7: Recordkeeping
- Module 8: Training Non-Certified Renovation Workers

Activities and Exercises - The course includes activities and exercises to help you identify methods for reducing the amount of dust you create, and containing and cleaning up the dust you do create. Many of the exercises and activities take place in small groups, so you will have an opportunity to share your experiences and ideas with others in the class.

Appendices - This manual has nine appendices that provide extra information that will help contractors.
- Appendix 1 - EPA's Renovation, Repair, and Maintenance Program Final Rule (40 CFR Part 745)
- Appendix 2 - U.S. Department of Housing and Urban Development (HUD) Requirements
- Appendix 3 - *Renovate Right: Important Lead Hazard Information for Families, Child Care Providers and Schools*
- Appendix 4 - *Small Entity Compliance Guide to Renovate Right*
- Appendix 5 - *Steps to LEAD SAFE Renovation, Repair, and Painting*
- Appendix 6 - Hands-on Exercises
- Appendix 7 - State and Local Regulations
- Appendix 8 - Regulatory Status of Waste Generated by Contractors and Residents from Lead-Based Paint Activities Conducted in Households
- Appendix 9 - For More information

Test - Renovators must pass the test administered at the end of the course in order to earn certification. Failure to pass the test means you must retake the course.

You Will Learn...

- Why lead-based paint is a problem during renovations.
- What the EPA and HUD regulations require of Certified Firms and Certified Renovators.
- How to determine if lead-based paint affects work.
- How to begin the work.
- How to set up the work area to contain dust.
- How to work in a lead-safe manner.
- How to clean the work area and verify cleanliness.
- How to dispose of waste safely.
- How to document your work.

Feb 09

4

Module 1: Teaches the health problems related to lead, why lead is a problem you need to deal with, and who is put at risk if renovations are not handled correctly.

Module 2: Teaches what EPA and HUD rules require of Certified Firms and Certified Renovators.

Module 3: Teaches how to determine if lead-based paint affects your work, and how to educate owners and residents in target housing, or owners and adult representatives in child-occupied facilities about how the work will affect lead in their property. This module also discusses how to plan the work so that it is lead safe.

Module 4: Teaches how to properly set up the work area so that dust and debris created by your work do not contaminate the property and leave behind lead dust.

Module 5: Teaches how to work in a lead-safe manner and what practices are prohibited by the EPA and/or HUD rules; provides information on personal protective equipment.

Module 6: Teaches how to effectively clean up dust generated by the work performed in the home or child-occupied facility, and teaches Certified Renovators how to conduct a cleaning verification. This section also contains information about how to dispose of renovation waste.

Module 7: Teaches the requirements in the EPA and HUD Rules for creating and maintaining documentation of the work.

Module 8: Teaches the Certified Renovator how to train non-certified renovation workers in lead safe practices while on the job.

This Course...

- Meets EPA and HUD requirements.
- Produces EPA Certified Renovators.
- Demonstrates your commitment to safety.

BUT,

- Is not an abatement course.
- Does not satisfy OSHA training requirements.
- May not satisfy state, local or tribal training requirements.

♺EPA
United States
Environmental Protection
Agency

Feb 09   5

The Value of this Training
- This course meets EPA and HUD requirements for lead-safe work practices training under the RRP Rule.
- Renovators obtain EPA certification after successful completion of the course.
- Completing this training demonstrates your company's competence to prospective clients and can be a marketing advantage that distinguishes your company from the competition.

Lead Abatement Training
- Lead abatement refers to work that is done for the specific purpose of permanently removing lead-based paint and lead-based paint hazards from a home. This course **is not** an abatement course designed to address the removal, encapsulation or enclosure of lead-based paint or lead-based paint hazards. This course **is not** an Operations and Maintenance course designed to manage lead-based paint in place using interim controls. To perform lead abatement work requires additional specialized training.

OSHA
- OSHA has training requirements for workers that employers should be aware of. For more information on OSHA requirements, visit www.osha.gov/Publications/osha3142.pdf.

State, Local, and Tribal Requirements
- Many states, localities and Indian tribes have their own lead-based paint requirements, including specific training and certification requirements. Check with your State, local or tribal housing and environmental agencies to obtain information about such requirements.

Module 1: Why Should I Be Concerned About Lead Paint?

Module 1: Why Should I be Concerned about Lead Paint?

Overview

- What is lead-based paint?
- What health risks and health effects are related to lead exposure?
- Why is lead-contaminated dust a problem?

Feb 09   1-1

Upon completion of this module, you will be able to explain:

- What lead-based paint is and why it is a problem for renovators.

- The health risks of lead to children and adults.

- Why we are concerned with lead-contaminated dust.

What Is Lead-Based Paint?

- Federal standards define lead-based paint as:
  - Any paint or surface coatings that contain lead equal to or in excess of 1.0 milligram per square centimeter or more than 0.5 percent by weight.
  - Some states and localities regulate paint with lower concentrations of lead.
  - It is the primary source of lead-contaminated dust in housing.
- Why was lead used in paint?
  - Lead was added for color and durability.
- Lead-based paint was banned in 1978.

Feb 09

1-2

Federal standards define lead-based paint.

- Lead-based paint is any paint or surface coatings that contain lead equal to or in excess of 1.0 milligram per square centimeter or more than 0.5 percent by weight.
- Paint with concentrations of lead lower than the definition above can still cause health problems. Even paint with a small amount of lead can account for a lot of lead in airborne or settled dust.
- Information on how to determine if a property contains lead-based paint is provided in Module 3.

Some states and localities regulate paint with lower concentrations of lead.

- You should check with your state and local health departments to see if they have requirements that are more stringent than the Federal requirements.

Why was lead added to paint?

- Lead was added for color and durability.
- Lead was also added to some other surface coatings, such as varnishes and stains.

Lead-based paint was banned from residential use in 1978

- In 1978, the Consumer Products Safety Commission banned the sale of lead-based paint for residential use. In practice, this means that homes built in 1978 could still have used lead-based paint, because existing supplies of paint containing lead would still have been available.
- This is why the year of construction is such an important consideration.

Health Risks of Lead

- Very hazardous to children.
  - Damages the brain and central nervous system; can cause decreased intelligence, reading and learning difficulties, behavioral problems, and hyperactivity.
  - Damage can be irreversible, affecting children throughout their lives.
- Hazardous to pregnant women.
  - Damage to the fetus.
- Also hazardous to workers and other adults.
  - High blood pressure.
  - Loss of sex drive and/or capability.
  - Physical fatigue.
- Lead exposure causes permanent damage.

United States
Environmental Protection
Agency

Feb 09   1-3

Children under six are most at risk from small amounts of lead.

- Children are at a greater risk than adults because their bodies are developing. During normal and frequent playing or hand-to-mouth activity, children may swallow or inhale dust from their hands, toys, food or other objects.
- In children, lead can cause:
  - Nervous system and kidney damage.
  - Decreased intelligence, attention deficit disorder, and learning disabilities.
  - Speech, language, and behavior problems.

Among adults, pregnant women are especially at risk from exposure to lead.

- Lead is passed from the mother to the fetus and can cause:
  - Miscarriages
  - Premature births
  - Brain damage
  - Low birth weight

Health effects of lead in adults include:

- High blood pressure.
- Fertility problems in men and women.
- Digestive problems.
- Nerve disorders.
- Memory and concentration problems.
- Sexual disorders.
- Muscle or joint pain.

Symptoms Of Lead Poisoning are Not Always Obvious

- Symptoms are easily misinterpreted by medical personnel, thus delaying effective treatment and increasing the likelihood of permanent physical and mental damage.
- Only sure way to determine lead poisoning is to take a blood lead level (BLL) test.

Feb 09   1-4

Lead poisoning does not always have obvious symptoms.

- The symptoms of lead poisoning are often non-specific, and are frequently attributed to other causes.
- Specific symptoms that people with lead exposure sometimes complain of include:
    - Headache
    - Stomach ache
    - Irritability
    - Fatigue
    - Loss of appetite
    - Joint and/or muscle pain
- Because many symptoms are non-specific or similar to flu symptoms, parents may not be alerted to get immediate medical attention for their children. This is critical for young children. The longer a young child stays untreated, the higher the risk of permanent brain damage.
- Workers with an occupational exposure to lead need to inform their doctors in order to give them all the background needed for an adequate evaluation of symptoms as possibly related to lead exposure.
- The best way to determine if lead is present in the body is by testing blood.
- The amount of lead in blood is measured in micrograms per deciliter (µg/dl) of the blood, a very small unit of measurement. A microgram is one millionth of a gram. That is like one penny out of $10,000. For reference, a standard size paper clip weighs about one gram, or one million times more than a microgram. A microgram is a very small amount of lead. Remember how small this amount of lead is as it applies to dust cleanup when we get to **Module 4: Contain Dust During Work, Module 5: During the Work,** and **Module 6: Cleaning Activities and Checking Your Work.**

Why are Dust and Debris a Problem?

- Renovation activities that disturb lead-based paint create dust and debris. Debris becomes dust.
- Lead-contaminated dust is poisonous.
- Very small amounts of lead-contaminated dust can poison children and adults.
  - Children swallow dust during ordinary play activities.
  - Adults swallow or breathe dust during work activities.
- Workers can bring lead-contaminated dust home and poison their families.

United States
Environmental Protection
Agency

Feb 09   1-5

Dust and debris from renovation, repair, and painting jobs in pre-1978 housing and child-occupied facilities may contain lead.

- Pre-1978 paint may contain lead.
- Renovation, repair and painting jobs disturb paint that may contain lead. Any activity involving surface preparation, such as hand-scraping, power sanding, the use of heat guns above 1100° Fahrenheit, and open flame burning, can generate lead dust. More complicated tasks such as removing building components and demolishing walls also can create a lot of dust.

Small amounts of lead-contaminated dust can poison children and adults.

- A tiny amount of lead can be extremely harmful.
- Leaded-dust particles are often so small that you cannot see them, yet you can breathe or swallow them. These smaller, inhaled or swallowed dust particles are more easily absorbed by the body than larger particles, and can therefore more easily cause poisoning.
- Leaded dust may be breathed or swallowed by children, residents and workers.
- Through normal hand-to-mouth activities, children may swallow or inhale dust on their hands, toys, food, or other objects. Children may also ingest paint chips.
- Adults can swallow or breathe dust during work activities.
  - When workers perform activities such as scraping and sanding by hand, or use a power sander or grinding tool, dust is created. The dust goes into the air that they breathe.
  - If workers eat, drink, smoke or put anything into their mouths without washing up first, they may swallow the leaded dust present.

A Little Dust Goes a Long Way

- You can't see it.
- It's hard to sweep up.
- And, it travels.

One gram of lead-based paint can contaminate a large area!

Feb 09

1-6

A little dust goes a long way.

- **You can't see it.** Even a floor that looks clean can have leaded dust on it. Only a laboratory test can tell you for sure if an area is contaminated with lead.

- **It's hard to sweep up.** Normal cleaning methods will not pick up all the dust in a work area. Sweeping is not enough. You need to use water, detergent and a HEPA vacuum to clean up dust effectively.

- **It travels.** Once dust is released, it is easily tracked around, inside and outside the work area. And, an exterior painting job can contaminate the inside of a home as the dust, chips and leaded soil are tracked inside.

Later in this course we will discuss in detail the EPA and HUD dust-lead hazard and clearance standards. The limits are included here to reinforce the idea that a very small amount of lead can cause health problems. These numbers represent the amount of lead measured in micrograms (1 millionth of a gram) that is allowed in an area one foot wide and one foot long (one square foot). More than this amount of lead in the specified areas is hazardous.

EPA & HUD use these standards when clearance is performed:

- Floors   40 $\mu g/ft^2$
- Interior window sills   250 $\mu g/ft^2$
- Window troughs   400 $\mu g/ft^2$

NOTE: States and localities may enforce lower standards.

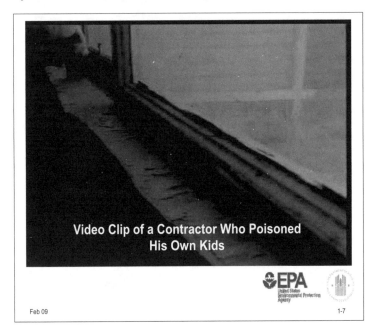

Contractor discusses how lead safe work practices could have protected his kids from becoming lead poisoned.

The video shown at this point in the course is of Kevin Sheehan, a lead contractor, who discusses how he poisoned his family while working on older houses which contained lead-based paint. Kevin discusses the need for lead safety precautions during renovation work, shares the lessons he has learned, and reveals what can be done to keep people safe during work in older homes with lead-based paint.

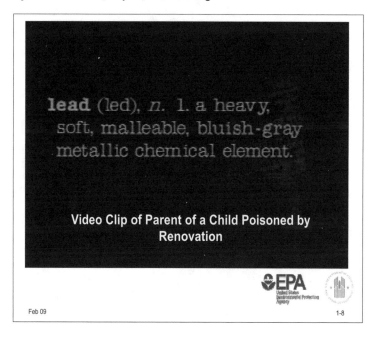

Parent Discusses Child Poisoned by Renovation Undergoing Treatment.

The video shown at this point in the course shows Maurci Jackson, a parent whose child became lead poisoned, discussing how hard it was to watch her daughter undergo "chelation" treatments to remove lead from her body. Maurci shares her fears about her child's future health after being lead poisoned and her frustration that lead poisoning is completely preventable if those who disturb lead-based paint would just considered the consequences of working with lead improperly. She emphasizes the need for lead safety precautions and planning to prevent lead poisoning.

Note: Chelation treatment is a series of medical procedures that remove lead from the body.

Now You Know...

- What lead-based paint is and the adverse health effects of lead.
- Dust is the problem.
- Lead poisoning is hard to spot and the effects can be permanent.
- Kids are most at risk for lead poisoning.
- Lead poisoning is preventable.

United States
Environmental Protection
Agency

Feb 09   1-9

Module 2: Regulations

Module 2: Regulations

U.S. Environmental Protection Agency (EPA):
- Established accredited training and certification programs for workers, supervisors, inspectors and risk assessors conducting evaluation or abatement of lead-based paint.
- Established requirements for pre-renovation education.
- Promulgated the Renovation, Repair, and Painting Program Final Rule (RRP Rule).

U.S. Department of Housing and Urban Development (HUD):
- Established actions in Federally-assisted target housing.
- Established Federal grant programs.
- Established guidelines for lead-based paint evaluation and control; established the Lead Safe Housing Rule.

U.S. Occupational Safety and Health Administration (OSHA):
- Established worker protection standards.

&EPA
United States
Environmental Protection
Agency

Feb 09   2-1

U. S. Environmental Protection Agency (EPA):
- EPA has established training requirements for people involved in lead abatement (the permanent removal of lead). **Certified Renovators may not perform lead-based paint abatement unless they are Certified Lead Abatement Workers or Certified Lead Abatement Supervisors.**
- Lead abatement is defined as any measure or set of measures designed to permanently remove or cover lead-based paint or lead-based paint hazards. Abatement includes, but is not limited to: (1) The removal of paint and dust, the permanent enclosure or encapsulation of lead-based paint, the replacement of painted surfaces or fixtures, or the removal or permanent covering of soil, when lead-based paint hazards are present in such paint, dust or soil; and (2) All preparation, cleanup, disposal, and post-abatement clearance testing activities associated with such measures. (40 CFR 745.223).
- Abatement does not include renovation, remodeling, landscaping or other activities, when such activities are not designed to permanently eliminate lead-based paint hazards, but are designed to repair, restore, or remodel a given structure or dwelling, even though these activities may incidentally result in a reduction or elimination of lead-based paint hazards. Furthermore, abatement does not include interim controls, operations and maintenance activities, or other measures and activities designed to temporarily, but not permanently, reduce lead-based paint hazards. (40 CFR 745.223).
- Module 3 has information on the pre-renovation education requirements.
- Details on the RRP Rule are in the slides following.

U. S. Dept. of Housing and Urban Development (HUD):
- If you work in Federally-assisted target housing, certain actions are required to address lead hazards. In these cases, the workers must have proper training. See Appendix 2 for more information on the HUD requirements for worker training and lead hazard reduction in Federally-assisted housing.
- HUD has a grant program to state and local governments for funding lead hazard reduction activities.
- Check with nearby states and localities to find out if there are any local programs (which may be state or Federally funded) that are designed to address lead hazards.

U. S. Occupational Safety and Health Administration (OSHA): OSHA has a Lead in Construction Standard which outlines worker protection requirements. Your employer should be aware of these. For more information, on the OSHA Lead in Construction Rule, see 29 CFR 1926.62 (http://www.osha.gov/Publications/osha3142).

State and Local Regulations: State and local regulations may also apply to the renovation work you do. Where applicable, these requirements will be covered at the end of this module.

The RRP Rule

Addresses activities that disturb lead-based paint in target housing and child-occupied facilities. It requires:

- Renovators to be certified through training.
- Firms to be certified.
- Training providers to be accredited.
- Lead-safe work practices during renovations.
- Pre-renovation education in target housing and child-occupied facilities.

· On or after April 22, 2010, firms working in pre-1978 homes and child-occupied facilities must be certified and use lead-safe work practices during renovations.

· EPA may authorize states, territories and tribes to enforce the Rule.

$\oplus$EPA
United States
Environmental Protection
Agency

Feb 09

2-2

EPA's Renovation, Repair and Painting Final Rule:

- Published April 22, 2008, under the authority of the Toxic Substances Control Act (section 402(c)(3) of TSCA).
- After April 22, 2010, the final rule addresses lead-based paint hazards created by renovation, repair and painting activities that disturb lead-based paint in "target housing" and "child-occupied facilities."

    Target Housing is a home or residential unit built on or before December 31, 1977, except:
    - Housing designated for the elderly or persons with disabilities (unless any child who is less than 6 years of age resides or is expected to reside in such housing).
    - Any zero-bedroom dwelling (e.g. studio apartments, hospitals, hotels, dormitories, etc).

    A Child-Occupied Facility is a pre-1978 building that meets all three of the criteria below:
    - Visited regularly by the same child, under 6 years of age.
    - The visits are on at least two different days within any week (Sunday through Saturday period), provided that each day's visit lasts at least 3 hours.
    - Combined weekly visits last at least 6 hours, and the combined annual visits last at least 60 hours.

    Child-occupied facilities may be located in a public or commercial building or in target housing. These facilities include schools, child care facilities, and daycare centers.

- State Authorization: EPA may authorize states, territories and tribes to enforce all aspects of the RRP Rule. Such states are called "Agreement states." EPA enforces the Rule in non-Agreement states.

The Rule is effective April 22, 2010:

- Training providers must be accredited.
- Renovation firms must be certified.
- Renovators and dust sampling technicians must be trained and certified.
- Non-certified workers must work under and be trained on-the-job by a Certified Renovator.
- Work practices must be followed for work covered by the rule.
- Renovators must educate owners/occupants (Module 3).

The RRP Rule: Exclusions

- Renovation activities where affected components do not contain lead-based paint.
- Emergency renovations (requires cleanup and cleaning verification).
- Minor repair and maintenance activities. *Note: This exclusion does not apply to window replacement, demolition or activities involving prohibited practices.*
- Renovations performed by homeowners in their own homes.

⊕EPA
United States
Environmental Protection
Agency

Feb 09   2-3

The Renovation, Repair, and Painting rule does not apply to renovation work that meets the following exclusions.

- If the renovation only affects components that do not contain lead-based paint, the rule does not apply to renovation of these components.
- EPA has established limits (see below) for minor repairs or maintenance. Work that does not exceed these limits is exempt from the work practice requirements in the Rule. The EPA limits for minor repairs and maintenance are larger than the HUD limits (see the HUD box below).

Minor repair and maintenance activities have been defined in the Rule.

- EPA has defined minor repair and maintenance activities as below.
    1. Interior work disturbing less than 6 square feet (6 ft²) per room of painted surface is exempt from the work practices requirements in the Rule. Cleanup and cleaning verification are not required after minor repair and maintenance activities, unless they involve window replacement, demolition, or prohibited practices.
    2. Exterior work disturbing less than 20 square feet (20 ft²) of painted surface is exempt from the work practices requirements in the Rule. Cleanup and cleaning verification are not required after minor repair and maintenance activities, unless they involve window replacement, demolition, or prohibited practices.
    3. Minor repair and maintenance activities do not include window replacement, demolition or activities involving prohibited practices.
    4. The entire surface area of a removed component is the amount of painted surface disturbed. Work, other than emergency renovations, performed within a 30-day period must be considered the same job when determining the amount of paint disturbed.

The HUD Lead Safe Housing Rule applies to every home built prior to 1978 that receives Federal housing assistance, typically provided through state and local governments, where greater than HUD's *de minimis* amounts of painted surfaces will be disturbed. HUD's *de minimis* amounts are: 2 square feet of interior lead-based paint, 20 square feet of exterior lead-based paint or 10% of the total surface area on an interior or exterior type of component with a small surface area that contains lead-based paint. Examples include window sills, baseboards, and trim.

Lead Safety for Renovation, Repair, and Painting

The RRP Rule: "Opt-Out" Provision

Not in Effect

- Homeowners may sign a statement to opt out of the work practice requirements in the Rule, if all of the following are true:
  - The owner resides in the house;
  - No child under 6 years old resides in the house and the house is not a child-occupied facility;
  - No pregnant woman resides in the house;
  - No child-occupied facility exists on the property; and,
  - The owner signs a written acknowledgement that the Certified Firm is not required to use work practices found in the Rule.

Feb 09

Certified Firms have the knowledge and training necessary to prevent lead contamination of the home through the use of safe work practices in the home where lead will be disturbed. EPA strongly encourages those homeowners who qualify to opt out of the work practice requirements to seriously consider the use of Certified Firms when performing renovations that disturb known or presumed lead-based paint.

Prior to the decision to opt out of the lead-safe work practices requirements, the homeowner must receive the *Renovate Right* pamphlet as required under the Pre-Renovation Education Rule. Once informed about the safety issues related to disturbing lead during renovation, the homeowner must meet all four qualifications to be eligible to opt out of the work practice requirements in the Rule.

1. The owner must live in the residence to be renovated; and,
2. There must not be children under 6 years of age residing in the home; and,
3. There must not be a pregnant woman residing in the home; and,
4. No child-occupied facility is present on the property; and,
5. The homeowner must sign a statement that the Certified Firm is not required to follow the work practices requirements found in the Rule.

 HUD does not allow owners to opt out of lead-safe work practices in its assisted housing. The HUD Lead Safe Housing Rule applies to every home built prior to 1978 that receives Federal housing assistance where greater than 2 square feet of interior or 20 square feet of exterior lead-based paint will be disturbed during renovation, repair or painting.

The RRP Rule: Firm Certification

- On or after April 22, 2010, all covered renovations must be performed by Certified Firms, using Certified Renovators and other trained workers.
- To become certified, firms must <u>submit an application, and pay a fee</u>, to EPA. Firms may begin to apply for certification on October 22, 2009.
- Certifications will be good for <u>5 years</u>.
- Certification allows the firm to perform renovations in any non-authorized state or Indian tribal area.

&EPA
United States
Environmental Protection
Agency

Feb 09   2-5

- On or after October 22, 2009, firms may apply to EPA to become certified.

- On or after April 22, 2010, no firm working in target housing or child-occupied facilities, where lead-based paint will be affected by the work, may perform, offer or claim to perform renovations without Firm Certification from EPA, or an EPA-authorized agreement state, territory, or Indian tribe.

- One EPA renovation firm certification is all that is needed for a renovation firm to work in any non-authorized state/territory/tribal area. Firm certification is not the same as the personal certification attained by each renovator's successful completion of this course.

- States, territories and tribes may seek authorization from EPA to operate their own programs. Also, states, territories and tribes, whether authorized by EPA or not, can establish additional requirements for firms working within their jurisdictions. Be sure to determine if your state, territorial or tribal government has additional regulations that may affect renovation in your community.

The RRP Rule: Firm Responsibilities

- Ensure overall compliance with the RRP Rule.
- Ensure that all renovation personnel are Certified Renovators or have been trained on-the-job by Certified Renovators.
- Assign a Certified Renovator to all jobs.
- Meet pre-renovation education requirements.
- Meet recordkeeping requirements.

Feb 09   2-6

- The Certified firm must ensure that everyone on the renovation, repair or painting job is trained to perform lead-safe work practices during the work. EPA requires all persons on the job to be trained. The person responsible for lead-safe work practices must be a Certified Renovator. Other firm employees (non-certified renovation workers), working on the job, must be trained on-the-job by Certified Renovators, or must be Certified Renovators themselves. This could be accomplished by:
    - Having all employees trained as Certified Renovators; or,
    - Having at least one person trained as a Certified Renovator, who will then train the rest of the employees in lead-safe work practices. Note that this training must be performed by a Certified Renovator.
- The Certified Firm must designate a Certified Renovator: to conduct set-up activities; to insure that the renovation is performed in accordance with work practice standards; to verify work and cleanup activities using the cleaning verification procedure; and, to train non-certified renovation personnel on-the-job in lead-safe work practices.
- The Certified Firm must ensure that the renovation is performed in accordance with the work practice requirements in the Rule.
- The Certified Firm is responsible for complying with pre-renovation education requirements.
- The Certified Firm is also responsible for keeping all records including:
    - Pre-renovation education documentation (proof of receipt, proof of delivery, waivers, etc.);
    - Documentation of lead-based paint;
    - Training and certification records; and,
    - Cleaning verification records.

Note: Recordkeeping is covered in detail in Module 7.

The RRP Rule: Individual Certification

- To become a Certified Renovator, an individual must take an EPA-approved <u>8-hour training course</u> from an EPA-<u>accredited training provider</u>.
- The course completion certificate serves to certify renovators (no application to EPA is required).
- Refresher training is required every <u>5 years</u>.
- <u>Workers do not need certification</u> so long as on-the-job training is received from a Certified Renovator and the work is not HUD-regulated.

EPA
United States
Environmental Protection
Agency

Feb 09   2-7

On or after April 22, 2010, all renovations must be directed by Certified Renovators. Individuals may become Certified Renovators by completing an EPA-approved 8-hour training course in lead-safe work practices taught by an EPA-accredited training provider. Successful completion of that course will result in a 5 year certification as a Certified Renovator. To maintain certification, Certified Renovators must take an EPA-approved 4-hour refresher course taught by an EPA-accredited training provider, before their certification expires.

No application or fee is required to become a Certified Renovator. Instead, the course completion certificate serves as the renovator certification. A "copy" of the initial and/or refresher course completion certificate must be available on-site during the work.

States, territories and tribes may establish requirements for individual renovators working within their jurisdictions. Be sure to determine if your state, territorial or tribal government has additional regulations that may affect what you must do and where you may work.

HUD requires instructor-led training for all workers unless they are supervised by a certified abatement supervisor (who, under the RRP Rule, must also be a Certified Renovator).

The RRP Rule: Certified Renovator Responsibilities

- Perform work and direct lead-safe work practices.
- Provide on-the-job training to non-certified workers.
- Keep a copy of the initial and/or refresher training certificates onsite.
- Use EPA-recognized test kits to identify lead-based paint.
- Be physically present while posting signs, containing work areas, and cleaning work areas.
- Be available by telephone when off-site.
- Maintain the containment to keep dust and debris within the work area.
- Implement the cleaning verification procedure.
- Prepare and maintain required records.

Feb 09
2-8

The RRP Rule requires that an <u>individual</u> Certified Renovator be responsible for the renovation job regardless of the level of training and certification of the other persons working on the job. This <u>individual</u> Certified Renovator has the following responsibilities.

1. Perform work and direct the work of non-certified renovation workers.
2. Train all non-certified workers on-the-job in lead-safe work practices.
3. Maintain copies of initial and/or refresher training certifications onsite.
4. Conduct testing for lead-based paint using EPA-recognized test kits and report findings.
5. Remain onsite during the sign posting, work area setup, and cleanup phases of work.
6. When not on site, be available by telephone or pager.
7. Make sure that the containment is maintained in a way that prevents the escape of dust and debris. This responsibility implies a need to determine which work practices should be used to minimize dust.
8. Conduct the cleaning verification procedure to make sure that the work is complete and that the work area is ready to reoccupy.
9. Prepare a summary of the work, maintain training and certification records, and certify that all work was done in a lead safe manner.

The RRP Rule: Work Practice Standards

The Renovation, Repair, and Painting Final Rule covers setup of the work area, prohibited work practices, cleanup and the cleaning verification procedure.

- <u>Setup practices,</u> such as posting signs and containing the work area, will be covered in Module 4.
- <u>Prohibited practices</u> and dust reduction suggestions will be covered in Module 5.
- <u>Cleanup practices and cleaning verification procedures</u> will be covered in Module 6.
- <u>Recordkeeping</u> will be covered in Module 7.

Feb 09

2-9

 HUD has additional work practice requirements. See Slide 2-13.

The RRP Rule: Enforcement

- EPA may <u>suspend, revoke, or modify a firm's certification</u> if the Certified Firm or Certified Renovator is found to be in non-compliance.
- Those firms found to be non-compliant may be liable for civil penalties of up to <u>$32,500 for each violation</u>.
- Those firms who knowingly or willfully violate this regulation may be subject to fines of up to an <u>additional $32,500 per violation, or imprisonment, or both</u>.

⊕EPA

Feb 09

2-10

Enforcement:

- EPA has the authority to seek civil fines of $32,500 per offense and an additional criminal fine of $32,500 plus jail time for knowing and willful violations of the Renovation, Repair, and Painting Rule requirements.
- EPA can also revoke certification for of a Certified Firm or a Certified Renovator who violates Renovation, Repair, and Painting Rule requirements.
- Note that violators may be both Certified Renovation Firms and non-certified contractors who are not aware of or have ignored the requirement to become a Certified Renovation Firm.

HUD's Lead Safe Housing Rule

- Covers federally-owned or -assisted target HOUSING and federally-owned target housing being sold. Renovators should ask if the housing receives financial assistance.
  - If yes, the renovator should ask the owner to find out if the assistance is federal assistance.
- HUD's rule has evaluation and control requirements based on type of assistance:
  - Visual assessment, lead paint inspection;
  - Paint stabilization, interim control, abatement;
  - Ongoing lead-based paint maintenance.

Feb 09   2-11

HUD requirements for federally assisted housing are similar to those in the EPA rules with some exceptions. In this curriculum the differences between the HUD rules and the RRP Rules will be highlighted when they occur by special text boxes containing the HUD logo. These boxes are located at the bottom of pages on which an EPA requirement and a HUD requirement differ. Appendix 2, contains an overview of the HUD requirements, and a table detailing differences between the rules.

The HUD "Lead Safe Housing Rule" covers pre-1978 Federally-owned or assisted housing and Federally-owned housing which is being sold. Housing owned and operated by a Federal agency other than HUD may be covered by this regulation.

HUD's rule does not cover "Child-Occupied Facilities" unless they are part of a residential property covered by the rule. This differs from the EPA Renovation, Repair and Painting Rule, which covers housing and child occupied facilities, whether or not they are federally-assisted. Wherever the EPA regulations and HUD regulations differ, the more protective standard must be followed.

HUD has many programs that provide financial assistance, for example: rehabilitation, community development, acquisition assistance, etc. HUD requires addressing lead-based paint hazards (such as peeling paint, friction and impact surfaces, and high lead dust levels) by linking those activities to the HUD financial assistance. When asking clients if the housing is receiving federal assistance, renovators should recognize that the assistance may come through a state or local government, community development corporation or other local entity, so they may have to ask the client to check into the ultimate source of the assistance funds.

HUD does not recognize on-the-job worker training alone, and generally requires all individuals performing interim controls (see Slide 2-12) of lead hazards in Federally-owned and Federally-assisted housing to complete a HUD-approved training course. HUD's training requirements for work other than abatement are satisfied by successful completion of this EPA/HUD jointly approved Certified Renovator Course.

HUD's Lead Safe Housing Rule: Safe Work Practices

- HUD's rule requires lead safe work practices for:
  - Paint stabilization
  - Interim control of identified lead-based paint hazards
  - Rehabilitation (renovation)
  - Standard treatments
  - Ongoing lead-based paint maintenance
- HUD's de minimis level is smaller than the RRP Rule's minor repair and maintenance level

Feb 09   2-12

The HUD Lead Safe Housing Rule requires lead safe work for the activities listed on the slide. It specifies prohibited practices, requirements for protecting occupants, and preparing the work site. Special cleaning techniques must be used and clearance achieved.

Lead safe work practices are required during:
- Paint Stabilization – Renovation to repair non-intact painted surfaces (flaking, peeling, or otherwise damaged) by performing substrate repair (if needed), surface preparation and repainting. The result is an intact painted surface.
- Interim Controls - Interim controls are defined by HUD to include repairs, painting, temporary containment, specialized cleaning, clearance, ongoing lead-based paint maintenance activities, and the establishment and operation of management and occupant education programs.
- Rehabilitation – This is HUD's term for the renovation of properties.
- Standard Treatments - a set of measures that reduce all potential lead-based paint hazards in a dwelling unit when lead-based paint is presumed to be present (no lead-based paint evaluation is performed); all deteriorated paint is treated as a lead-based paint hazard.
- Ongoing Maintenance – Normal maintenance activities.

In Federally-owned/assisted target housing, all areas of deteriorated paint in the work area must be repaired. Work affecting less than the small – "*de minimis*" – amounts listed below is not required to follow the lead safe work practices and clearance requirements in the HUD Rule. HUD's "*de minimis*" limits are smaller than the limits for minor repair and maintenance activities in the EPA's Renovation, Repair and Painting Rule. HUD's "*de minimis*" amounts are:
- 2 square feet in any one interior room or space.
- 20 square feet on exterior surfaces.
- 10% of the total surface area of small interior or exterior component type.

HUD's clearance requirements are covered in Module 6. In general, clearance is required after all work above HUD's *de minimis* amounts, and is performed by a certified professional, such as a Lead Inspector, Lead Risk Assessor, or Dust Sampling Technician, who is independent of the Certified Renovation Firm. State and local jurisdictions may have different clearance requirements than HUD's and EPA's; the most stringent requirements must be used.

Lead Safety for Renovation, Repair, and Painting

HUD's Rule Addresses:

- Training (usually classroom training for workers)
- Occupant protection and worksite preparation
- Prohibited methods (3 in addition to RRP Rule's)
- De minimis levels (smaller than RRP Rule's)
- Lead safe work practices
- Specialized cleaning
- Clearance testing (covered in Module 6)
- Occupant notification (within 15 days)

&EPA

The HUD Lead Safe Housing Rule (LSHR) covers renovation work in Federally-assisted or owned target housing, and specifically addresses the following lead safe activities.

Training: EPA requires that Certified Renovators be responsible for renovation projects. Because of this requirement, there are now two major training options for renovation work under the LSHR:

- All renovation workers on the job are trained as Certified Renovators; or,
- The designated Certified Renovator is also a Certified Lead Abatement Supervisor, and all workers who are not certified renovators have on-the-job training in lead-safe work practices (see Module 8).

Occupant Protection and Worksite Preparation: Occupants have to be kept out of the work area during the renovation work, and must be relocated from the unit during longer renovation projects. EPA-recognized test kits may not be used to test for lead-based paint (LBP); only a Certified Lead Inspector or Risk Assessor may determine whether LBP is present.

Prohibited Practices: HUD prohibits the same practices as the EPA RRP Rule, plus three more:

- Heat guns that char paint;
- Dry scraping or sanding except within 1 ft. of electrical outlets; and,
- Use of a volatile stripper in poorly ventilated space.

De minimis levels: HUD has a smaller *de minimis* threshold for interior work than EPA's limit for minor repair and maintenance activities. See the notes on the previous slide for details.

Clearance Testing: HUD requires a clearance examination after renovation work above the *de minimis level,* in homes regulated by the LSHR. HUD requires a clearance examination by a party independent of the renovator, and, therefore, does not allow acceptance of the Certified Renovator's visual inspection or use of the cleaning verification procedure. When the HUD LSHR applies to your work (see Appendix 2), a clearance examination must be performed by a certified professional such as Lead Inspector, Lead Risk Assessor, or Dust Sampling Technician. Some state and local authorities have different clearance requirements and standards.

Occupant Notification: HUD requires notices to be distributed to occupants within 15 days after LBP or LBP hazards in their unit (and common areas, if applicable) are identified, and within 15 days after completion of the hazard control work in their unit or common areas.

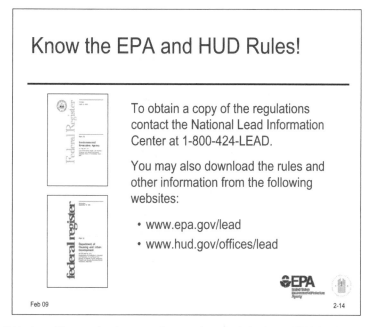

Know the EPA and HUD Rules!

To obtain a copy of the regulations contact the National Lead Information Center at 1-800-424-LEAD.

You may also download the rules and other information from the following websites:

- www.epa.gov/lead
- www.hud.gov/offices/lead

Feb 09   2-14

Individuals and firms performing renovation, repair, and painting in pre-1978 dwellings and child-occupied facilities should understand the EPA Renovation, Repair, and Painting Final Rule. The EPA Renovation, Repair, and Painting Final Rule can be found in Appendix 1.

Individuals performing renovation, remodeling, and rehabilitation in pre-1978 housing that is Federally-assisted, need to understand the HUD Lead Safe Housing Rule. Appendix 2 contains more information on the HUD Lead Safe Housing Rule.

State and Local Regulations

- States and localities may have different regulations than EPA and HUD for renovations in target housing.
- Check with your state and local housing and environmental agencies to obtain information about such requirements.
- Appendix 7 is reserved for copies or summaries of state and local regulations.

Feb 09

2-15

Reserved for student notes on state and local regulations for renovation that differ from the EPA and HUD regulations.

Now You Know...

- That the EPA Renovation, Repair, and Painting Program Final Rule (RRP Rule) applies to renovation in housing and child-occupied facilities built before 1978 that contain lead-based paint.
- To always take into account the requirements and responsibilities of certification for Certified Firms and Certified Renovators, and to re-certify every 5 years.
- To comply with setup of the work area, prohibited work practices, cleanup and the cleaning verification procedure requirements in the Rule.
- To determine whether your renovation job is regulated by EPA, HUD, both, or neither.

⊜EPA
United States
Environmental Protection
Agency

Module 3: Before Beginning Work

Module 3: Before Beginning Work

Overview

This module teaches you:

- To educate owners and residents.
- That the use of lead-based paint was widespread.
- To determine if lead-based paint is present.
- To use EPA-recognized test kits to check for lead-based paint.
- How to decide which rule(s) apply.

Feb 09   3-1

Module Overview

- The module also considers the important questions that must be asked at the beginning of a job to establish whether a job is covered by the RRP Rule and/or the HUD Rules, and what requirements apply.

Educate Owners and Residents

The Pre-Renovation Education Rule:

- Requires Renovation Firms to provide the *Renovate Right* pamphlet to owners/residents prior to renovation activities in pre-1978 housing and child-occupied facilities.
- Specifies requirements for educating residents/occupants and delivering the *Renovate Right* pamphlet that vary by type of property and the area being renovated.

Under the RRP Rule, Certified Firms MUST:

- Give homeowners/residents and child-occupied facility owners/adult representatives copies of the *Renovate Right* pamphlet.
- Let parents/guardians of children using a child-occupied facility know about the renovation and how to get a copy of the *Renovate Right* pamphlet.
- Get confirmation of receipt of the *Renovate Right* pamphlet from owners, or evidence that the pamphlet was delivered to tenants/residents.
- Keep all records for at least 3 years.

Feb 09

3-2

Exclusions: The Pre-Renovation Education Rule covers the same renovation activities that are covered by the Renovation, Repair, and Painting Rule. The same exclusions apply, except that the owner/occupant cannot opt out of pamphlet delivery. (Refer to Module 2 for more information on exclusions.)

Work in Homes: No more than 60 days before beginning a renovation, Certified Renovation Firms must distribute the *Renovate Right* pamphlet to the owners and residents of the pre-1978 housing to be renovated.
- Firms must either obtain the owner's written acknowledgment or proof that the pamphlet was sent by certified mail, return receipt requested, at least 7 days before the renovation began.
- For tenants, Certified Firms must either obtain a written acknowledgment of receipt, or document that the firm delivered the pamphlet and was unable to obtain a written acknowledgment.
- All proof of receipt/mailing/delivery records must be kept for 3 years after completion of the renovation.
- Sample forms to document confirmation of receipt are included in the *Renovate Right* pamphlet.

Work in Common Areas: No more than 60 days before beginning a renovation, Certified Renovation Firms must provide the *Renovate Right* pamphlet to the owner of pre-1978 housing being renovated. Firms must provide written notification to all residents in the affected units of the property being renovated, must notify affected residents about where information is posted if work in nearby common areas will affect them. The following information should be posted about work in common areas:
- Describing the nature and location of the work;
- Listing the work start and end dates; and,
- Providing the *Renovate* Right pamphlet or information on how to obtain a free copy of the pamphlet.
This information may be provided to tenants by mail, hand-delivery, or by posting signs containing this information where they are likely to be seen by the residents of all affected units.

Work in Child-Occupied Facilities: No more than 60 days before beginning a renovation, Certified Renovation Firms must distribute the *Renovate Right* pamphlet to the owner of the building and to an adult representative of the child-occupied facility, following the same documentation requirements as for homes. Firms must also provide notification to parents and guardians of children using the child-occupied facility, following the same requirements as for tenants affected by renovations in common areas.

To obtain copies of the *Renovate Right* pamphlet visit the EPA website at www.epa.gov/lead, or contact the National Lead Information Center at 1-800-424-LEAD (5323). The pamphlet may be copied for distribution as needed to comply with pre-renovation education requirements.

How Widespread is Lead-Based Paint in Housing?

Year House Was Built	Percent of Houses with Lead Based Paint
Before 1940	86 percent
1940-1959	66 percent
1960-1978	25 percent
All Housing	35 percent

⊜EPA
United States
Environmental Protection
Agency

Feb 09

3-3

Source of data in table above: *American Healthy Homes Survey: Draft Final Report for Peer Review: Lead and Arsenic Findings, October 7, 2008.*

Homes built in 1978 and earlier

Approximately 34 million pre-1978 housing units contain paint that meets the Federal definition of "lead-based paint" (Source: *American Healthy Homes Survey: Draft Final Report for Peer Review: Lead and Arsenic Findings, October 7, 2008*).

- EPA's RRP Rule assumes that any house built before 1978 contains lead-based paint, unless the house has been tested for lead-based paint and the results indicate that the house does not contain lead-based paint.
- Components most likely to be coated with lead-based paint include windows and doors (interior and exterior), as well as exterior walls and porches.

Homes built before 1960

Homes built before 1960 are more likely than homes built after 1960 to contain lead-based paint and are also more likely to have deteriorated paint surfaces due to age. In addition, concentrations of lead in paint were higher prior to the 1950's when paint companies began to use less lead in paint they manufactured.

Consider:
- 86% of pre-1940 homes contain lead-based paint on at least one surface.
- 66% of homes built from 1940 to 1959 contain lead-based paint on at least one surface.

Note: Determining the age of the property may require some investigation. If the owner does not know or have access to records, property information in many localities can be accessed from review of court registration or tax records held by the office of the tax assessor in the community or county where the property is located. If you don't know the age of the building, assume it was built before 1978.

How to Determine if Lead-Based Paint is Present

- Paint testing must be performed prior to renovation on all surfaces to be affected by the work, or you must presume the paint is lead-based. Any testing must be performed by the appropriate qualified professional.

Type of Paint Testing for Renovations	Who can do the testing?
EPA-recognized test kits	Certified Renovators
X-Ray Fluorescence instruments (surface-by-surface)	Certified lead-based paint inspectors or risk assessors
Paint chip sampling and laboratory testing	Certified lead-based paint inspectors or risk assessors

United States
Environmental Protection
Agency

Feb 09

3-4

Surface-by-Surface or Limited Testing: Lead-based paint can only be identified by testing paint. A surface-by-surface evaluation of painted surfaces (a lead inspection) and all paint-chip sampling must be conducted by a Certified Lead Inspector or Certified Lead Risk Assessor. Whether paint testing is accomplished by an inspection or by limited testing, the results of testing only apply to the work if the surfaces covered by the renovation are covered by the testing report. A property owner may provide a report from a Certified Lead Inspector/Risk Assessor that proves no lead-based paint is present, in lieu of testing affected surfaces. If no testing result is available, test the paint or presume lead-based paint is present.

EPA-Recognized Test Kits: Check the EPA website at www.epa.gov/lead for information on EPA-recognized test kits and how to use them. EPA is currently reviewing more sensitive test kits which may come on the market. All test kits currently on the market are colorimetric tests for lead; that is, they change color when lead is present. Different test kit chemicals produce different colors when lead is present. All paint layers must be tested when using test kits. Make sure to follow the manufacturer's instructions when using this testing method. If there is no color change on the paint film tested, lead-based paint is not present and lead-safe work practices are not required on that surface. Test kit sampling is intrusive and damages each surface tested. Common kit types include:

- Rhodizonate-based test kits that produce a pink to red color when lead is present. This test cannot be used on paint colors such as reds, oranges and pinks which make seeing any color change difficult. Rhodizonate test kits should not be used to test paint on drywall and plaster surfaces; and,
- Sulfide-based test kits that produce a dark grey to black color when lead is present. Dark colored paints, like dark greens blues and, especially, black make seeing any color change difficult. Sulfide test kits should not be used to test paint on metal surfaces.

X-Ray Fluorescence Testing: Requires a special instrument and a specially-trained Certified Lead Inspector or Certified Lead Risk Assessor. The instrument tests by bombarding the paint film with gamma radiation that causes the lead in the paint to emit x-rays that can be read by a sensor in the instrument. The amount of lead in the paint is directly related to the x-rays read by the sensor. A computer program in the instrument calculates how much lead is in the paint film. This testing method is non-intrusive and is the most used.

Paint-Chip Collection for Laboratory Analysis: Paint-chip testing requires intrusive sampling. All paint layers are removed from the surface being tested. The resulting sample is sent to an EPA-recognized laboratory where it is analyzed to determine how much lead is present. Paint chips may only be collected by Certified Lead Inspectors or Certified Lead Risk Assessors. Laboratory charges are based on turnaround time, and it usually requires a day or two to get results. Intrusive sampling makes repair of tested surfaces necessary.

Using EPA-Recognized Test Kits to Check for Lead-Based Paint

- **EPA-recognized test kits:**
  - Until 9/01/10, EPA will only require the use of test kits that verify the absence of lead-based paint.
  - After 9/01/10, test kits must be able to determine whether or not lead-based paint is present.
- **Submit a testing report of results from use of an EPA-recognized test kit to the client as soon as possible, but no later than 30 days after completing the renovation.**

Feb 09

3-5

If test kits are used, you must use an EPA-recognized test kit.

- Until September 1, 2010, EPA is only requiring the use of test kits that determine that lead-based paint is not present on the surfaces tested. If a color change does not occur, lead-safe work practices are not required. If a color change occurs, the change does not with certainty mean that lead-based paint is present. However, the surface must still be presumed to be coated with lead-based paint.
- To be EPA-recognized after September 1, 2010, a test kit must be able to identify lead-based paint. At that time, a test kit positive test result will mean that lead-based paint is present in the coating and that lead-safe work practices must be followed when that surface is disturbed. A negative test result will mean that lead safe-work practices are not required.
- If the test kit gives a positive result on any of the tested surfaces, lead-safe work practices must be used. Alternatively, sampling may be performed by a Certified Lead Inspector or Risk Assessor to determine whether or not lead-based paint is present.
- If test kits are used, Certified Renovators must use an EPA-recognized test kit in order to test affected surfaces. EPA-recognized test kits will be listed on the EPA website at www.epa.gov/lead.

What should be tested?

- Each building component to be renovated or disturbed by renovation must be tested, unless the component is a part of a larger component system and is representative of the whole system. In this case, a single component may represent the larger system. For instance, a stair tread may represent the whole stair system if the painting history of both is similar. If the painting histories are similar and the tested tread shows a negative test for lead-based paint, then the RRP Rule does not apply to the stair system.

Reporting

- When EPA-recognized test kits are used, the Certified Firm must provide a report to the client within 30 days after completion of the renovation. The date of testing, identification of and contact information for the Certified Firm and Certified Renovator performing the testing, test kit manufacturer's name and kit identification, locations of surfaces tested, descriptions of the surfaces tested, and the results of testing must be included in the report to the owner.

Test Kit Hands-on

Purpose: The purpose of this hands-on exercise is to teach Certified Renovators how to correctly use EPA-recognized test kits to determine if lead-based paint is present on components and surfaces affected by renovation work.

Feb 09

3-6

Skill Set #1: Using EPA-Recognized Test Kits
<u>Time</u>: **15 minutes**
Feb 09

Supplies needed:
- EPA-recognized test kit(s) w/ manufacturer's instructions
- Kit-specific supplies as required in the manufacturer's instructions
- Disposable plastic drop cloth 2' by 2'
- Tape (duct, painters, and masking)
- Disposable, non-latex gloves
- Disposable shoe covers
- Manufacturer provided test verification card with lead-based paint layer
- Disposable wet cleaning wipes
- Heavy duty garbage bags
- Painted wood surface with no lead-based paint layer
- *Test Kit Documentation Form*
- *Participant Progress Log*
- Pen or pencil
- Digital camera (*Optional*)
- Numbered index cards (*Optional*)
- EPA vacuum with attachments (for cleanup after sampling)

Note to Instructor: *It is strongly suggested that instructors prepare plastic bags containing all materials needed for the hands-on exercises, prior to the exercise, in order to meet the time limits allocated to Skill Set #1.*

Purpose: The purpose of this hands-on exercise is to teach students how to correctly use EPA-recognized test kits to determine if lead-based paint is present on components and surfaces affected by renovation work.

Note to Instructor: *Read the purpose of this activity to students and remind them to document all areas where the paint color or substrate reactions may cause an incorrect result. These surfaces should not be tested with a test kit, but should either be tested by Certified Inspectors or Certified Risk Assessors; or must be assumed to contain lead-based paint.*

Demonstration: The course instructor must show and explain all of the steps involved in the use of EPA-recognized test kits. The demonstration should not take longer than 5 minutes including the time needed to hand out materials.

Evaluating the Students: Allow students to practice the eight steps on the following page. Watch each student follow the steps. Make corrections and suggestions as the exercise proceeds and determine if additional practice is necessary. This should take no longer than 10 minutes. Students must complete all required steps to be "Proficient". Evaluate the work of each student and once the student can use a test kit correctly, the instructor should write the word "Proficient" in the field on the Participant Progress Log that corresponds to Skills Set #1 and that particular student's name.

Skill Set #1: Using EPA-Recognized Test Kits - Continued

Purpose: The purpose of this hands-on exercise is to teach Certified Renovators how to correctly use EPA-recognized test kits to determine if lead-based paint is present on components and surfaces affected by renovation work.

Skills Practice:

Step 1: Read the manufacturer's instructions

Step 2: Write required information and observations about the test location on the *Test Kit Documentation Form.**

Step 3: (Optional) Secure a small disposable plastic drop cloth (2ft x 2 ft) on the floor beneath the test location with masking tape.

Step 4: Put on disposable non-latex gloves and shoe covers.

Step 5: Follow the manufacturer's instructions for use of the test kit to conduct the test.* Perform one test on the test card provided by the manufacturer, to observe a positive test result; conduct one test of a painted wood surface with no lead-based paint layer, to observe a negative test result.*

Step 6: Use one wet cleaning wipe to remove residual chemicals left on the surface tested. Use a second cleaning wipe to remove any visible debris or dust on the floor beneath the sample collection area and place the used cleaning wipe in the trash bag.*

Step 7: Check documentation for completeness and note the result of the testing on the *Test Kit Documentation Form.**

Step 8: (Optional) Number the test location in sequence on the *Test Kit Documentation Form*, then select the corresponding numbered index card and tape it next to the test location with masking tape and take a picture of the numbered test location to photo-document conduct and possibly the result of the test.

   *Indicates required skills that must be accomplished for a "Proficient" rating.

Interpreting the Results of Test Kit Sampling:

The manufacturer's instructions will indicate the targeted indicator color change for lead in paint. Once the test is conducted, note the result and refer to the manufacturer's guidelines for interpreting the result. All painted surfaces that show the manufacturer's listed color change for lead in paint (a positive test result) must be treated as lead-based paint until additional testing performed by a Certified Lead Inspector or Risk Assessor proves it is not.

Documenting Test Kit Results:

A report of the findings from use of the test kit must be submitted to the person contracting the work within 30 days following the completion of the renovation work. The completed *Test Kit Documentation Form* should be kept by the Certified Firm for 3 years after the work is completed.

Owner Information

Name of Owner/Occupant: _____

Address: _____

City: _____   State: _____   Zip code: _____   Contact #: (____) ____-_____

Email: _____

Renovation Information

Fill out all of the following information that is available about the Renovation Site, Firm, and Certified Renovator.

Renovation Address: _____   Unit# _____

City: _____   State: _____   Zip code: _____

Certified Firm Name: _____

Address: _____

City: _____   State: _____   Zip code: _____   Contact #: (____) ____-_____

Email: _____

Certified Renovator Name: _____   Date Certified: /   /

Test Kit Information

Use the following blanks to identify the test kit or test kits used in testing components.

Test Kit #1

Manufacturer: _____   Manufacture Date: _____/_____/_____

Model: _____   Serial #: _____

Expiration Date: _____

Test Kit #2

Manufacturer: _____   Manufacture Date: _____/_____/_____

Model: _____   Serial #: _____

Expiration Date: _____

Test Kit #3

Manufacturer: _____   Manufacture Date: _____/_____/_____

Model: _____   Serial #: _____

Expiration Date: _____

Test Kit Documentation Form

Page __ of __

Renovation Address: _____ Unit# _____

City: _____ State: _____ Zip code: _____

Test Location # ____ Test Kit Used: (Circle only one) Test Kit # 1 Test Kit # 2 Test Kit # 3

Description of test location: _____

_____

Result: Is lead present? (Circle only one) YES NO Presumed

Test Location # ____ Test Kit Used: (Circle only one) Test Kit # 1 Test Kit # 2 Test Kit # 3

Description of test location: _____

_____

Result: Is lead present? (Circle only one) YES NO Presumed

Test Location # ____ Test Kit Used: (Circle only one) Test Kit # 1 Test Kit # 2 Test Kit # 3

Description of test location: _____

_____

Result: Is lead present? (Circle only one) YES NO Presumed

Test Location # ____ Test Kit Used: (Circle only one) Test Kit # 1 Test Kit # 2 Test Kit # 3

Description of test location: _____

_____

Result: Is lead present? (Circle only one) YES NO Presumed

Test Location # ____ Test Kit Used: (Circle only one) Test Kit # 1 Test Kit # 2 Test Kit # 3

Description of test location: _____

_____

Result: Is lead present? (Circle only one) YES NO Presumed

Test Location # ____ Test Kit Used: (Circle only one) Test Kit # 1 Test Kit # 2 Test Kit # 3

Description of test location: _____

_____

Result: Is lead present? (Circle only one) YES NO Presumed

Test Location # ____ Test Kit Used: (Circle only one) Test Kit # 1 Test Kit # 2 Test Kit # 3

Description of test location: _____

_____

Result: Is lead present? (Circle only one) YES NO Presumed

Using Decision Logic Charts

- Using the following pages, you will practice use of the decision logic charts found in the *Small Entity Compliance Guide to Renovate Right*.

- The decision logic charts will assist you in making decisions regarding how the EPA RRP Rule applies to your work.

- Determine if the property is Federally-assisted and if it is, then determine what to do next.

EPA
United States
Environmental Protection
Agency

Feb 09   3-7

The information presented in the *Small Entity Compliance Guide to Renovate Right* flow charts is intended to assist you in understanding what RRP Rule requirements apply to the renovation you are about to perform and whether the HUD Rule also applies to the project. You will find the *Small Entity Compliance Guide to Renovate Right* flow charts on the following pages in this module. For a complete copy of the *Small Entity Compliance Guide to Renovate Right* see Appendix 4.

The *Small Entity Compliance Guide to Renovate Right* flow charts walk you step-by-step through a decision tree which asks you a series of ordered yes-or-no questions. To use the flow charts, begin at the top of flow chart 1, ask yourself each question. Following the yes-or-no answer arrows to the next appropriate question box. At some point you will come to an arrow with directions about continuing to another flow chart. Follow the direction to whichever flow chart the pathway takes you to, skipping flow charts that do not apply. Whenever a text box gives direction about what to do, write it down to develop a list of actions that must be taken for RRP Rule compliance.

Appendix 2 provides a summary of HUD requirements that apply to work done in homes that receive Federal assistance. Information found in Appendix 2 provides assistance in determining whether the property receives Federal housing assistance and what requirements apply if it does. If the property is pre-1978 and does receive Federal housing assistance, both the HUD Lead Safe Housing Rule and the EPA RRP Rule apply to your renovation work.

EPA's Lead Program Rule At-A-Glance

FLOW CHART 1: Do the Requirements Apply to the Renovation?

If you will be getting paid to do work that disturbs painted surfaces in a pre-1978 home, apartment building, or child-occupied facility, answer the questions below to determine if the EPA lead program requires you to distribute the lead pamphlet and/or if you will need to comply with training, certification, and work practice requirements when conducting the work.

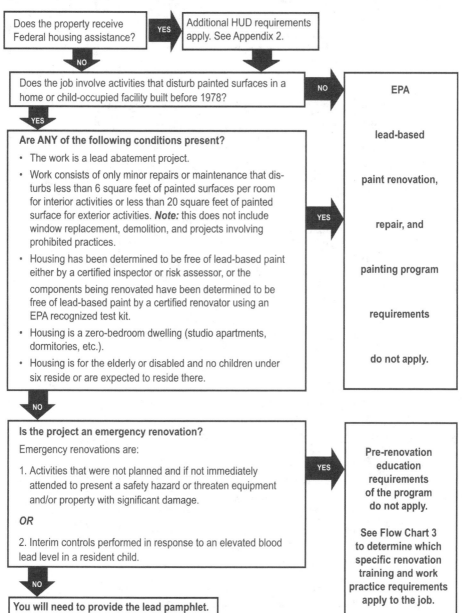

Does the property receive Federal housing assistance? — **YES** → Additional HUD requirements apply. See Appendix 2.

NO ↓

Does the job involve activities that disturb painted surfaces in a home or child-occupied facility built before 1978? — **NO** → EPA lead-based paint renovation, repair, and painting program requirements do not apply.

YES ↓

Are ANY of the following conditions present?

- The work is a lead abatement project.
- Work consists of only minor repairs or maintenance that disturbs less than 6 square feet of painted surfaces per room for interior activities or less than 20 square feet of painted surface for exterior activities. *Note:* this does not include window replacement, demolition, and projects involving prohibited practices.
- Housing has been determined to be free of lead-based paint either by a certified inspector or risk assessor, or the components being renovated have been determined to be free of lead-based paint by a certified renovator using an EPA recognized test kit.
- Housing is a zero-bedroom dwelling (studio apartments, dormitories, etc.).
- Housing is for the elderly or disabled and no children under six reside or are expected to reside there.

YES → EPA lead-based paint renovation, repair, and painting program requirements do not apply.

NO ↓

Is the project an emergency renovation?

Emergency renovations are:

1. Activities that were not planned and if not immediately attended to present a safety hazard or threaten equipment and/or property with significant damage.

OR

2. Interim controls performed in response to an elevated blood lead level in a resident child.

YES → Pre-renovation education requirements of the program do not apply.

See Flow Chart 3 to determine which specific renovation training and work practice requirements apply to the job.

NO ↓

You will need to provide the lead pamphlet. See Flow Chart 2 for specific requirements.

FLOW CHART 2: How Do I Comply with the Pre-Renovation Education Requirements?

Requirements to distribute pre-renovation educational materials vary based on the location of the renovation. Select the location below that best describes the location of your project, and follow the applicable procedure on the right.

Renovations in Owner-Occupied Dwelling Units	Deliver lead pamphlet to owner before renovation begins and obtain confirmation of receipt. *OR* Mail lead pamphlet to owner 7 days before renovation begins and document with certificate of mailing.

Renovations in Tenant-Occupied Dwelling Units	1. Provide lead pamphlet to owner using either procedure described in the box at the top of this page. 2. Provide lead pamphlet to tenant by either method below: (a) Deliver pamphlet to dwelling unit before renovation begins and document delivery with either a confirmation of receipt of lead pamphlet or a self-certification of delivery. *OR* (b) Mail lead pamphlet to tenant at least 7 days prior to renovation and document with a certificate of mailing.

Renovations in Common Areas of Multi-Family Housing Units	1. Provide owner with lead pamphlet using either procedure described in the box at the top of this page. 2. Notify tenants and make pamphlet available, or post signs describing the renovation. The signs must include the pamphlet or information on how to review a copy. 3. Maintain written documentation describing notification procedures. 4. Provide supplemental renovation notice if changes occur in location, timing, or scope of renovation occurring.

Renovations in Child Occupied Facilities (COFs)	1. Provide the owner of the building with the lead pamphlet using either: (a) The procedure described in the box at the top of this page. *OR* (b) If the child-occupied facility is not the building owner, provide the lead pamphlet by either method below: (i) Obtain a written acknowledgment that an adult representative received the pamphlet; or certify in writing that a pamphlet was delivered. *OR* (ii) Obtain a certificate of mailing at least 7 days before the renovation. 2. Provide the parents or guardians of children using the child-occupied facility with information by either of these methods: (a) Mail or hand-deliver the lead pamphlet and renovation information to each parent or guardian. *OR* (b) Post signs describing the renovation. The signs must include the pamphlet or information on how to review a copy.

See Flow Chart 3 for information about specific training and work practice requirements for the job.

FLOW CHART 3: Do the Renovation Training and Work Practices Apply?

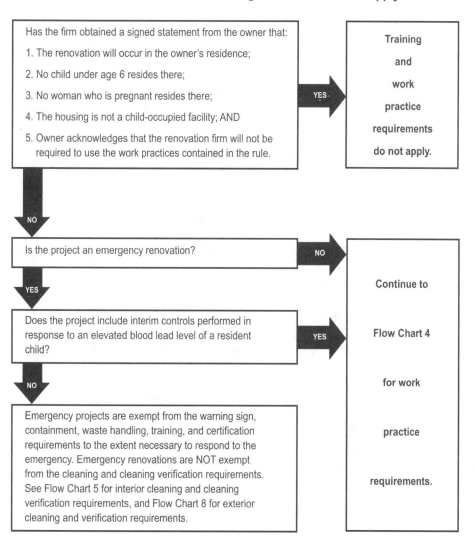

Has the firm obtained a signed statement from the owner that:

1. The renovation will occur in the owner's residence;

2. No child under age 6 resides there;

3. No woman who is pregnant resides there;

4. The housing is not a child-occupied facility; AND

5. Owner acknowledges that the renovation firm will not be required to use the work practices contained in the rule.

YES →

Training and work practice requirements do not apply.

NO ↓

Is the project an emergency renovation?

NO →

YES ↓

Does the project include interim controls performed in response to an elevated blood lead level of a resident child?

YES →

Continue to Flow Chart 4 for work practice requirements.

NO ↓

Emergency projects are exempt from the warning sign, containment, waste handling, training, and certification requirements to the extent necessary to respond to the emergency. Emergency renovations are NOT exempt from the cleaning and cleaning verification requirements. See Flow Chart 5 for interior cleaning and cleaning verification requirements, and Flow Chart 8 for exterior cleaning and verification requirements.

FLOW CHART 4: Work Practice Requirements

General

(A) Renovations must be performed by certified firms using certified renovators.

(B) Firms must post signs clearly defining the work area and warning occupants and other persons not involved in renovation activities to remain outside of the work area. These signs should be in the language of the occupants.

(C) Prior to the renovation, the firm must contain the work area so that no dust or debris leaves the work area while the renovation is being performed.

(D) Work practices listed below are prohibited during a renovation:

    1. Open-flame burning or torching of lead-based paint;

    2. Use of machines that remove lead-based paint through high speed operation such as sanding, grinding, power planing, needle gun, abrasive blasting, or sandblasting, unless such machines are used with HEPA exhaust control; and

    3. Operating a heat gun on lead-based paint at temperatures of 1100 degrees Fahrenheit or higher.

(E) Waste from renovations:

    1. Waste from renovation activities must be contained to prevent releases of dust and debris before the waste is removed from the work area for storage or disposal.

    2. At the conclusion of each work day and at the conclusion of the renovation, waste that has been collected from renovation activities must be stored to prevent access to and the release of dust and debris.

    3. Waste transported from renovation activities must be contained to prevent release of dust and debris.

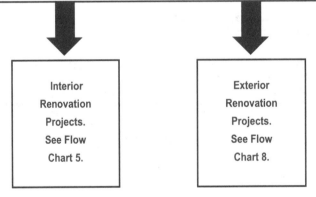

Interior Renovation Projects. See Flow Chart 5.

Exterior Renovation Projects. See Flow Chart 8.

FLOW CHART 5: Work Practice Requirements Specific to Interior Renovations

The firm must:

(A) Remove all objects from the work area or cover them with plastic sheeting with all seams and edges sealed.

(B) Close and cover all ducts opening in the work area with taped-down plastic sheeting.

(C) Close windows and doors in the work area. Doors must be covered with plastic sheeting.

(D) Cover the floor surface with taped-down plastic sheeting in the work area a minimum of six feet beyond the perimeter of surfaces undergoing renovation or a sufficient distance to contain the dust, whichever is greater.

(E) Use precautions to ensure that all personnel, tools, and other items, including the exteriors of containers of waste, are free of dust and debris when leaving the work area.

(F) After the renovation has been completed, the firm must clean the work area until no dust, debris or residue remains. The firm must:

1. Collect all paint chips and debris, and seal it in a heavy-duty bag.

2. Remove and dispose of protective sheeting as waste.

3. Clean all objects and surfaces in the work area and within two feet of the work area in the following manner:

a. Clean walls starting at the ceiling and working down to the floor by either vacuuming with a HEPA vacuum or wiping with a damp cloth.

b. Thoroughly vacuum all remaining surfaces and objects in the work area, including furniture and fixtures, with a HEPA vacuum.

c. Wipe all remaining surfaces and objects in the work area, except for carpeted or upholstered surfaces, with a damp cloth. Mop uncarpeted floors thoroughly using a mopping method that keeps the wash water separate from the rinse water, or using a wet mopping system.

Cleaning verification is required to ensure the work area is adequately cleaned and ready for re-occupancy. See Flow Chart 6 for instructions on performing cleaning verification for interior projects.

FLOW CHART 6: Interior Cleaning Verification: Visual Inspection and Optional Clearance Testing

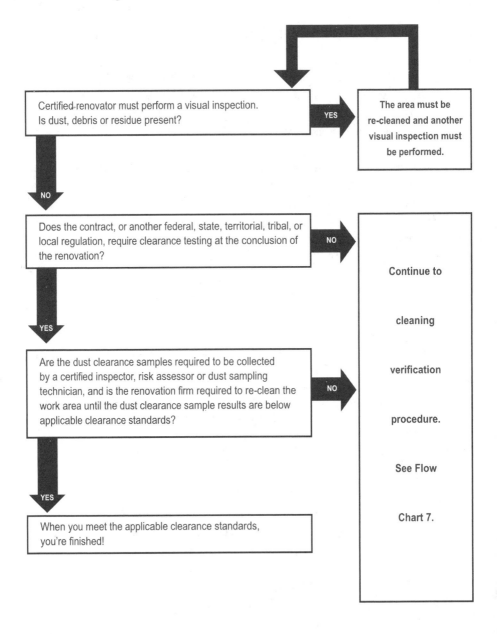

Certified renovator must perform a visual inspection. Is dust, debris or residue present?

YES → The area must be re-cleaned and another visual inspection must be performed.

NO ↓

Does the contract, or another federal, state, territorial, tribal, or local regulation, require clearance testing at the conclusion of the renovation?

NO → Continue to cleaning verification procedure. See Flow Chart 7.

YES ↓

Are the dust clearance samples required to be collected by a certified inspector, risk assessor or dust sampling technician, and is the renovation firm required to re-clean the work area until the dust clearance sample results are below applicable clearance standards?

NO → Continue to cleaning verification procedure. See Flow Chart 7.

YES ↓

When you meet the applicable clearance standards, you're finished!

FLOW CHART 7: Interior Cleaning Verification: Floors, Countertops, and Window Sills

Note: For areas greater than 40 square feet, separate the area into sections and use a new disposable cleaning cloth for each section.

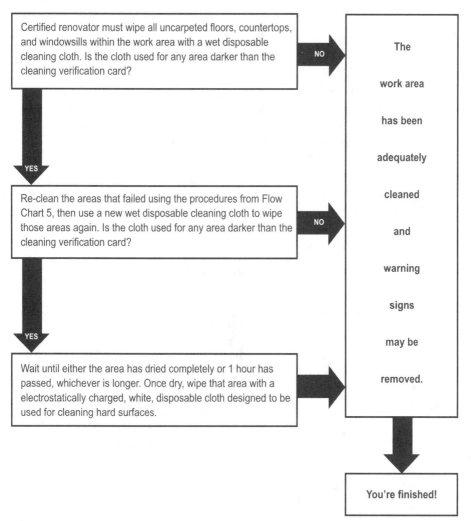

Certified renovator must wipe all uncarpeted floors, countertops, and windowsills within the work area with a wet disposable cleaning cloth. Is the cloth used for any area darker than the cleaning verification card?

NO

The work area has been adequately cleaned and warning signs may be removed.

YES

Re-clean the areas that failed using the procedures from Flow Chart 5, then use a new wet disposable cleaning cloth to wipe those areas again. Is the cloth used for any area darker than the cleaning verification card?

NO

YES

Wait until either the area has dried completely or 1 hour has passed, whichever is longer. Once dry, wipe that area with a electrostatically charged, white, disposable cloth designed to be used for cleaning hard surfaces.

You're finished!

FLOW CHART 8: Work Practice Requirements Specific to Exterior Renovations

The firm must:

(A) Close all doors and windows within 20 feet of the renovation.

(B) Ensure that doors within the work area that will be used while the job is being performed are covered with plastic sheeting in a manner that allows workers to pass through while confining dust and debris.

(C) Cover the ground with plastic sheeting or other disposable impermeable material extending a minimum of 10 feet beyond the perimeter or a sufficient distance to collect falling paint debris, whichever is greater.

(D) In situations such as where work areas are in close proximity to other buildings, windy conditions, etc., the renovation firm must take extra precautions in containing the work area, like vertical containment.

(E) After the renovation has been completed, the firm must clean the work area until no dust, debris or residue remains. The firm must:

    1. Collect all paint chips and debris, and seal it in a heavy-duty bag.

    2. Remove and dispose of protective sheeting as waste.

    3. Waste transported from renovation activities must be contained to prevent release of dust and debris.

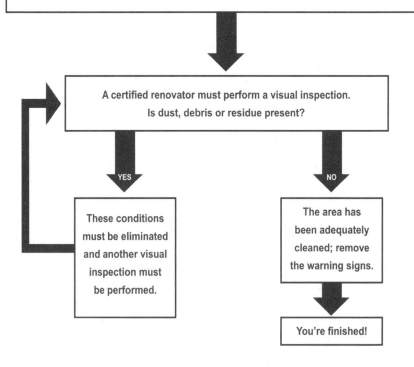

A certified renovator must perform a visual inspection.
Is dust, debris or residue present?

YES — These conditions must be eliminated and another visual inspection must be performed.

NO — The area has been adequately cleaned; remove the warning signs.

You're finished!

Now You Know...

To properly plan a renovation, you must:

- Educate owners and residents.
- Determine if lead-based paint is present.
- Determine what requirements from the EPA and HUD Rules apply to your renovation activities.

Feb 09

3-8

Module 4: Contain Dust During Work

Module 4: Contain Dust During Work

Overview
- **What is containment?**
- **Containing dust for interior activities.**
- **Containing dust for exterior activities.**

Feb 09

4-1

Upon completion of this module you will be able to:
- Establish containment systems that will keep dust inside of the work area to allow you to clean more efficiently at the end of the day and at completion of the job;
- Identify containment requirements for interior renovations; and,
- Identify containment requirements for exterior renovations.

What Is Containment?

- "Containment" is a system of temporary barriers used to isolate a work area so that no dust or debris escapes while the renovation is being performed.
- Benefits of containment.
  - Protects residents and workers.
  - Prevents spread of dust to rest of house/building or neighboring properties.
  - Easier cleaning at the end of the job.
- Containment is required.

Feb 09

4-2

What is containment?

- In general, there are many degrees of containment, ranging from simple plastic sheeting on the floor surrounding a small work area to a fully enclosed space. Some types of containment are more effective than other types.
- For purposes of this training, "containment" is what is required under the RRP Rule to prevent dust and debris from spreading beyond the work area to non-work areas.

Containing the work area includes:

- Removing objects and furniture from the work area, or covering them with plastic sheeting.
- Covering floors (or the ground) with plastic sheeting a minimum of 6 feet (10 feet for exterior work) beyond surfaces being renovated, repaired or painted.
- Closing, and using plastic sheeting to seal, all windows, doors and air ducts in the work area.
- Covering doors used to enter the work area with plastic sheeting in a manner that allows workers to pass through but contains dust and debris within the work area.

Containment is required by the RRP Rule because it:

- **Reduces the risk to you and residents**. Following the work area setup requirements of this module will protect you, your co-workers and residents by confining lead-contained dust and debris to a defined and demarcated area. Confining the lead is an important consideration in avoiding exposure. Reducing the risk to you and co-workers is also dependent upon use of personal protective equipment.
- **Facilitates efficient cleaning of the work area.** The pre-work setup process is essential to keeping lead-contaminated dust confined to the work area where it can be easily cleaned. Proper containment of the work area helps to limit the area you need to clean after the job is complete. Knowing exactly where to clean is an important factor in saving time (and money) spent on cleanup.

Keep Dust Within the Containment

- **Consider how much dust the renovation will generate.**
- **Containment design is a function of the work practices to be used and the expected amount of dust to be generated during the renovation.**
- **Plan the size and configuration of containment to keep the generated dust within containment.**
- **You are responsible for making sure dust does not migrate out of containment.**

❤EPA
United States
Environmental Protection
Agency

Feb 09   4-3

If you do not plan and contain the work area correctly, the dust and debris created by renovation can spread beyond the minimum contained area required by the RRP Rule. This means that:
- For interior locations, dust may migrate more than 6 feet from the surface being renovated; or,
- For exterior locations dust may migrate more than 10 feet from the surface being renovated.
Controlling dust and debris may require more extensive containment than is specified in the rule if the job is particularly dusty. Plan accordingly.

In general, renovations that involve only a small amount of paint disturbance create less dust than jobs that involve larger areas of paint disturbance. However, in addition to the size of the area of paint disturbed, the work practices (e.g., sanding) and equipment used will also affect how much dust is created and how the dust migrates. The location of the work activity also has a bearing on the amount of dust that is distributed. For example, small areas of ceiling work can spread dust over the entire room and are very difficult to control.

Required containment is similar for all jobs, but jobs that generate more dust and debris may require protection of larger areas. While the Rule does not <u>require</u> vertical containment, such systems may be helpful in limiting the size of the area affected by the work and may reduce the area that must be cleaned at the end of the job. Pre-engineered containment systems (purchased and home-made) are very helpful in cutting time spent on the job erecting containment and are easier to install than hanging plastic sheeting with tape. These systems also allow the contractor to create a sealed room within a room where the dust can be completely contained to a limited and controlled area.

Examples of dusty jobs include:
- Hand scraping large areas.
- Removing paint with a low temperature heat gun and scraper.
- Removing dry residue and paint after using chemical strippers.
- Demolishing painted surfaces.
- Removing building components with painted surfaces that are in poor condition.

Remember, <u>you are responsible</u> for making sure that dust and debris remain inside of the contained work area. When planning containment, keep in mind how, how much, and where the work practices to be used will create dust, and plan accordingly.

Interior Containment: Limit Access and Post Signs

- Notify residents to stay away from the work area.
- Do not allow residents or pets near the work area.
- Do not allow eating, drinking, or smoking in the work area.
- Post warning signs.

Feb 09   4-4

Restrict access to the work area and notify residents to stay away while work is underway.

- Restricting access to the work area will protect residents, especially children and pregnant women, from unnecessary exposures to leaded dust and will minimize the spread of dust to non-work areas.
- Before the job starts, notify the residents not to enter the work area and to stay away from the vicinity of the entrance to the work area as much as possible. Residents and pets coming and going can easily track lead-contaminated dust into non-work areas throughout the home. Non-work areas will likely not be cleaned up promptly or properly.
- Restricting exposure is especially important for small children under 6 years old and for pregnant women. Be sure to explain to residents that restricting access is for their own protection, and that small children and pregnant women are most at risk of health problems from exposure to lead.
- You must provide an indication of how long you will be working in a particular area so that residents can plan ahead to obtain items that they may need from the work area before you begin working.

Do not allow eating, drinking, or smoking in the work area.

- This is primarily for worker protection, but is also important if residents are living near the work area. Post signs that prohibit eating, drinking and smoking in the work area. Dust in the air can land on food or be inhaled when smoking. If food is set on a dust-contaminated surface, it can easily pick up the lead-contaminated dust, which is then ingested when the food is consumed.

Post warning signs.

- Before beginning the renovation, post a sign in the residents' native language to warn them and other persons not involved in renovation activities to remain outside of the work area. Signs must remain in place and be readable through completion of the renovation and the post-renovation cleaning verification.
- A warning sign must be posted: at each entry to a work area; or, at each main and secondary entryway to a building from which occupants have been relocated; or, for exterior work, where it is easily read 20 feet (6 meters) from the edge of the worksite.

Interior Containment: Remove or Cover Belongings

- Remove belongings.
- Cover immovable objects in protective sheeting, including:
  - Furniture;
  - Carpet; and,
  - Lamps and other fixtures.
- Seal edges and seams.

United States
Environmental Protection
Agency

Feb 09   4-5

Where Practicable Remove Belongings and Furniture from the Work Area.

- It is desirable to remove all objects from the work area including furniture, rugs and window coverings. Removal is the best option for protecting occupant items from contamination and for reducing post-renovation cleanup time (and cost).

If It Can't Be Moved Out of the Work Area, Cover It.

- Cover all objects that were not removed from the work area in protective sheeting. Seal the seams and edges with tape. Completely cover all immovable fixtures, furniture, carpets and other personal items with protective sheeting.
- Secure protective sheeting to the floor with tape so that no dust can get onto the covered items.
- Protective sheeting such as disposable heavy-duty plastic sheeting is commonly used in many remodeling jobs. Protective sheeting can be bought at most hardware stores.

Interior Containment: Cover Floors

Required:
- Cover all work area floors with plastic sheeting.
- Cover floors a minimum of 6 feet in all directions around the paint being disturbed.

Recommended:
- Lay plastic sheeting in high traffic areas.
- Take special precautions for carpets.
- Use a disposable tack pad at the edge of protective sheeting.
- If using chemical stripper, add 2nd plastic layer.

Feb 09

4-6

Cover Floors

- Use protective sheeting to cover all work area floors including installed carpet. The protective sheeting must extend a minimum of 6 feet to the left, right and front – and in some cases to the back – of the area where work will be performed. It should be tightly secured to baseboard or flooring using duct tape (where appropriate), painters tape or masking tape. The corner edge of the protective sheeting should be reinforced using duct tape or a staple.

- Take special precautions with carpets in the work area. Carpets are a major dust collection medium and it is very difficult to clean the dust out of them once contaminated. When the work area includes carpets, you must cover all carpeted areas that are in the work area with at least one layer of sealed plastic sheeting.

- Consider covering shoes with removable shoe covers, wiping off the tops and soles of shoes with a damp paper towel each time you step off the sheeting, and/or using a disposable tack pad that removes dust from the soles of shoes. Immediately place used paper towels in a covered garbage bin. Disposable tack pads can be found at many hardware stores or bought through a supply catalog. A tack pad is a sticky pad that you walk on to remove dust from the soles of your shoes. The disposable tack pad can be taped to an outer corner of the sheeting. Replace disposable tack pads at least daily.

- You may find that using a HEPA vacuum to clean off shoes and clothing is necessary in controlling carry-away dust when personnel leave the work area. This is called a "dry decon" and works well.

- A second smaller layer of protective sheeting should be used with chemical strippers. This second layer should be taped to the top of the first layer. Place the second layer immediately below the work area. This layer will capture splashes and waste, and allows the mess made by chemical strippers to be cleaned up immediately after use.

- Use precautions to ensure that all personnel, tools and other items, including the exteriors of waste containers, are free of dust and debris before removing them from the work area. A container of cheap hand or baby wipes is quite useful for such cleaning.

Interior Containment: Close Windows, Doors, HVAC

Depending on what work is to be done:
- Close all windows in the work area.
- Close and seal all doors in the work area.
- Close and seal all HVAC vents in the work area.
- Turn off the HVAC unit (recommended).

United States
Environmental Protection
Agency

Feb 09   4-7

Close Windows

- Close all windows within the work area.
- When conducting window replacements from the inside, consider attaching plastic sheeting to the exterior of the window to prevent spread of dust and debris to the ground and other surfaces under the window. If window replacement affects both interior and exterior surfaces, then setup containment for both the interior and exterior work areas.
- For dusty jobs, it is strongly recommended that you seal work area windows with protective sheeting to prevent dust from getting into the trough or on the sill, making it harder to clean.
- When sealing windows, cut plastic sheeting layer slightly larger than the window that you are covering.
- Attach the plastic sheeting with tape over the window to completely seal it.
- Make sure that the tape or the sheeting does not cover part of the area on which you are working.

Close and Seal Doors

- Close all doors including closet and cabinet doors in the work area, and cover with plastic sheeting.
- Doors used as an entrance to the work area must be covered with plastic sheeting or other impermeable material in a manner that allows workers to pass through while confining dust and debris to the work area.
- As an alternative to putting up plastic, doors may be shut and then sealed closed with painter's tape.

Close and Seal HVAC Vents

- Heating ventilating and air conditioning (HVAC) systems distribute air throughout the building and thus can also carry dust to other rooms. If possible, turn off the HVAC system for the work area. Close the HVAC supply and return vents in the work area and then cover them tightly with plastic sheeting to prevent air from blowing the dust out of the contained work area and to prevent dust from getting into the HVAC system.

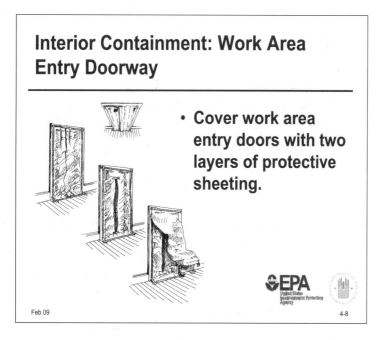

Interior Containment: Work Area Entry Doorway

- Cover work area entry doors with two layers of protective sheeting.

Feb 09

4-8

- A physical barrier, such as a cone or warning tape, can be placed outside the entry to remind residents to stay away from the work area, especially in buildings where more than one family lives. The double layers of plastic on the entry door and other barriers serve as a reminder to residents that people and pets should not enter the work area, and also signals that the area has not yet been cleaned up.

When the work area boundary includes a door used to access the work area, cover the door with two layers of protective sheeting as described below.

- Set up a two-layer entry barrier with closable flaps at the entry to the work area so that workers can pass through but dust and debris stay in the work area. Covering the door with this two-layer system will help contain the dust within the work area. Follow the steps below.
  1) Cut the first plastic sheeting layer slightly wider and longer (three inches) than the door frame.
  2) Make a small "S" fold at the top of the sheeting and tape it to the top of the door frame. Make a similar "S" fold at the bottom of the sheeting and tape it to the floor. This will ensure that the plastic is not taut.
  3) Secure the top corners to the door frame for reinforcement.
  4) For exiting and entering the room, tape a vertical line about the size of a man from floor to header on both sides of the plastic. Cut a long vertical slit through the tape, in the middle of the protective sheeting. Leave about 6 inches at the top and bottom uncut. Reinforce the top and bottom of the slit with tape to prevent the plastic from tearing.
  5) Tape a second layer of protective sheeting to the top of the door frame. This layer is cut slightly shorter than the door frame so that it will hang down flat against the first sheet of plastic.
  6) Tape and secure the top corners of the second layer to the door frame and the first layer. Leave it to hang over the first layer. Weight the bottom of the flap with a dowel to keep it in place. If needed, another weighted flap can be added to the other side of the door to provide a third layer of plastic sheeting.
- **See Appendix 5** *Steps to LEAD SAFE Renovation, Repair and Painting* **for more information on how to put the two layer system in place.**

Overview of Interior Containment Steps

The goal of these interior containment practices is to prevent dust and debris from escaping the work area.

- Limit access and post signs.
- Remove (preferred) or cover belongings.
- Cover floors.
- Close and seal windows, doors and HVAC system.
- Construct a work area entry doorway.

United States
Environmental Protection
Agency

Feb 09

4-9

RRP Rule: Interior Containment General Requirements:

- Posted signs: These must be posted on all sides of the work area to define the work area, must be in the primary language of occupants, must be posted before the beginning of the renovation, and must remain until cleaning verification is achieved.
- Contain the work area: Before renovation, isolate the work area to prevent the escape of dust. During work, maintain the containment integrity and ensure that containment does not interfere with occupant and worker egress from the home or work area.
- Remove or cover furniture/objects: Remove (preferred) objects like furniture, rugs, window coverings; or cover them with plastic sheeting with all seams and edges taped.
- Cover floors: Cover floors including carpets in the work area with taped down plastic sheeting or other impermeable material to 6 feet beyond the perimeter of surfaces undergoing renovation or to a distance sufficient to contain dust, whichever is greater.
- Close and seal doorways and close windows: Close and seal doorways and close windows in the work area with plastic sheeting or other impermeable material. Doors used as entrances to the work area must be covered with plastic sheeting that allows workers to pass through while confining dust to the work area.
- Cover duct opening: Close and cover all HVAC vents in the work area with taped down plastic sheeting or other impermeable materials (e.g., magnetic covers).
- Remove dust and debris from everything leaving the work area: Use precautions to ensure that all personnel, tools and all other items are free from dust and debris before being removed from the work area.

Exterior Containment: Establish the Work Area

- **Cover the ground with protective sheeting.**
  - If space permits, extend a minimum of 10 feet from the work area.
  - Play special attention and cover nearby vegetable gardens and children's play areas.
- **Limit access, place signs.**
  - Establish a 20 foot perimeter around the work area if space permits.

Feb 09   4-10

Cover the ground with protective sheeting

- If space permits, lay protective sheeting on the ground below the work area to at least 10 feet from the house. This creates a visible work area and helps remind residents and passers-by that they should not enter the work area unless they have a compelling need. Extend the work area farther if needed to collect dust and debris; for example, when paint on the second story of a building is being disturbed. Note: Black and clear disposable plastic sheeting can kill plants by making them too hot. Consider using white plastic sheeting instead.
- Remember children often play in the dirt and may put their hands in their mouths while playing. Dirt, dust or debris on their hands will go into their mouths and may be swallowed.
- **Remove toys and other items from the work area** and cover all play areas including sandboxes. Protect items that cannot be moved with plastic sheeting.
- **Staple or tape the protective sheeting to the wall** of the building, or use a 2x4 wrapped in protective sheeting to hold the material next to the wall. Use heavy objects (e.g., rocks) to weight the other edges of the protective sheeting to the ground so that it won't blow in the wind.
- **When using ladders on plastic sheeting** consider placing a sturdy piece of plywood on the plastic and then set the ladder on the plywood. This will prevent the ladder from puncturing the plastic and will provide a stable surface for the ladder. If plywood is used, take special care to secure it to the ground so that it does not move. This could be done by staking the plywood and later sealing the holes in the plastic with duct tape.

Limit work area access

- Limit access to the work area by placing orange cones or saw horses and warning tape around a 20 foot perimeter of the work area. Ropes with signs at regular intervals could also be used instead of barrier tape. This will help to discourage residents and passersby from entering the work area. Keep pets out of the work area.

Exterior work area daily cleaning

- Cleaning the exterior work area is crucial to prevent the spread of dust and debris. Picking up all debris throughout the day and the use of temporary, plastic-sheeting drop cloths can facilitate easy cleanup. Note that the plastic drop cloths do not take the place of protective sheeting on the ground.

Exterior Containment: Close Windows and Doors

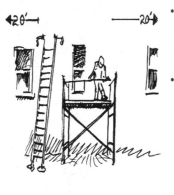

- Close all nearby doors and windows that are within 20 feet of the work area.
- Use two layers of plastic sheeting on doors in the work area that are being used during the job.

United States
Environmental Protection
Agency

Feb 09   4-11

Close and cover all nearby windows and doors.

- All windows and doors within 20 feet of the work area should be closed to prevent dust from entering the home. Renovators have an obligation to keep the dust and debris from the renovation contained within the work area and contained within the boundaries of the property on which they are working. If the windows and doors of apartments or condominiums are within 20 feet of the work area, consider requesting that the owners or residents of those affected units close the affected windows and doors in order to comply with the RRP Rule. If this is an unavailable option, other methods of restricting dust and debris to the work area and the work-site property must be considered. These other methods include construction of a vertical containment wall at the property line.

- On multi-story buildings, close all doors and windows within 20 feet of the renovation on the same floor as the renovation, and close all doors and windows on all floors directly below the area designated as the work area.

Establish two layers of plastic sheeting on the doors in work areas being used during the job.

- In the exterior work area, there will be times when a door into the house needs to be used to access interior work areas. When this occurs, cover this door with disposable plastic sheeting or other impermeable material in a manner that allows workers to pass through while confining dust and debris to the work area. The steps for placing two layers of plastic sheeting in a doorway are covered in the student notes on page 4-8.

Exterior Containment: Extra Precautions

- **Extra precautions taken to prevent the spread of dust.**
- **Extending work area.**
- **Vertical containment.**
- **Avoid working in windy conditions, where possible.**

 United States Environmental Protection Agency

Feb 09

4-12

Situations Requiring Extra Precautions

Some situations may require extra precautions to avoid the spread of dust to the rest of a property or to adjacent properties. These situations might include work in high winds that can carry dust out of the work area and work conducted on upper levels of a building during which even light winds can spread dust beyond the containment as it falls.

Extend the Work Area

The simplest solution may be to extend the area of ground covered by plastic sheeting.

Vertical Containment

If conditions are windy, if space is limited or if adjacent properties are relatively close to the work area, vertical containment systems may need to be constructed. Examples of vertical containment systems include plastic sheeting attached to scaffolding and plastic sheeting attached to vertical wood boards.

Avoid High Winds Where Possible

Be wary of windy conditions. On days with high winds, it is not advisable to perform dust creating activities. The HUD Rule restricts exterior work in winds in excess of 20 miles per hour. The EPA RRP Rule does not specifically address wind speed, but when the wind is strong enough to move dust and debris, special precautions need to be taken to keep the work area contained. That may mean creating a wind screen of plastic at the edge of the ground-cover plastic to keep dust and debris from migrating. More frequent cleanup of exterior work areas is also not addressed specifically, but frequent cleanup will help the renovator comply with the requirements to contain the work area and prevent dust and debris from getting outside of the work area. Ultimately, <u>you are responsible</u> for preventing dust and debris from leaving the work area, so take appropriate precautions to make that happen when wind is a factor.

Overview of Exterior Containment Steps

- **Establish the work area.**
- **Close all windows and doors.**
- **Establish, as necessary, additional. containment to prevent spread of dust to adjacent properties.**

Feb 09   4-13

RRP Rule: Exterior Containment General Requirements:

- <u>Posted signs:</u> Signs must be placed on all sides of the work area to define the area, must be posted in the primary language of occupants, and must be posted before the beginning of the renovation and remain until cleaning verification is achieved.
- <u>Contain the work area:</u> Before renovation, isolate the work area to prevent the escape of dust. During work maintain the containment integrity and ensure that containment does not interfere with occupant and worker egress from the building or work area.
- <u>Close doors and windows:</u> Close all doors and windows within 20 feet of the work area. For multi-story buildings close all windows and doors on the same floor within 20 feet of the work area and all windows on all floors below that are the same horizontal distance from the renovation.
- <u>Doors used as entrances to the work area:</u> Cover doorway openings with plastic sheeting that allows workers to pass through while confining dust to the work area.
- <u>Cover the ground:</u> Cover the ground with plastic sheeting or other impermeable material extending 10 feet beyond the perimeter of surfaces undergoing renovation or to a sufficient distance to contain dust, whichever is greater, unless the property line prevents 10 feet of such ground cover.
- <u>Ensure that dust and debris do not contaminate or migrate to adjacent areas or properties:</u> In certain situations, the renovation will require extra precautions for containing the exterior work area to ensure that dust and debris does not contaminate other properties. Examples of these situations may include high wind, over-spray issues, or short distances between properties that require vertical containments to keep dust in the work area. The RRP Rule establishes performance standards that the contractor must meet, but does not specify how the contractor must meet them. This allows the contractor flexibility in how to comply with the requirement to ensure that no dust or debris leaves the work area.

Hands-on Exercises: Interior and Exterior Containment

- **Practice the following Skills:**
  - Skill Set #2: Setting up Barriers, Signs and Flapped Entry Doors.
  - Skill Set #3: Cover and Move Furniture.
  - Skill Set #4: Establish Interior Containment.
  - Skill Set #5: Establish Exterior Containment.
- **Work in groups of 2 to 6.**
- **Choose the right tools and materials.**

Feb 09

4-14

Setting Up

This exercise gives you a chance to practice setting up the work area signs, barriers and containments. The slide provides basic instruction.

- Follow the instructions in each skill set. Your instructor may choose to also demonstrate skills.
- Form into groups of 2 to 6 students. The student-to-instructor ratio should not exceed 12 for this part of the training.
- Your instructor will assign your group to an area to perform setup activities as if for a job.
- Choose the right tools and set up the work area to provide proper containment.

Skill Set #2: Setting up Barriers, Signs and Flapped Entry Doors

Time: 10 minutes

Feb 09

Supplies needed:

- Barrier tape
- Warning signs
- Doorway to use for work area entry setup
- Utility knife and razor blades, or scissors
- Heavy duty plastic sheeting
- Duct tape, masking tape, and/or painter's tape
- Stapler and staples
- Broom handle, or dowels, or 1" x 1" x 30" wood or metal stock
- Optional: Pre-engineered containment systems may also be used for this exercise.

Note to Instructor: It is strongly suggested that instructors prepare plastic bags containing all materials needed for the skills practice prior to the exercise in order to meet the time limits allocated to Skill Set #2.

Purpose: The purpose of this hands-on exercise is to show students the proper steps in determining where to place critical barriers, and to give them practice in erecting barriers and posting signs to isolate the work area from access by unauthorized personnel.

Note to Instructor: Read the purpose of this activity to students. Remind them that these setup steps must be completed before the disturbance of more than 6 ft^2 per room of lead-based paint, or, whenever window replacement or demolition is to be accomplished.

Demonstration: The course instructor must show and explain all of the steps involved in establishing a critical barrier and in placement of signage. Critical barriers are plastic sheeting barriers secured over openings, doors, and windows that must remain in place until cleaning verification or clearance is achieved in order to keep dust inside of the work area. While they are not always required, they can assist with controlling the spread of dust to other areas of the home. Use students to assist in the erection of the demonstration critical barriers. Note: In the interest of time, use precut barriers for installation in the doorway. Velcro attached barriers may be used for demonstration and practice. Velcro sign attachments may also be used.

Evaluating the Students: The instructor should allow students to practice the steps on the following page while watching each student follow the steps. Make corrections and suggestions as the exercise proceeds and determine if additional practice is necessary. *Option: Have students say the steps as they work.* Students must complete all required Steps to be "Proficient". Evaluate the work of each student and once the student has completed all required elements of the exercise correctly record the performance as "Proficient" in the field on the Participant Progress Log that corresponds to Skill Set #2 and that particular student's name.

Skill Set #2: Setting up Barriers, Signs, and Flapped Entry Doors - Continued

Skills Practice:

Step 1:   Ask occupants to leave and remain out of the room where work will be done.

Step 2:   Have them stay out until the cleaning verification procedure is complete or until clearance is passed. Install barrier tape to establish a controlled perimeter.

Step 3:   Post a "Do Not Enter" sign at the doorway to the work area.* Also post a sign that states that no eating, drinking, or smoking is allowed the doorway to the work area.*

Step 4:   Cover the work area entry doorway with 2 layers of plastic sheeting, by doing the following:*

Step 5:   Cut first plastic sheeting layer slightly wider and longer than (about 3 inches longer) than the door frame.*

Step 6:   Make a small "S" fold at the top of the plastic sheeting and tape so that all layers are secured to the top of the door frame.* Make a similar "S" fold at the bottom of the plastic sheeting and tape so that all layers are secured to the floor.* This will ensure that the plastic sheeting is not tight and allows it to give instead of tearing when people move through it. Secure both sides of the plastic sheeting to the door frame with tape.

Step 7:   Staple top corners to the door frame for reinforcement.*

Step 8:   For exiting and entering the room, use duct tape to create a vertical line about the size of a man from floor to header in the middle of the plastic sheeting on both sides.* Cut a long vertical slit through the duct tape; leave about 6 inches at the top and the bottom uncut.* Reinforce the top and bottom of the slit with horizontal duct tape to prevent the plastic sheeting from tearing.*

Step 9:   Tape a second layer of plastic sheeting to the top of the door frame.* This layer is cut slightly shorter than the door frame so that it will hang down flat against the first sheet of plastic sheeting.

Step 10:   Weight the bottom of the second layer of plastic sheeting by taping a dowel rod to the bottom of the second layer of plastic sheeting with duct tape. This creates a self-sealing flap over the doorway and seals the opening that was cut in the plastic sheeting during step 8.

*Indicates required skills that must be accomplished for a "Proficient" rating.

Skill Set #3: Cover or Remove Furniture

<u>Time</u>: **10 minutes**

Feb 09

<u>Supplies needed:</u>

- Heavy duty plastic sheeting
- Cutting tool (e.g., razor knife, box cutter or scissors)
- Tape (duct, painters, and masking)

<u>Purpose:</u> The purpose of this hands-on exercise is to show students the proper steps for determining when and how to cover or remove furniture and belongings from a work area.

> ***Note to Instructor:*** *Read the purpose of this activity to students. Remind them that these setup steps must be completed before the disturbance of more than 6 ft² per room of lead-based paint, or, whenever window replacement or demolition is to be accomplished. Also remind them that the best solution to the problem of moving furniture and belongings is to notify residents to remove them prior to the work. Remind them also that it is better to remove personal property than to cover it. Provide students with the opportunity to observe/practice both methods (covering and removal).*

<u>Demonstration</u>: The course instructor should explain all of the steps involved in covering and/or removing furniture and belongings from the work area. Use students to demonstrate moving chairs out of the work area. Then cover a table with plastic sheeting and secure the plastic sheeting with tape so that no part of the table is exposed. Discuss placing other items under the table for maximized efficiency in preparing the work area. The demonstration should not take longer than 3 minutes including the time needed to hand out materials.

<u>Evaluating the Students:</u> The instructor should allow students to practice the steps on the following page while watching each student follow the steps. Make corrections and suggestions as the exercise proceeds and determine if additional practice is necessary. *Option: Have students say the steps as they work.* Students must complete all required Steps to be "Proficient". Evaluate the work of each student and once the student has completed all required elements of the exercise correctly record the performance as "Proficient" in the field on the Participant Progress Log that corresponds to Skill Set #3 and that particular student's name.

Skill Set #3: Cover or Remove Furniture – Continued

Skills Practice:

Step 1:   Move all the furniture out of the work area.

Note: If the training area is small, designate an area against one wall that is "out of the work area", where furniture removed from the work area can be placed. In a classroom setting, move the chairs and most of the tables to the designated area, and cover the tables.

Step 2:   Have the students team into groups of 2 to 6 per group. Cover several of the tables where students were sitting. This is done as follows:

Step 3:   Cut a piece of plastic sheeting large enough to cover the table and to overlap the floor by 3-6 inches.*

Step 4:   Secure the plastic sheeting to the table and/or the floor with tape.*

Step 5:   If the table will not need to be moved during the work, the plastic sheeting can be secured to the floor using duct tape or masking tape as is appropriate to the surface.*

Step 6:   If the table will need to be moved during the work, wrap the table with plastic sheeting including the legs and secure the plastic sheeting to the table with tape. Take care when applying tape so that there is no damage to the finished surfaces of the furniture.*

Note: Students should understand that they are to remove or cover all window treatments, furniture and rugs within 6 feet of surfaces that will be renovated, repaired or painted. Removal of furniture is recommended whenever possible.

*Indicates required skills that must be accomplished for a "Proficient" rating.

Skill Set #4: Establish Interior Containment

Time: 10 minutes

Feb 09

Supplies needed:
- Orange cones
- Rope and/or barrier tape (bright color preferable)
- Warning signs
- Tape measure
- Tape (duct, painters, and masking)
- Heavy duty plastic sheeting
- Cutting tool (e.g., razor knife, box cutter or scissors)
- Magnetic covers
- Disposable tack pad

Purpose: The purpose of this hands-on exercise is to show students the proper steps in covering floors, and closing and sealing the doors, windows and HVAC in the work area.

> *Note to Instructor: Read the purpose of this activity to students. Remind them that these setup steps must be completed before the disturbance of more than 6 ft^2 per room of lead-based paint, or, whenever window replacement or demolition is to be accomplished.*

Demonstration: The course instructor should explain all of the steps involved in covering and sealing floors and other horizontal surfaces in the work area, and in closing and sealing doors and windows between the work area and non-work areas. Use students to demonstrate closing and taping the windows and doors with masking tape. Remind them that they are trying to keep dust from escaping the work area.

Evaluating the Students: Allow students to practice the steps for covering the floors, closing and sealing windows, and closing and sealing doors. Watch each student follow the steps on the following page. Make corrections and suggestions as the exercise proceeds and determine if additional practice is necessary. *Option: Have students say the steps as they work.* Students must complete all required Steps to be "Proficient". Evaluate the work of each student and once the student has completed all required elements of the exercise correctly, record the performance as "Proficient" in the field on the Participant Progress Log that corresponds to Skill Set #4 and that particular student's name.

Skill Set #4: Establish Interior Containment - Continued

Skills Practice:

Step 1: At each non-entry doorway leading from the work area, place an orange cone, barrier tape, and a "Do Not Enter" sign.*

Step 2: Close all doors and windows leading to/from the work area.*

Step 3: Tape the seams around each door and window casing with painter's tape, masking tape, or duct tape.*

Step 4: Cut plastic sheeting so that it covers all exposed surfaces within 6 feet of the component(s) that are to be affected by the work.*

Step 5: Secure the plastic sheeting to the floor and walls as appropriate with tape.*

Step 6: Use plastic sheeting floor runners to avoid stepping on the carpet or floors when walking out of the work area. Secure them to the floor with tape.*

Step 7: Close and cover all air and heat diffusers and intakes with magnetic covers, tape, or plastic sheeting and tape.* Also, if possible, turn off the HVAC system while working.* HVAC units may be turned on after cleaning verification or clearance has been achieved.

Step 8: Stage all of the tools, supplies and equipment you will need to conduct the renovation, repair or painting work on the plastic sheeting in the work area to avoid contaminating the work area.*

Step 9: Place a disposable tack pad at the corner of the plastic sheeting nearest the entry door to control tracking dust off of the plastic sheeting.*

*Indicates required skills that must be accomplished for a "Proficient" rating.

Skill Set #5: Establish Exterior Containment

<u>Time</u>: **15 minutes**
Feb 09

<u>Supplies needed:</u>
- Orange cones
- Rope and/or barrier tape (bright color preferable) and fencing stakes
- Warning signs
- Heavy duty plastic sheeting
- Tape (duct, painters, and masking)
- Cutting tool (e.g., razor knife, box cutter or scissors)
- Tape measure
- Disposable tack pad

<u>Purpose:</u> The purpose of this hands-on exercise is to show students the proper steps for restricting entry to the exterior work area, and to protect the ground under and around the work area from becoming contaminated.

> **<u>Note to Instructor:</u>** *Read the purpose of this activity to students. Remind them that these setup steps must be completed before the disturbance of more than 20 ft^2 of paint on components that have been determined to be lead-based paint, or, whenever window replacement or demolition is to be accomplished.*

<u>Demonstration:</u> The course instructor should explain all of the steps involved in restricting access to and containing dust within the work area. Emphasize to students that proper setup will restrict access, and will keep dust and debris from escaping the work area.

<u>Evaluating the Students:</u> Allow students to cover the ground and establish barriers to prevent unauthorized access to the work area. Watch each student follow the steps on the following page. Make corrections and suggestions as the exercise proceeds and determine if additional practice is necessary. *Option: Have students say the steps as they work.* Students must complete all required Steps to be "Proficient". Evaluate the work of each student and once the student has completed all required elements of the exercise correctly, record the performance as "Proficient" in the field on the Participant Progress Log that corresponds to Skill Set #5 and that particular student's name.

Skill Set #5: Establish Exterior Containment - Continued

Skills Practice:

Step 1:   At each non-entry doorway leading into the work area, place an orange cone, barrier tape, and a "Do Not Enter"sign.*

Step 2:   Close all doors and windows within 20 feet of the work area.*

Step 3:   Place plastic sheeting as ground cover a minimum of 10 feet in all directions from the actual location of a paint disturbance.*

Step 4:   Weigh down the edges of the plastic sheeting with 2x4s or bricks or stake down the edges of the plastic sheeting.*

Step 5:   Secure the plastic sheeting to the floor and walls with tape or furring strips and tacks.*

Step 6:   Place barrier fencing or a rope around the perimeter of the work area 20 feet from the work area and on all exposed sides.*

Step 7:   Establish an entry point to the work area and place a "Do Not Enter, No Food or Drinks or Smoking Allowed"sign.*.

Step 8:   Curb the edges of the plastic sheeting to prevent dust from blowing off.* Curbs can be made by running a low rope near the ground and draping the plastic sheeting over the top of the rope. The rope should be only a few inches above the ground. A staked 2x4 may also be used to raise the edges of the plastic sheeting instead of the rope method.

Step 9:   Stage all of the tools, supplies, and equipment you will need to conduct the renovation, repair, or painting work on the plastic sheeting in the work area to avoid contaminating the work area.*

Step 10:   Place a disposable tack pad at the corner of the plastic sheeting nearest the entry door to control tracking dust off of the plastic sheeting.*

*Indicates required skills that must be accomplished for a "Proficient" rating.

Debrief of Hands-on Exercise

- How did it go?
- What were some of the hard parts?

Feb 09

4-15

Debrief of Hands-on Exercises.

Consider the questions above. Discuss as a class.

Now You Know...

- How to setup for a job
  - Interior containment
  - Exterior containment

Feb 09

4-16

Now you know how to set up for a job. The next module will discuss the conduct of lead-safe work practices during the job.

Module 5: During the Work

Module 5: During the Work

Overview:

- Traditional renovations create airborne dust.
- Prohibited practices.
- Protect yourself and make a personal protective equipment toolkit.
- Control the spread of dust.
- Hands-on exercise (Skill Set #6).

Feb 09

5-1

Requirements in the EPA RRP Rule:

The RRP Rule prohibits the use of certain practices. These prohibited practices are discussed in this module. This module also contains recommendations regarding how to reduce dust during work activities that are not specifically required or addressed in the RRP Rule. The practices you choose to use in the contained work area must not include prohibited practices. Beyond this you are free to use whatever practices get the job done, provided that all dust and debris you generate stays in the work area and does not migrate to other areas or properties. The recommendations in this section will assist you by reducing the amount of dust released during work. Dust reduction in the work area will make the workplace safer for employees, and will make cleaning easier.

Upon completion of this module, you will know:

- What work practices are prohibited under the RRP Rule because they create dangerous amounts of dust and paint chips;
- What practices to use to control dust, debris or paint chips; and,
- What tools you will need.

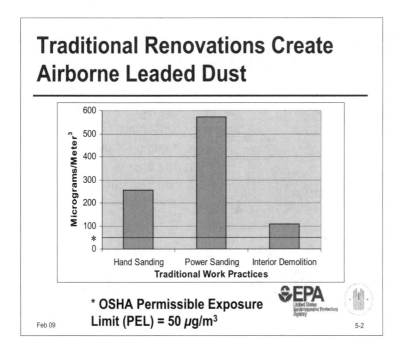

The data above are from *Lead Exposure Associated with Renovation and Remodeling Activities: Summary Report*, Prepared by Battelle for the U.S. Environmental Protection Agency, May 1997, EPA 747-R-96-005.

Traditional work practices create large amounts of dust!

- This chart shows amounts of lead dust created by three common construction practices: hand sanding, power sanding, and interior demolition. **The RRP Rule prohibits the use of power sanding, grinding, planing and cutting without attached HEPA-filtered local capture ventilation because these practices produce so much dust.**

- By using safe work practices, you can control and significantly reduce the amount of dust created on the job. Controlling leaded dust at the source of generation is important because dust released into the air will eventually become settled dust on the ground. Later in this chapter, you will learn safe work practices that can replace these prohibited work practices. In this section you will also find best practice recommendations for reducing dust in the work area.

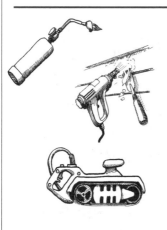

Prohibited Practices

- Open-flame burning or torching.
- Heat gun above 1100° F.
- Power sanding, power grinding, power planing, needle guns, abrasive blasting and sandblasting, without HEPA vacuum attachment.

 United States Environmental Protection Agency

Feb 09   5-3

The EPA Renovation, Repair, and Painting Rule does not specifically address what measures must be taken to reduce the amount of dust generated on the job. Rather, the rule lists three Prohibited Practices that must not be used on the job.

1. Open-flame burning or torching.
2. Heat gun above 1,100° F (degrees Fahrenheit).
3. The use of machines that remove lead-based paint through high-speed operation such as sanding, grinding, planing, needle gun, abrasive blasting, or sandblasting is prohibited unless such machines are used with attached HEPA-filtered local capture ventilation.

A key to minimizing the spread of dust and paint chips is not to use certain traditional work practices known to create large amounts of dust and debris.

- **Open-flame burning or torching of paint and using a heat gun above 1,100° F** create very fine leaded dust particulates ("fume") that are dangerous for workers to breathe. The small leaded dust particles created by burning and heating also settle on surrounding surfaces and are very hard to clean up.

- **Power sanding, power grinding, power planing, needle guns, abrasive blasting, and sandblasting** create a large amount of dust that floats in the air and then settles on surfaces inside and outside of the work area. These activities are prohibited unless equipped with attached HEPA-filtered local capture ventilation devices to control the dust-laden exhaust.

See Appendix 5 *Steps to LEAD SAFE Renovation, Repair and Painting* for more information.

 The practices listed on the slide are also prohibited in pre-1978 properties with lead-based paint that receive Federal housing assistance. The HUD Rule also prohibits extensive dry scraping and sanding by hand, and paint stripping in a poorly ventilated space using a volatile paint stripper. States, localities or tribes may also prohibit these practices.

Specialized Tools

- **Large jobs may require special considerations to get the job done, like:**
  - Power sanders, grinders and planers, needle guns, and abrasive and sand blasters, each with required HEPA-filtered capture attachments.
  - Pneumatic and battery powered tools to protect against shock hazards.
  - Specialized planning and containment.

Feb 09

5-4

Only power tools equipped with attached HEPA-filtered local capture ventilation may be used when lead-based paint is present or presumed to be present.

- Electric power tools such as sanders, grinders, circular saws, reciprocating saws, planers and drills produce dust and debris. Because they are electric, wet methods are not safe. Pneumatic and battery powered tools prevent shock hazards. Attached HEPA-filtered tools or the use of vacuum attached shrouds on these tools contain the dangerous leaded dust and paint chips that are generated by their use.

- Tools with attached HEPA-filtered capture ventilation collect and filter dust and debris as it is created. A shroud at the head of the tool helps to contain the dust and paint chips as the vacuum draws away dust and debris for safe storage in the vacuum canister. This makes the job cleaner and safer.

- Abrasive blasting is very effective at removing large areas of paint quickly, but these practices require special HEPA filtration equipment that contains the blast medium, dust and paint chips without releasing dust into the air or into the containment.

Containment is even more important when using specialized tools.

- Proper containment and cleaning are crucial even when using HEPA-filtered specialized tools. These tools generate a lot of dust inside a localized negative pressure (vacuum) environment. If the vacuum fails or if the vacuum seal created by the shroud is broken, large volumes of dust can be released. Nonetheless, HEPA-filtered specialized tools can reduce dust levels when used properly, and can aid work production by shortening the cleaning time and lowering cost.

- See the Shopping List of tools and supplies found in Appendix 5 *Steps to LEAD SAFE Renovation, Repair and Painting* for more information.

Protect Yourself

- Workers should wear:
  - Disposable painter's hat.
  - Disposable coveralls.
    - Repair tears with duct tape.
    - Dispose of in plastic bag.
  - Disposable N-100, R-100 or P-100 respirator.
- Wash face and hands frequently and at the end of each shift.
  - Washing helps to reduce hand-to-mouth ingestion of leaded dust.
- OSHA may require more protection depending on what work is done.

 United States Environmental Protection Agency

Feb 09

5-5

Workers should protect themselves.

- **Painter's hats** are an inexpensive way to keep dust and paint chips out of workers' hair. Painter's hats can be easily disposed of, and should be disposed of at the end of each day or at the end of the job.

- **Disposable coveralls** are a good way to keep dust off workers' street clothes and reduce the chance of carrying dust away as they come and go. The coveralls can be removed when workers leave the work site and stored in a plastic bag overnight. Remember to use a HEPA vacuum to remove dust and debris from coveralls or other outerwear (a "dry decon") before exiting the work area. To keep costs down, consider buying extra large coveralls in bulk and sizing down to fit workers using duct tape. Some coveralls have a hood to keep dust out of hair.

- **Respiratory protection.** Employers should consider that workers should wear respiratory protection, such as a disposable N-100, R-100 or P-100 respirator, to prevent them from inhaling leaded dust. These respirators are particulate-filtering respirators and would not be appropriate as protection from chemical stripping compounds. OSHA provides additional information on respirators in 29 CFR 1910.134.

- **You must wash your hands and face at the end of each shift. Workers should wash** their hands and faces periodically to avoid ingesting leaded dust. It is required that you wash well before eating, drinking or smoking. It is **forbidden for anyone to eat, drink, or smoke in the work area**. Some of the dust that settles on the face around the mouth invariably finds its way into the mouth. Workers should also wash at the end of the day before getting in their car or going home. They shouldn't take leaded dust home to their families.

- Personal protection is especially important on high dust generating jobs when lead-based paint or lead-contaminated dust is disturbed, and while cleaning is being performed. However, the same level of protection is not necessary during the planning, testing or setup phases of the work when lead is not being disturbed.

- The protective equipment listed above is meant to show what is needed during activities that disturb lead-based paint and lead-contaminated dust. Depending upon work practices used, OSHA rules may require employers to take further steps to protect the health of workers on the job.

- OSHA provides additional information on working with lead in their Safety and Health Regulations for Lead in the Construction Industry (29 CFR 1926.62).

Control the Spread of Dust

- When you leave the work site, clean yourself and your tools.
  - Remove shoe coverings and HEPA vacuum or wipe shoes.
  - Walk on disposable tack pads to remove dust from your soles.
  - HEPA vacuum and remove coveralls, and HEPA vacuum your clothes.
  - Remove gloves if used, and carefully wash your hands and face.
  - Dispose of all used disposable clothing in plastic bags.
- At the end of the day don't take lead home to your family on your clothes or in your car.
  - HEPA vacuum clothes, shoes, etc.
  - Change your clothes, and dispose of or place dusty work cloths in a plastic bag to wash separately from household laundry.

Don't hug your family until you get clean!
  - Wash your hands and face.
  - Shower as soon as you get home.

Feb 09

5-6

Precautions to take when leaving the work site

- When you leave the work site (the area covered by protective sheeting or the work room), take precautions to prevent spreading dust and paint chips on your clothes and shoes to other parts of the residence.

- Every time you leave the plastic sheeting around the surfaces being renovated, remove the disposable shoe covers and wipe or vacuum your shoes before you step off the plastic sheeting. A large disposable tack pad on the floor can help to clean the soles of your shoes.

- Every time you leave containment, HEPA vacuum and remove your disposable coveralls and disposable shoe covers. Clean and/or vacuum your shoes, and wash your hands and face.

- At the end of the day:

  - Change your clothes and wash yourself to reduce the risk of contaminating your car and taking leaded dust home to your family.

  - Before leaving the worksite, remove any protective clothing, HEPA vacuum dust from non-protective clothing, and thoroughly wash your hands and face. Throw away disposable clothing or place clothing in a plastic bag to stop dust from getting on other clothes at home.

  - If you cannot clean yourself at the work site get a piece of plastic to protect the floor and seat of your car from lead contamination.

  - As soon as you arrive home, take a shower and be sure to thoroughly wash your hair, especially before playing with children. Wash your work clothes separately from regular household laundry to stop lead from getting on your other clothes.

  - Be clean before you come in contact with family members, especially children. Remember the video about the contractor who lead-poisoned his own kids.

Cleaning During the Job

- **A clean work site reduces the spread of dust and paint chips.**
- **Clean as you work.**
  - **HEPA vacuum horizontal surfaces.**
  - **Remove debris frequently.**
  - **Remove paint chips as they are created.**
  - **As building components are removed, wrap and dispose of them immediately.**
- **Clean frequently (in stages, at least daily).**

United States
Environmental Protection
Agency

Feb 09   5-7

Clean the work site frequently.

- Cleaning the work site frequently as the job progresses will reduce the spread of dust and paint chips. Daily cleaning need not be as thorough as the final cleaning. It should, however, keep debris, dust and paint chips from piling up and spreading beyond the immediate work site.

Daily cleaning during the job includes:

- **Removing debris frequently.** Seal and dispose of construction debris as it is created.

- **Vacuuming horizontal surfaces frequently.** HEPA vacuum dust and paint chips that settle on surfaces, including protective sheeting. As workers come and go during the work day, this debris is easily spread. Periodic cleaning throughout the work day helps minimize the spread of dust.

- **Collect paint chips as they are created.** When removing paint, paint chips can spread outside the immediate work area as workers come and go from the work site. To keep paint chips from spreading beyond the work site, make sure that they are collected as they are created. Periodically HEPA vacuum and dispose of paint chips.

- **Wrapping and disposing of removed components.** When removing painted components such as windows, trim and cabinets, wrap them in plastic sheeting and dispose of them in stages. This will prevent the spread of debris and keep residents, especially children, from coming into contact with leaded dust created by the work.

- **Safe Waste Disposal.** All renovation waste from the work area must be contained prior to its removal, storage, or disposal to prevent releases of dust and debris. Chutes for removing waste from the work area must be covered. At the conclusion of each work day, collect waste and store it in containment, in an enclosure, or behind a barrier that prevents the release of, and access to, dust and debris. When transporting waste from the renovation work area it must be contained to prevent the release of dust and debris.

How often should cleaning during the job take place?

- The goal is to keep dust and debris under control, not to maintain a completely spotless site at all times. Every job is different; so clean when it makes sense to, without hindering progress. Remove large amounts of dust, paint chips, and debris frequently, at least daily.

Exercise: Personal Protective Equipment

- **Watch the instructor dress a volunteer in personal protective equipment.**
  - Skill Set #6 – Protective Equipment (10 Min).
- **Practice putting on and taking off personal protective equipment.**
- **Dispose of used equipment properly and clean up.**

Feb 09   5-8

Personal Protective Equipment

This exercise gives you a chance to learn and practice the proper steps for putting on and taking off personal protective equipment, disposing of used equipment, and decontaminating yourself. The slide provides basic instruction.

Skill Set #6: Personal Protective Equipment
Time: 10 minutes
Feb 09

Supplies needed:
- Disposable coveralls
- Disposable non-latex gloves
- Disposable foot covers
- Eye protection
- Leather or canvas work gloves
- N-100 respirators
- Disposable waste bags
- Duct tape
- Hand washing facilities and hand soap

Purpose: The purpose of this hands-on exercise is to show students the proper steps for putting on (donning) and taking off (doffing) personal protective equipment, and the steps for decontaminating and disposing of used equipment.

Note to Instructor: *Read the purpose of this activity to students.*

Demonstration: The course instructor should explain all of the steps involved in putting on personal protective equipment while actually dressing a volunteer student in personal protective equipment. Emphasize to students that this equipment prevents their exposure to lead as well as prevents the contamination of areas outside of the work area.

Evaluating the Students: Watch each student as they follow the steps on the next page. Make corrections and suggestions as the exercise proceeds and determine if additional practice is necessary. *Option: Have students say the steps as they work.* Students must complete all required Steps to be "Proficient". Evaluate the work of each student and once the student has completed all required elements of the exercise correctly record the performance as "Proficient" in the field on the Participant Progress Log that corresponds to Skills Set #6 and that particular student's name.

Skill Set #6: Personal Protective Equipment – Continued

Skills Practice:

Step 1:   Put on (don) a set of protective coveralls.*

Step 2:   Put on disposable gloves.*

Step 3:   Put on boot covers over shoes.*

Step 4:   Put on safety glasses.*

Step 5:   Put on work gloves.*

Step 6:   When dressed in this Personal Protective Equipment, discuss the use of respirators and show the proper method for putting on and securing the respirator in place.
Note: Students should not wear a respirator if they are not currently enrolled in the training firm's respiratory protection program. Watch the demonstration but do not try on a respirator if this note applies you.

Step 7:   Remove the work gloves and place them in a marked waste bag.*

Step 8:   Remove the boot covers by pulling them off from the heel and rolling the cover inside out as it is rolled toward the toes. Once removed, place them in a marked waste bag.*

Step 9:   Remove your suit by unzipping it and rolling it dirty side in to prevent releasing dust. Once removed, place the suit in a marked waste bag.*

Step 10:   Remove your disposable non-latex gloves by grasping the cuff of one glove and peeling the glove inside out off of the hand. Hold the glove that was removed in the palm of the gloved hand. Place one finger under the cuff of the gloved hand and remove this glove by peeling it off of the gloved hand inside out and over the balled up glove you had already removed. Once removed, you should have one glove inside the other, with the dirty side contained. Dispose of the gloves in the marked waste bag.*

Step 11:   Wash your hands, face and shoes with soap and water. Dry your hands and face with a disposable towel.*

*Indicates required skills that must be accomplished for a "Proficient" rating.

Now You Know...

- What work practices produce dust.
- What work practices are prohibited by EPA and HUD.
- How to work safely around lead-based paint and leaded dust.
- Proper use of personal protective equipment.

Feb 09

5-9

The practices you learned in this module will help you make less dust as you work.

In the next module, we'll talk about how to conduct final cleaning of the work area, and how to verify that the cleaning is complete.

Module 6: Cleaning Activities and Checking Your Work

Module 6: Cleaning Activities and Checking Your Work

Overview
- **What is effective cleanup?**
- **Interior cleaning techniques.**
- **Exterior cleaning techniques.**
- **How to check your work.**
- **Cleaning verification procedure.**
- **Clearance testing.**
- **Safe disposal practices.**

Feb 09

6-1

What you will learn in this module:
This module will cover all the topics listed on the slide above.

- The goal of cleaning is to leave the work area as clean as or cleaner than when you arrived so that, as a result of your work, leaded dust is not left behind to poison the residents.
  - At the end of this module, you will know how to check your work to ensure the work area is clean enough to pass the visual inspection and cleaning verification procedure, or pass a clearance examination.
- By using the techniques described in this module, you will be able to clean a work area quickly and efficiently. Remember, approaching a cleanup is similar to approaching a job. Proper preparation and planning will help make your cleaning efforts more effective and efficient.
- Always schedule time at the end of each day to thoroughly clean the work area.

What is Effective Cleanup?

- Keeping dust from getting back into areas already cleaned.
- Using proper cleaning techniques.
- Cleaning all surfaces, tools and clothing.
- Checking your work.
  - Usually will involve performing cleaning verification.
  - Could include a clearance examination.
- Safe and secure disposal of waste.

Feb 09
6-2

Containment

- Effective cleaning begins with proper preparation and containment. Cleaning will be much easier and efficient if proper containment has kept all dust and debris confined to the work area. While cleaning, keeping dust in the area that is being cleaned is also important. You don't want to have cleaned areas become re-contaminated after cleaning.

Proper cleaning techniques

- Follow a "top to bottom, back your way out" approach so that you don't have to re-enter an area that has already been cleaned. Start cleaning high to low. You should be careful not to spread dust to other areas while cleaning. Follow an ordered sequence of cleaning to ensure that you do not contaminate other areas. For example, if floors are cleaned before the countertops you must walk on the floors to get to the countertops and this risks re-contaminating the floors. Never re-enter areas already cleaned. Also, countertops are higher than floors and can drop dust onto the floors.

Cleaning all surfaces

- The term "all surfaces" includes all vertical surfaces such as walls and windows, and all horizontal surfaces such as floors, door tops and moldings, window troughs, and window sills. Cleaning should proceed from high to low, i.e., from top of wall to window to floor.

Checking your work

- Conduct a visual inspection after cleaning is completed. Look for paint chips, dust and debris.
- Perform cleaning verification until all areas pass when compared to the cleaning verification card.
- A dust clearance examination may replace cleaning verification when required by Federal, state, tribal, or local law, or by the owner.

Safe and secure disposal of waste

- Bag and "gooseneck seal" all waste in heavy duty plastic bags. Safely dispose of all waste in accordance with Federal, state and local regulations. See slides 6-9 and 6-10 for information on disposal.

Interior Cleaning Requirements

- Collect all paint chips and debris, and seal in heavy duty plastic bags.
- Mist, remove, fold (dirty side in) and tape or seal protective sheeting. Dispose of sheeting as waste.
- Plastic sheeting between non-contaminated rooms and work areas must remain in place until after cleaning and removal of other sheeting.
- HEPA vacuum or wet wipe walls from high to low, then HEPA vacuum remaining surfaces and wipe with a damp cloth.
- Clean 2 feet beyond the contained work area.
- Use disposable wipes or change cloths frequently.
- For carpet or rug, use HEPA vacuum with beater bar.
- HEPA vacuum and wet mop uncarpeted floors - two-bucket mopping method or wet mopping system.

Feb 09   6-3

Pick up

- Always begin cleaning activities by picking up visible paint chips and debris with a wet disposable cloth without dispersing any of it, and sealing this material in a heavy-duty bag.
- When the job is complete, mist the sheeting, fold it (dirty side in), and either seal it with tape, or seal it in a heavy-duty bag. Always fold dirty side inwards, and seal with tape or place in a heavy duty plastic bag. If it is placed in a heavy-duty bag, "gooseneck-seal" the bag and dispose of the bag with the rest of your waste. Dispose of all sheeting as waste by using the correct folding and disposal procedure, after it has been vacuumed.

Clean with a Plan

- Start cleaning at the far end of the work area and work back to the exit.
- Clean walls with a HEPA vacuum or by wiping with a damp disposable cloth: Start with the tops of the walls, tops of doors and door frames and work down to the floor.
- Thoroughly vacuum all remaining surfaces and objects, including furniture and fixtures, in the work area. The HEPA vacuum must be equipped with a beater bar when vacuuming carpeting or rugs.
- Wipe all surfaces and objects that remained in the work area, except carpeted or upholstered surfaces, with a damp cloth.

Clean the floor last

- Clean with a wet mopping system or a two-sided bucket and mop.
- Clean the entire work area and the area within 2 feet of the work area.
- If using the two-bucket mopping system, repeat the process using a new mop head and clean water. Remember, always keep one bucket for cleaning solution and the other bucket for wringing out the cloth or mop head. You must keep wash and rinse water separate. Change the rinse water often.

• Check your work

- Before a Certified Renovator visually inspects the work area, check your work to determine whether dust, debris or residue is still present. If dust, debris or residue is still present, these conditions must be corrected before the visual inspection is performed.

Visual Inspection Procedure

1. **Conducted by Certified Renovator.**
2. **Put on disposable foot covers before entering the work area.**
3. **Make sure there is adequate lighting in the work area.**
   - Turn-on all of the lights or use a bright, white-light flashlight.
4. **Systematically look for dust and debris on every horizontal surface in the work area and 2 feet beyond.**
   - Work from the farthest area from the entry to the entry.
   - Closely examine each surface.
5. **If you find visible dust or debris, then re-clean the work area and repeat step 4.**
6. **Once you have carefully looked at all of the surfaces and found no dust or debris, proceed to the cleaning verification procedure or clearance.**

United States
Environmental Protection
Agency

Feb 09

6-4

- <u>Visual inspection after cleaning is required by the RRP Rule.</u> Visual inspection is just the first step.
- A visual inspection must be conducted by a Certified Renovator once cleaning is complete, and prior to the cleaning verification or clearance examination of the work area.
- In a visual inspection, the Certified Renovator looks for visible paint chips, dust and debris.
- Make sure that adequate lighting is provided during the cleaning and visual inspection of the work area. You cannot see dust and small paint chips without adequate lighting.
- Inspect the entire work area and the area 2 feet beyond the work area on all sides of the containment.
- <u>Visual inspection of the work area alone will not verify that the work area has been cleaned adequately – visual inspection is only the first step.</u> In many instances, leaded dust is not visible to the naked eye and will not be detected during a visual inspection. Once the visual inspection has been completed and no visible dust and debris are present, the work area must pass either the cleaning verification procedure or a clearance examination in order for the project to be completed in compliance with the RRP Rule.
- Whether the cleaning verification procedure or clearance examination is conducted will be based on regulatory requirements or terms in the renovation contract.

Cleaning Verification (CV) Procedure

- Wipe each window sill within the work area. Use a single wet disposable cleaning cloth per window sill.
- Wipe uncarpeted floors and all countertops with wet disposable cleaning cloths. Wipe up to a maximum of 40 ft^2 per cloth.
- Compare each wipe to the CV card. If the cloth matches or is lighter than the CV card, the surface has passed cleaning verification and no further action is required.
- If the cloth is darker than the CV card, re-clean and repeat the CV process.
- If the second wet cloth fails, wait 1 hour or until surfaces are dry, and then wipe with an electrostatically-charged white disposable cleaning cloth designed to be used for cleaning hard surfaces. This completes the cleaning verification.

EPA
United States
Environmental Protection
Agency

Feb 09   6-5

After visual inspection, one of two activities must be conducted. A Certified Renovator must perform cleaning verification or other certified professionals must conduct a clearance examination. The steps for the cleaning verification procedure are explained below.

Window Sills

- Using a single, wet, disposable cleaning cloth, wipe the entire surface of each window sill in the work area.

Wipe Countertops and Floors

- Wipe the entire surface of each countertop and uncarpeted floor within the work area with wet disposable cleaning cloths. Floors must be wiped using a wet cleaning system, including a long handle device with a head to which a wet disposable cleaning cloth is attached. The cloth must remain damp at all times while being used to wipe the floor.
- If the surface of a countertop or floor within the work area is greater than 40 square feet, the surface within the work area must be divided into roughly equal sections that are each less than 40 square feet. Wipe each surface section separately using a new wet disposable cleaning cloth.

Interpret the Cleaning Verification Procedure.

- Compare each wipe representing a specific surface section to the cleaning verification card. If the cloth used to wipe each surface section within the work area matches or is lighter than the cleaning verification card, that surface section has been adequately cleaned.
- If the cloth is darker than the cleaning verification card, re-clean that surface section, then use a new wet disposable cleaning cloth to wipe the surface section. If the cloth matches or is lighter than the cleaning verification card, that surface section has been adequately cleaned.
- If the second cloth does not match and is not lighter than the cleaning verification card, re-clean the surface and wait for 1 hour or until the surface section has dried completely, whichever is longer. Then wipe the surface section with an electrostatically charged white disposable cleaning cloth designed to be used for cleaning hard surfaces. The cleaning verification procedure is now complete and the surface is considered clean.
- When cleaning verification has been completed for all of the surfaces in the work area (including window sills), warning signs may be removed.

Dust Clearance Examination

A dust clearance examination may be performed instead of cleaning verification.

- **<u>A clearance examination must be a conducted by a Certified Lead Inspector, Risk Assessor, or Dust Sampling Technician.</u>**
- **If clearance fails, the renovation firm must re-clean the work area until dust standards comply with applicable state, territorial, tribal and local standards.**

Feb 09   6-6

Clearance Examination (Dust Clearance Testing) – Optional under the RRP Rule

- Dust clearance testing may be performed to check the effectiveness of the cleaning efforts. Clearance is an option under the EPA Renovation, Repair, and Painting Rule and is required by the HUD Rule in many cases.
- Dust clearance testing is performed to check the effectiveness of cleaning efforts.
- In some cases, dust clearance testing may be required as part of "clearance" (a regulation-defined process to ensure that a work area is not contaminated with leaded dust after work is completed). Cleaning verification need not be performed if dust clearance testing is required at the conclusion of a renovation. In such cases, dust clearance testing may only be performed by a Certified Lead Inspector, Risk Assessor, or Dust Sampling Technician. The Certified Renovation Firm is required to re-clean the work area until dust-lead levels in the work area meet the clearance standards. Some state, local, and tribal laws may require a clearance examination following renovation and remodeling work, to levels that differ from the Federal clearance standards. The selection of a CV or a clearance examination will be based on regulatory requirements or the renovation contract.

Clearance is required in many pre-1978 properties receiving Federal housing assistance. The clearance examination may be scheduled by the agency administering the assistance. A clearance examination is performed by a trained person <u>independent</u> of the renovation firm performing the work. Ask your client or contact the agency administering the assistance to the property to find out if a clearance examination is required at the end of the job and to find out who will schedule it. Remember, if the property fails clearance, the unit must be re-cleaned and another clearance examination performed. Sometimes the cost of re-cleaning and the additional clearance examination will be the responsibility of the contractor. Cleaning well the first time will saves both time and money.

Exterior Cleanup Requirements

- Clean all surfaces in the work area until no visible dust, debris, or residue remains.
- Remove all dust and debris without dispersal, and seal in heavy plastic bags.
- Remove protective plastic sheeting and mist before folding it dirty side inward.
- Check your work.
  - Focus on areas such as window sills, bare soil, and children's play areas.
  - Look for dust, debris and paint chips.

United States
Environmental Protection
Agency

Feb 09   6-7

Specific exterior jobs
- If work takes place on an exterior porch or stairwell, HEPA vacuuming, wet cleaning and mopping, in addition to a thorough visual inspection, should be used to clean the work area. For such jobs, the cleanup can be similar to cleanup after interior jobs. Collect and dispose of any dust and debris with the rest of your waste.

Remember
- Lead contaminated soil can poison children.
- Avoid dry raking and shoveling, and spreading dust. However, raking and shoveling the soil is appropriate if it is misted first.

Protective sheeting
- Collect all dust and debris on the sheeting and place in plastic bags.
- Mist sheeting, fold dirty side inward, and dispose of as waste. This is especially important since you will not be cleaning the ground afterward. Remember that you are responsible to make sure you do not leave dust and debris behind.
- The Certified Renovator should visually inspect the plastic after cleaning for dust and debris. Remember the Certified Renovator is required to certify that the work area was cleaned properly at the end of the job.
- Protective sheeting is to be disposed of as waste.

Visual inspection
- A thorough visual inspection of the work area should be conducted after any exterior job. Any visible paint chips, wood chips and other debris from the work area should be collected and disposed of with the rest of your waste.
- Focus your visual inspection on areas such as exterior porches, outside play areas, bare soil and ground, and window sills, but don't ignore or neglect other areas.

Exterior – Check Effectiveness of Cleaning

- **Visual inspection**
  - A Certified Renovator conducts a visual inspection after any cleaning.
  - Determines if any visible dust and debris are present in and beyond the boundaries of the work area.
- If visible dust or debris are found, collect and dispose of all paint chips, dust, and debris identified during the visual inspection.
- After re-cleaning, the Certified Renovator conducts another visual inspection.
- When all areas pass, warning signs may be removed.

United States
Environmental Protection
Agency

Feb 09

6-8

Checking your work

- A thorough visual inspection is the main part of checking your cleanup after an exterior job. You should collect and dispose of any paint chips, wood chips and debris found during the visual inspection.
- A visual inspection is conducted after completing cleanup, to check your work.
- The Certified Renovator must perform the visual inspection to determine whether dust, debris or residue is still present on surfaces in or below the work area, including window sills and on the ground.
- If dust or residue is present, clean again, and then repeat the visual inspection.
- Warning signs may be removed after passing visual inspection.

 Clearance on exterior jobs. For exterior jobs, HUD requires only a visual assessment of the work area to pass clearance. No dust or soil testing is required. If you follow procedures taught in this course you will satisfy HUD requirements.

Disposal

- What should I do with my waste?
- At the work site:
  - **Place waste in heavy duty plastic bag.**
  - **"Gooseneck seal" the bag with duct tape.**
  - **Carefully dispose of waste in accordance with Federal and other regulations.**
  - **HEPA vacuum the exterior of the waste bag before removing it from the work area.**
  - **Store waste in a secure area.**

United States
Environmental Protection
Agency

Feb 09   6-9

At the Work Site

- Always collect, bag and seal all waste at the work site and in the work area. HEPA vacuum or wipe the exterior of waste bags before removing them from the work area. Do not carry your waste to another room or another area before bagging and sealing it. Store all waste in a secure container or dumpster until disposal. Limit on-site storage time. Avoid transporting waste in an open truck or in a personal vehicle. Some examples of waste include protective sheeting, HEPA filters, paint chips, dust, dirty water, used cloths, used wipes, used mop heads, used protective clothing, used respirators, used gloves, and architectural components. Architectural components that are too big to fit into bags must be wrapped in plastic and sealed with tape prior to removal from the work area. If needed, "double-bag" your waste to help prevent the waste from escaping if the bag is cut or ripped.

Waste Water

- Water used for cleanup should be filtered and dumped in a toilet if local rules allow. Never dump this water down a sink or tub, down a storm drain or on the ground. Filtering waste water through a 5-micron filter may be necessary when lead-contamination such as paint chips and dust may be present in the water. **Check with your local water treatment authority, and in Federal and state regulations for more information.**

Always dispose of waste water in accordance with Federal, state and local regulations.

 HUD recommends that when building components are recycled or sold, painted building components should be stripped before re-installation. If components are not stripped, they should never be reinstalled in housing.

Disposal – Federal, State and Local Information

- According to Federal law:
  - In housing: Waste must be disposed of as normal household waste.
  - In non-residential child-occupied facilities: If waste exceeds 220 lbs, treat all debris as hazardous.
- Always check local requirements!

United States
Environmental Protection
Agency

Feb 09   6-10

Waste Disposal Issues

Because EPA considers most residential renovation and remodeling as "routine residential maintenance", the waste generated during these activities is classified as solid, non-hazardous waste, and should be taken to a licensed solid waste landfill. This does not apply to commercial, public or other non-residential child-occupied facilities.

- If you generate any hazardous waste, you should determine whether you generate more than 220 pounds of hazardous waste per job site per month. If you have less than 220 pounds per location per month, manage the waste as solid, non-hazardous waste. If you generate more than 220 pounds of hazardous waste, you should contact your state and local regulators to find out how to properly dispose of it.

- Some **possible** examples of **hazardous waste** include: paint chips; vacuum debris; sludge or chemical waste from strippers; and, HEPA filters.

- Some **possible** examples of **non-hazardous waste** may include: disposable clothing; respirator filters; rugs and carpets; protective sheeting; and, solid components with no peeling paint.

- All waste should be sealed in heavy duty heavy duty plastic bags and handled carefully.

- Large architectural components should be wrapped and sealed in plastic sheeting, and disposed of along with other waste.

- **Always check Federal, state and local requirements before disposing of waste. Some states have enacted more stringent waste management and disposal requirements than Federal regulations. You need to become aware of how Federal, state and local requirements affect the management and disposal of renovation waste in your area.**

Exercise: Cleaning and the Cleaning Verification Procedure

- Work in groups of 2-6.
- Assignments:
  - Skill Set #7: Interior Final Cleaning
  - Skill Set #8: Exterior Final Cleaning
  - Skill Set #9: Bagging Waste
  - Skill Set #10: Visual Inspection
  - Skill Set #11: Cleaning Verification Procedure
- Choose the tools and supplies you need to clean the work area.
- Clean your work area.
- You have 40 minutes.

Feb 09   6-11

Exercise: Cleanup and Cleaning Verification

This exercise gives you a chance to demonstrate cleanup, visual clearance, cleaning verification, and proper waste-bagging techniques. The slide provides basic instruction.

- Stay in your groups of 2 to 6 students, in your work area.
- Choose the right tools. Tools available include buckets, mops, water, detergent, HEPA vacuum, wipes, plastic sheeting, plastic bags, tape, etc.
- Clean up the dust.
- Bag the waste.
- Check your work.
- Verify cleaning.

Skill Set #7: Interior Final Cleaning
Time: 10 minutes
Feb 09

Supplies needed:
- Heavy duty plastic sheeting
- Duct tape
- HEPA vacuum with attachments and a powered beater bar
- Garden sprayer
- Cutting tool (e.g., razor knife, box cutter or scissors)
- Disposable wet cleaning wipes
- Heavy duty plastic bags
- Two-sided mop bucket with wringer (or equivalent), disposable mop heads, long handled mop to which disposable cleaning cloths can be attached; or, a wet mopping system.

Purpose: The purpose of this hands-on exercise is to show students the proper steps for cleaning the interior work area after the completion of the work and prior to the visual inspection and cleaning verification procedure, or a clearance examination.

> ***Note to Instructor:*** *Read the purpose of this activity to students. Remind them that they are trying to completely clean all visible dust and debris in the work area, and that their work will be checked. Remind them that this level of cleanliness is achievable, but does require attention and careful execution.*

- The course instructor should explain all of the steps involved in cleaning the work area. Emphasize to students that there are no short cuts to passing the visual inspection.

- Recommended personal protective equipment during final cleaning activities is a set of disposable coveralls, disposable gloves, and shoe covers.

- If plastic sheeting is not already in place from previous exercises, have plastic sheeting for the floor or carpets put down.

Evaluating the Students: Watch each student follow the steps on the following page. Make corrections and suggestions as the exercise proceeds and determine if additional practice is necessary. Students must complete all required Steps to be "Proficient". Evaluate the work of each student and once the student has completed all required elements of the exercise correctly, record the performance as "Proficient" in the field on the Participant Progress Log that corresponds to Skills Set #7 and that particular student's name.

Skill Set #7: Interior Final Cleaning - Continued

Skills Practice:

Step 1:   Wrap and seal, or bag all components and other large materials and then remove them from the work area.*

Step 2:   Clean off the plastic sheeting using a HEPA vacuum (this procedure is not required, but it is faster than wiping up dust and debris by hand). Mist the plastic sheeting and fold dirty side inward. Either seal the edges of the folded plastic sheeting with tape or place it in a heavy-duty plastic bag. Dispose of the protective sheeting.*

Step 3:   Remove all waste from the work area and place in appropriate waste containers.*

Step 4:   Clean all surfaces within the work area and in the area 2 feet beyond the work area until no dust or debris remains. Start cleaning at the top of the walls and work down toward the floor, HEPA vacuum or wet wipe all wall surfaces in the work area. HEPA vacuum all remaining surfaces in the work area, including furniture and fixtures. Use the upholstery attachment for the window surfaces and the crevice tool along the edge of the walls. Use the HEPA vacuum with a beater bar for carpeting. Work from the end farthest from the work area entrance back to the entrance, making sure never to step back into areas that have already been cleaned.*

Step 5:   Next, wipe all remaining surfaces and objects in the work area except for carpeted and upholstered surfaces, with a disposable wet cleaning wipe. Also mop uncarpeted floors using a two-bucket method or wet mopping system. Work from the end farthest from the work area entrance back to the entrance, making sure never to step back into areas that have already been cleaned. For carpeted areas, conduct a second pass with the HEPA vacuum using the beater bar attachment instead of wiping with a wet cleaning cloth.*

Step 6:   If the property is HUD-regulated, repeat Step 4 for walls, countertops and floors, and then continue to Step 7. Otherwise, continue to Step 7.

Step 7:   After completion of cleaning procedures, check your work. Conduct a careful visual inspection of the work area for visible dust and debris. If visible dust or debris is found, repeat Steps 4 and 5 as needed to make sure no visible dust or debris is present, and then re-check your work with a thorough visual inspection of the work area. When there is no visible dust or debris present, proceed to step 8.*

Step 8:   Notify the Certified Renovator in charge of the project that the work area is ready for visual inspection.*

*Indicates required skills that must be accomplished for a "Proficient" rating.

Skill Set #8: Exterior Final Cleaning

Time: 10 minutes
Feb 09

Supplies needed:
- Heavy duty plastic sheeting
- Heavy duty plastic bags
- Tape (duct, painters, and masking)
- Cutting tool (e.g., razor knife, box cutter or scissors)
- Flashlight.
- Disposable wet cleaning wipes
- HEPA vacuum with attachments
- Two-sided mop bucket with wringer (or equivalent), disposable mop heads, long handled mop to which disposable cleaning cloths can be attached; <u>or</u>, a wet mopping system.

Purpose: The purpose of this hands-on exercise is to show students the proper steps for cleaning an exterior work area after the completion of the work and prior to the visual inspection and (if required) the cleaning verification procedure or a clearance examination.

> **Note to Instructor:** *Read the purpose of this activity to students. Remind them that they are trying to clean all visible dust and debris within the work area, and that their work will be checked. Remind them that this level of cleanliness is achievable, but does require attention and careful execution.*

- The course instructor should explain all of the steps involved in cleaning the work area. Emphasize to students that there are no short cuts to passing the visual inspection.

- Recommended personal protective equipment during cleaning activities is a set of disposable coveralls, disposable gloves, and shoe covers.

- If plastic sheeting is not already in place from previous exercises, have plastic sheeting for the floor or carpets put down.

Evaluating the Students: Watch each student follow the steps on the following page. Make corrections and suggestions as the exercise proceeds and determine if additional practice is necessary. *Option: Have students say the steps as they work.* Students must complete all required Steps to be "Proficient". Evaluate the work of each student and once the student has completed all required elements of the exercise correctly, record the performance as "Proficient" in the field on the Participant Progress Log that corresponds to Skills Set #8 and that particular student's name.

Skill Set #8: Exterior Final Cleaning - Continued

Skills Practice:

Step 1:   Wrap and seal or bag all components and other large materials and then remove them from the work area.*

Step 2:   Clean off the plastic sheeting using a HEPA vacuum (this procedure is not required, but it sure is faster than wiping up dust and debris by hand). Mist the plastic sheeting and fold dirty side inward. Either seal the edges of the plastic sheeting with tape or place it in a heavy-duty plastic bag. Dispose of plastic sheeting.*

Step 3:   Remove all waste from the work area and place in appropriate waste containers.*

Step 4:   Clean all surfaces in the work area and areas within 2 feet beyond the work area until no visible dust, debris, or paint chips remain.*

Suggested Cleaning Procedure For Exterior Cleanable Surfaces: Start cleaning at the top of the walls and work down to the floor, HEPA vacuum or wet wipe all cleanable surfaces in the work area, including furniture and fixtures. Use the HEPA vacuum with the upholstery attachment for windows and use the crevice tool along the walls. Work from the end farthest from the work area entrance back to the entrance, making sure never to step back into areas that have already been cleaned.

Step 5:   After completion of cleaning, check your work. This is done by conducting a careful visual inspection of the work area for visible dust, debris, or paint chips on hard surfaces, and for visible dust, debris, or paint chips in the soil areas under the work area protective sheeting. If dust or debris is found, re-clean, and then re-check your work with a thorough visual inspection of the work area. Once there is no visible dust, debris, or paint chips present, proceed to step 6.*

Step 6:   Notify the Certified Renovator in charge of the project that the work area is ready for visual inspection.*

*Indicates required skills that must be accomplished for a "Proficient" rating.

Skill Set #9: Bagging Waste

<u>Time</u>: **10 minutes**
Feb 09

Supplies needed:

- Used plastic sheeting and used personal protective equipment (from previous exercises)
- Dust and debris (from previous exercises)
- Heavy duty plastic sheeting
- Heavy duty plastic bags
- Cutting tool (e.g., razor knife, box cutter or scissors)
- HEPA vacuum with attachments
- Duct tape

Purpose: The purpose of this hands-on exercise is to show the students the proper steps to bag and gooseneck waste, wrap large pieces of debris, and remove waste from the work area.

> ***Note to Instructor:*** *Read the purpose of this activity to students.*

- **Demonstration:** The course instructor should demonstrate the proper gooseneck technique for sealing waste bags.

- **Optional Bagging Relay Race:** This exercise can be conducted as a relay race. Divide students into teams and have each team member select a waste bag, load it with simulated waste material, make a gooseneck in the waste bag, vacuum the bag and submit it as complete in the simulated waste storage area. This will allow the instructors to observe proficiency in the method of closing the bags and making goosenecks and provides a fun way to learn for the students.

Evaluating the Students: Watch each student make a gooseneck closure on a waste bag. Students must complete all required Steps to be "Proficient". Once the student has completed all required elements of the exercise correctly, record the performance as "Proficient" in the field on the Participant Progress Log that corresponds to Skills Set #9 and that particular student's name.

Skill Set #9: Bagging Waste - Continued

Skills Practice:

Note: This exercise requires that the waste materials generated throughout the exercises be stored in unsealed bags or in sheets of plastic.

Gooseneck Procedure for Waste Bags:

Step 1: Each student should get a waste bag and place some material in it that will be discarded as simulate waste. Do not overfill bags.

Step 2: Gather the open end of the bag just below the opening into one hand.*

Step 3: Twist the bag so that the neck of the bag twists in the same direction and forms an 8"-10" column.*

Step 4: Fold the twisted column over on itself, in a similar manner to how you would fold a hose over onto itself to cut off the flow of water.*

Step 5: Grasp the folded neck of the bag in one hand and wrap tape around the folded neck to secure the fold in place.*

Step 6: Now wrap the tape about 2 or 3 inches from the top of the fold, several times so that the bag cannot come open. The resulting bags neck looks like the neck of a goose folded back on itself (a goose neck seal).*

Step 7: Use the HEPA vacuum to remove any dust from the exterior of the bags. Carry the bags out of the work area to the appropriate waste container.*

Wrapping large pieces of debris:

Step 1: Cut a piece of plastic so that it can be wrapped around the debris to be disposed of.*

Step 2: Once wrapped in plastic, tape the seams of the package.*

Step 3: Wrap tape around the width of the package in three spots to keep the package from unraveling.*

Step 4: Use the HEPA vacuum to remove any dust from the exterior of the package and carry the wrapped debris out of the work area to the appropriate waste container.*

*Indicates required skills that must be accomplished for a "Proficient" rating.

Skill Set #10: Visual Inspection

<u>Time</u>: **5 minutes**
Feb 09

Supplies needed:

- Disposable foot covers
- Flashlight

Purpose: The purpose of this hands-on exercise is to show the students the proper steps for conducting a visual inspection of the work area prior to conduct of the cleaning verification procedure.

> *Note to Instructor: Read the purpose of this activity to students. Remind them that they are trying to verify that all visible dust and debris has been cleaned from the work area. Remind them that this level of cleanliness is achievable, but does require attention and careful execution. Also read the note to the students below.*

> ***Note to Students:*** If a clearance examination is to be performed, the Certified Renovator should still conduct a visual inspection before submitting to the two-part clearance examination. A clearance examination consists of a separate visual inspection and dust wipe testing. The two-part clearance examination is conducted by a Certified Lead Inspector, Certified Lead Risk Assessor, or Certified Sampling Technician.

Demonstration: The course instructor should explain all of the steps involved in performing a visual clearance in the work area. Emphasize to students that there are no short cuts to passing the visual inspection.

Evaluating the Students: Watch each student conduct a visual inspection and listen as they point out problems that must be fixed. Students must complete all required Steps to be "Proficient". Evaluate the work of each student and once the student has completed all required elements of the exercise correctly, record the performance as "Proficient" in the field on the Participant Progress Log that corresponds to Skills Set #10 and that particular student's name.

Skill Set #10: Visual Inspection - Continued

Skills Practice:

Step 1:   Put on disposable foot covers so that you do not track dust and debris into the work area, then enter the work area.*

Step 2:   Turn on all of the lights that are available in the work area. Bring a bright, white-light flashlight to make sure there is adequate lighting.*

Step 3:   Systematically look at every horizontal surface in the work area, working from the farthest area from the entry to the entry without recovering your tracks. Get close to the surfaces you are inspecting.*

Note: Remember this is a visual inspection, but the cleaning verification is going to wipe dust up to compare with the cleaning verification card. If you suspect a surface to be dirty, have it re-cleaned with a wet cleaning cloth.

Step 4:   If you find visible dust or debris, re-clean the work area and repeat step 3.*

Step 5:   Once you have carefully inspected all of the surfaces and have found no dust or debris, proceed to the cleaning verification procedure in Skill Set #11.*

*Indicates required skills that must be accomplished for a "Proficient" rating.

Skill Set #11: Cleaning Verification Procedure

Time: 15 minutes

Feb 09

Supplies needed:
- Baby powder or corn starch
- Disposable foot covers
- Flashlight
- Disposable non-latex gloves
- Disposable wet cleaning wipes
- Cleaning verification card, one per student to take away and retain
- Electrostatically charged, white, disposable cleaning cloths designed for cleaning hard surfaces
- Long-handled mop designed for wet cleaning wipes
- Tape measure
- Watch or clock

Purpose: The purpose of this hands-on exercise is to show the students the proper steps for conducting the cleaning verification procedure.

- The course instructor should explain all of the steps involved in performing the cleaning verification procedure.

Evaluating the Students: Watch each student conduct the cleaning verification procedure and listen as they point out problems that must be fixed. Students must complete all required steps to be "Proficient". Evaluate the work of each student and once the student has completed all required elements of the exercise correctly, record the performance as "Proficient" in the field on the Participant Progress Log that corresponds to Skills Set #11 and that particular student's name.

Skill Set #11: Cleaning Verification Procedure - Continued
Skills Practice:

Step 1:   As you enter the work area put on disposable foot covers so that you do not track dust and debris into the work area.*

Step 2:   Turn on all of the lights that are available in the work area. Make sure there is adequate lighting.*

For window sills:
Step 3:   While wearing gloves, wipe each window sill in the work area with a clean, white, damp cleaning wipe.*

Step 4:   Compare the cleaning wipe to the cleaning verification card. If the first wipe is the same as or whiter (lighter) than the cleaning verification card, the window sill is clean; continue to Step 6. If the first cleaning wipe is not the same as or whiter (lighter) than the cleaning verification card, re-clean the window sill, and, repeat Step 3 and then proceed to Step 5 (skip this step).*

Step 5:   Compare the second cleaning wipe to the cleaning verification card. If the second wipe is the same as or whiter (lighter) than the cleaning verification card, the window sill is clean; continue to Step 6. If the second cleaning wipe is not the same as and not whiter (not lighter) than the cleaning verification card, wait one hour or until the wet surface is dry (for the purposes of this exercise you do not wait). Then re-clean the surface with a dry, electrostatically charged, white, disposable cleaning cloth designed for use on hard surfaces. The window sill is now clean and has completed the cleaning verification procedure.*

For Floors and Countertops:
Step 6:   While wearing gloves, wipe each floor or countertop in the work area with a clean, white, damp cleaning wipe. For floors, use a long handled mop designed to hold a wet cleaning wipe. For floors, wipe no more than 40 square feet per wipe. For countertops wipe the whole surface of the countertop up to 40 square feet per wipe.*

Step 7:   Compare each floor and countertop cleaning wipe to the cleaning verification card. If the first wipe is the same as or whiter (lighter) than the cleaning verification card, the floor or countertop is clean. If the first cleaning wipe is not the same as and not whiter (not lighter) than the cleaning verification card, re-clean the floor section or countertop section, wipe the floor or countertop section with a wet cleaning wipe, and repeat Step 6 for that section and proceed to Step 8 (skip this step).*

Step 8:   Compare the second floor or countertop cleaning wipe to the cleaning verification card. If the second wipe is the same as or whiter (lighter) than the cleaning verification card, the floor or countertop section has been adequately cleaned. If the second cleaning wipe is not the same as and not whiter (not lighter) than the cleaning verification card, wait one hour or until the wet surface is dry (for the purposes of this exercise you do not wait). Then re-clean the surface with a dry, electrostatically charged, white, disposable cleaning cloth designed for use on hard surfaces. The floor or countertop section is now clean and has completed the cleaning verification procedure.*

Step 9:   Once the cleaning verification shows that all areas have been adequately cleaned, remove the signs and critical barriers around the work area.*

*Indicates required skills that must be accomplished for a "Proficient" rating

Now You Know...

- How to clean the work area systematically.
- How to check the effectiveness of cleaning.
- How to perform a visual inspection of the work area.
- How to perform the cleaning verification procedure.
- How to release the work area for clearance testing.
- How to properly dispose of waste.

Feb 09

6-12

The information on the slide above summarizes the topics covered in this module.

Module 7: Recordkeeping

Module 7: Recordkeeping

Overview:

- **In this section, you will learn about records required for each job.**
- **Records must be retained and made available to EPA, upon request, for 3 years following completion of renovation.**

Feb 09

7-1

Language of the RRP Rule is:

"Firms performing renovations must retain and, if requested, make available to EPA, all records necessary to demonstrate compliance…for a period of three years following completion of the renovation."

 HUD also has a 3-year record retention requirement for notices, evaluations, and clearance or abatement reports (24 CFR 35.175).

On-The-Job Records

- **Copies of Certified Firm and Certified Renovator certifications (must be kept on site).**
- **Lead-based paint testing results when an EPA-recognized test kit is used.**
- **Proof of owner/occupant pre-renovation education.**
- **Opt out certification by owner/occupant, when they qualify to and decide to opt out of the lead-safe work practice requirements.**
- **Non-certified worker training documentation (must be kept on site).**

♻EPA
United States
Environmental Protection
Agency

Feb 09   7-2

The Certified Firm must designate (in writing) a Certified Renovator to be responsible for each renovation job in target housing or a child-occupied facility. This is the logical person to organize and maintain on-the-job records during the work. On the jobsite, the records should be kept in a safe, secure, clean and dry place. Once the project is complete, some records can be filed with other firm records while others may need to be moved to the next job site.

Records to be maintained on site include:
- Copy of Certified Firm and Certified Renovator(s) certifications.
- Non-certified worker training documentation.

Records to be maintained to document the job:
- Copy of Certified Firm and Certified Renovator(s) certifications.
- Non-certified worker training documentation.
- Designation of a Certified Renovator to the job.
- Information on and results of use of EPA-recognized test kits provided by a Certified Renovator who acted as the representative of the Certified Firm at the job site and who conducted testing for the presence of lead-based paint on surfaces to be affected by the renovation.
- Lead-based paint inspection reports provided by a Certified Lead Inspector or Certified Lead Risk Assessor, if applicable.
- Proof of owner/occupant pre-renovation education
- Opt-out certification by owner-occupant, when they qualify to, and decide to, opt-out of lead safe work practice requirements.
- Any other signed and dated documents from the owner(s) and/or residents regarding conduct of the renovation and requirements in the EPA RRP Rule.
- All reports required from the Certified Firm and the Certified Renovator by the EPA RRP Rule.

Recordkeeping: Pre-Renovation Education Records

In Target Housing – Individual units:
- Must acquire either written proof of receipt by an adult occupant or proof of delivery/unsuccessful delivery of *Renovate Right, or*:
- Written proof of receipt of *Renovate Right* by owner or proof of mailing (if mailing, send 7 days prior to renovation).

In Target Housing - Common Areas (Two Options):
- Provide written notification to each affected unit and make *Renovate Right* pamphlet available on request; or:
- Keep copies or pictures of the signs and notices posted.

In Child-Occupied Facilities
- Written proof of receipt of *Renovate Right* by owner or proof of mailing required (If mailing, send 7 days prior to renovation).
- Maintain proof of receipt by owner or adult representative, or certify in writing that the *Renovate Right* pamphlet has been delivered to facility.
- Keep copies or pictures of the signs and notices posted.

Feb 09

&EPA
United States
Environmental Protection
Agency

7-3

In addition to the requirements above, maintain all records for pre-renovation education activities that contain information about the following:

In Target Housing – Individual Units:

- When contacts with the owner and occupants were attempted.

- Written proof of when contacts were made.

In Target Housing – Common Areas:

- Documentation of when and to whom written notification was delivered for each unit affected.

- What notices were posted, and when and where they were posted.

In Child-Occupied Facilities:

- When contacts with the owner and occupants were attempted.

- Written proof of when contacts were made.

- Whether and when contact was made with the owner or adult representative of the child-occupied facility.

- What notices were posted, and when and where they were posted.

Sample Confirmation of Receipt of *Renovate Right*

❏ **I have received a copy of the pamphlet, *Renovate Right: Important Lead Hazard Information for Families, Child Care Providers and Schools.***

Recipient Signature:_____ Printed Name: _____ Date:__/__/__

Self-Certification Option (for tenant-occupied dwellings only) - If the lead pamphlet was delivered but a tenant signature was not obtainable, you may check the appropriate box below.

❏ **Refusal to sign.**

❏ **Unavailable for signature.**

Gather the following information:

- Printed name and signature of person certifying lead pamphlet delivery.
- Date and time of lead pamphlet delivery.
- Unit address.

&EPA
United States
Environmental Protection
Agency

Feb 09

7-4

Future Sample Pre-Renovation Form

This sample form may be used by firms to document compliance with the requirements of the Federal Lead-Based Paint Renovation, Repair, and Painting Program after April 2010.

Occupant Confirmation

Pamphlet Receipt

—I have received a copy of the lead hazard information pamphlet informing me of the potential risk of the lead hazard exposure from renovation activity to be performed in my dwelling unit. I received this pamphlet before the work began.

Owner-occupant Opt-out Acknowledgment

—(A) I confirm that I own and live in this property, that no child under the age of 6 resides here, that no pregnant woman resides here, and that this property is not a child-occupied facility.

Note: A child resides in the primary residence of his or her custodial parents, legal guardians, foster parents, or informal caretaker if the child lives and sleeps most of the time at the caretaker's residence.

Note: A child-occupied facility is a pre-1978 building visited regularly by the same child, under 6 years of age, on at least two different days within any week, for at least 3 hours each day, provided that the visits total at least 60 hours annually.

If Box A is checked, check either Box B or Box C, but not both.

—(B) I request that the renovation firm use the lead-safe work practices required by EPA's Lead-Based Paint Renovation, Repair, and Painting Rule; or

—(C) I understand that the firm performing the renovation will not be required to use the lead-safe work practices required by EPA's Lead-Based Paint Renovation, Repair, and Painting Rule.

_____

Printed Name of Owner-occupant

_____   _____

Signature of Owner-occupant   Signature Date

Renovator's Self Certification Option (for tenant-occupied dwellings only)
Instructions to Renovator: If the lead hazard information pamphlet was delivered but a tenant signature was not obtainable, you may check the appropriate box below.

—**Declined** – I certify that I have made a good faith effort to deliver the lead hazard information pamphlet to the rental dwelling unit listed below at the date and time indicated and that the occupant declined to sign the confirmation of receipt. I further certify that I have left a copy of the pamphlet at the unit with the occupant.

—**Unavailable for signature** – I certify that I have made a good faith effort to deliver the lead hazard information pamphlet to the rental dwelling unit listed below and that the occupant was unavailable to sign the confirmation of receipt. I further certify that I have left a copy of the pamphlet at the unit by sliding it under the door or by (fill in how pamphlet was left). _____

_____   _____

Printed Name of Person Certifying Delivery   Attempted Delivery Date

_____

Signature of Person Certifying Lead Pamphlet Delivery

_____

Unit Address

Note Regarding Mailing Option — As an alternative to delivery in person, you may mail the lead hazard information pamphlet to the owner and/or tenant. Pamphlet must be mailed at least 7 days before renovation. Mailing must be documented by a certificate of mailing from the post office.

Sample Forms (continued)

Renovation Notice — *For use in notifying tenants of renovations in common areas of multi-family housing.*

The following renovation activities will take place in the following locations:

_____

Activity *(e.g., sanding, window replacement)*

_____

Location *(e.g., lobby, recreation center)*

The expected starting date is _____ and the expected ending date is _____.
Because this is an older building built before 1978, some of the paint disturbed during the renovation
may contain lead. You may obtain a copy of the pamphlet, *Protect Your Family From Lead in Your
Home,* by telephoning me at _____ . Please leave a message and be sure to include your
name, phone number and address. I will either mail you a pamphlet or slide one under your door.

_____   _____
Date   Printed name of renovator

_____
Signature of renovator

Record of Tenant Notification Procedures — *Procedures Used For Delivering Notices to Tenants of
Renovations in Common Areas*

Project Address:_____

Street (apt. #)_____

City _____   State_____ Zip Code _____

_____   _____
Owner of multi-family housing   Number of dwelling units

_____
Method of delivering notice forms *(e.g. delivery to units, delivery to mailboxes of units)*

_____
Name of person delivering notices

_____   _____
Signature of person delivering notices   Date of Delivery

Recordkeeping: Non-Certified Worker Training

- Worker's name.
- Description of lead safe work practices the worker is trained to perform.
- Completed and signed skills evaluation checklists.
- Date(s) of training.
- Name and signature of the Certified Renovator who conducted the training.

$EPA
United States
Environmental Protection
Agency

Feb 09

7-5

Documentation of Non-Certified Renovation Worker Training

The Certified Renovator who conducted the non-certified worker training must document the information taught to, and skill set proficiencies achieved by, each individual trainee. This training can be conducted in a classroom setting with simulated hands-on or on the job. Documentation may vary for each trainee as not all trainees may be assigned to conduct all lead-safe work practices and the training is only required to be task specific.

To simplify this documentation, your training manual includes a form that can be adapted for documenting hands-on and topical training for non-certified workers (See Appendix 6).

Recordkeeping: Test Kit Reporting

If an EPA-recognized test kit is used to test surfaces in the work area, the firm must:

- Submit a report to the person contracting for the work within 30 days after the end of the renovation, containing:
  - Manufacturer and model of the EPA-recognized test kit.
  - A description of of the components tested.
  - The location of components tested.
  - Results of the testing.
- Retain a copy of the test kit documentation form.

United States
Environmental Protection
Agency

Feb 09   7-6

Checking for Lead-Based Paint With EPA-Recognized Test Kits:
- Check www.epa.gov for a list of EPA-recognized test kits.
- Each component to be renovated or impacted by renovation must be tested. If all surfaces are found to be free of lead-based paint, the RRP Rule does not apply.
- If a set of affected components make up an integrated whole (such as a stair tread or riser within a single staircase; or, a window casing, apron, stool, header or trough in a window case system), then only one of the individual components from that set needs to be tested.

EPA-Recognized Test Kits:
- Until September 1, 2010, EPA is only requiring the use of test kits that determine that lead-based paint is not present on the surfaces tested. If a color change does not occur, lead-safe work practices are not required. If a color change occurs, while the change does not with certainty mean that lead-based paint is present, the surface must be presumed to be coated with lead-based paint.
- To be EPA-recognized after September 1, 2010, a test kit must be able to identify lead-based paint. At that time, a test kit positive test result will mean that lead-based paint is present in the coating and that lead-safe work practices must be followed when that surface is disturbed. A negative test result will mean that lead safe-work practices are not required. These kits may be available as early as September 2009.
- If the test kit positive indicator is present on any of the tested surfaces, lead-safe work practices must be used. Alternatively, sampling may be performed by a Certified Lead Inspector or Risk Assessor to prove by laboratory analysis that lead-based paint is not present.
- Certified Renovators must use an EPA-recognized test kit to test affected surfaces. EPA-recognized test kits are listed on the EPA website at www.epa.gov.

Reporting:
- When test kits are used, within 30 days of completing the renovation, the Certified Renovation firm must provide information on test kit manufacturers and models used for testing, a description of components tested including locations, and the results of testing, to the client who contracted for the renovation.
- Retain a copy of the test kit documentation form.

Recordkeeping: Post-Renovation Reporting

- At the end of each renovation, the Certified Renovator must sign a report including the following information:
  - Name of Certified Renovator assigned to lead the project;
  - Copy of Certified Renovator certification(s);
  - Certification from a Certified Renovator of non-certified worker training, and a list of the topics covered;
  - Certification of posting of warning signs;
  - Description of chemical spot testing, if any performed;
  - Certification by the Certified Renovator of work area containment, on-site waste containment and transport, proper post renovation work area cleaning, and of successful cleaning verification.
  - Clearance report, if performed.

Feb 09

7-7

Post-Renovation Reporting

The end of renovation report should describe the whole project from posting signs to cleaning verification or clearance. The report should name the Certified Renovator designated by the Certified Firm as responsible for lead-safe work practices on that project. Also include proof of certification for the designated Certified Renovator. The report also must have a signed statement from the Certified Renovator that covers the following areas:

- Proof of non-certified worker training;
- Proof of posting warning signs;
- Description of results from used of EPA-recognized chemical spot test kits;
- Description of work area containment;
- Description of on-site waste containment and transport;
- Proof of proper post-renovation work area cleaning;
- Records of inspections and/or risk assessments conducted by Certified Lead Inspectors or Risk Assessors, if applicable.
- Proof of successful cleaning verification.

If dust clearance sampling is performed in lieu of cleaning verification, provide a copy of the dust sampling report to the person who contracted for the renovation within 30 days of the completion of the renovation (see 40 CFR 745.86(d)).

Future Sample Renovation Recordkeeping Checklist

(effective April 2010)

Name of Firm:_____

Date and Location of Renovation:_____

Brief Description of Renovation:_____

Name of Assigned Renovator:_____

Name(s) of Trained Worker(s), if used: _____

Name of Dust Sampling Technician,
Inspector, or Risk Assessor, if used:_____

— Copies of renovator and dust sampling technician qualifications (training certificates, certifications) on file.
— Certified renovator provided training to workers on (check all that apply):
   — Posting warning signs   — Setting up plastic containment barriers
   — Maintaining containment   — Avoiding spread of dust to adjacent areas
   — Waste handling   — Post-renovation cleaning
   — Test kits used by certified renovator to determine whether lead was present on components affected
      by renovation (identify kits used and describe sampling locations and results):

   _____

— Warning signs posted at entrance to work area.
— Work area contained to prevent spread of dust and debris
   — All objects in the work area removed or covered (interiors)
   — HVAC ducts in the work area closed and covered (interiors)
   — Windows in the work area closed (interiors)
   — Windows in and within 20 feet of the work area closed (exteriors)
   — Doors in the work area closed and sealed (interiors)
   — Doors in and within 20 feet of the work area closed and sealed (exteriors)
   — Doors that must be used in the work area covered to allow passage but prevent spread of dust
   — Floors in the work area covered with taped-down plastic (interiors)
   — Ground covered by plastic extending 10 feet from work area—plastic anchored to building and
      weighed down by heavy objects (exteriors)
   — If necessary, vertical containment installed to prevent migration of dust and debris to adjacent
      property (exteriors)
— Waste contained on-site and while being transported off-site
— Work site properly cleaned after renovation
   — All chips and debris picked up, protective sheeting misted, folded dirty side inward, and taped for
      removal
   — Work area surfaces and objects cleaned using HEPA vacuum and/or wet cloths or mops (interiors)

— Certified renovator performed post-renovation cleaning verification (describe results, including the
   number of wet and dry cloths used): _____

   _____

   —If dust clearance testing was performed instead, attach a copy of report.

— I certify under penalty of law that the above information is true and complete.

_____   _____

Name and title   Date

Now You Know...

- To have records available at the work site of:
  - Training of Certified Renovators and non-certified renovation workers.
  - Certifications for the Certified Firm and Certified Renovators.
- To retain all records for at least 3 years after completion of the renovation.
- To keep records of:
  - Training and certifications for all renovation personnel, and for certification of the firm.
  - Distribution of required information.
  - Communications with and certifications from owners and residents.
  - Work activities in compliance to the Rule.
  - Post-renovation reports.

Feb 09

7-8

Module 8: Training Non-Certified Renovation Workers

Module 8: Training Non-Certified Renovation Workers

Certified Renovators are responsible for teaching lead-safe work practices to non-certified renovation workers.

Feb 09

8-1

The RRP Rule requires that you, the Certified Renovator, be responsible for instruction of non-certified renovation workers.

Teaching Lead Safe Work Practices Means:

- Training workers to properly use signs, dust barriers, dust minimizing work practices, and dust cleanup practices during the course of renovation, repair, and painting activities to prevent and/or reduce potentially dangerous dust-lead contamination in the home.

- To effectively train workers you need to:
  - Know lead safety yourself.
  - Show students what you know.
  - Review the shopping list in *Steps to LEAD SAFE Renovation, Repair, and Painting* and have appropriate materials at hand.

Feb 09

8-2

- Remember all the skills you mastered during the Skill Set exercises? You will be teaching non-certified workers to master them.
- The shopping list at the end of *Steps to LEAD SAFE Renovation, Repair and Painting* details all of the equipment and supplies you may need to conduct hands-on exercises during on-the-job training of non-certified renovators.
- All that follows is presented to aid you in conduct of the training.

The Role of the Certified Renovator

Certified Renovators:

- Perform lead safe work as described in the RRP Rule.
- Train all non-certified workers in lead safe practices.
- Provide onsite and regular direction for all non-certified workers during setup and cleanup.
- Are available by phone when not physically present at the work site during work.
- Maintain onsite proof of certification as a Certified Renovator and training records for all non-certified renovation workers.

EPA
United States
Environmental Protection
Agency

Feb 09   8-3

What Are the Responsibilities of a Certified Renovator? Certified Renovators are responsible for ensuring overall compliance with Renovation, Repair, and Painting Program requirements for lead-safe work practices at renovations to which they are assigned.

A Certified Renovator:

1. Must use an EPA-recognized test kit, when requested by the party contracting for renovation services, to determine whether components to be affected by the renovation contain lead-based paint (EPA will announce which test kits are "recognized" prior to April 2010. See www.epa.gov/lead).

2. Must provide lead-safe work practices training to non-certified workers so those workers can perform assigned tasks safely. This training can be provided by the Certified Renovator on-the-job or in the classroom, provided adequate hands-on practice is available. This training could also be conducted by a third party although the instructor must be a Certified Renovator.

3. Must be physically present at the work site when warning signs are posted, while the work area containment is being established, and while the work area cleaning is performed. (*Note: Use the terms Setup and Cleanup to describe this work*).

4. Must monitor work being performed by non-certified individuals to ensure that lead-safe work practices are being followed. This includes maintaining the integrity of the containment barriers and ensuring that no dust or debris migrates from the work area.

5. Must be available, either on-site or by telephone, at all times during performance of the renovation.

6. Must perform project cleaning verification.

7. Must have copies of their initial course completion certificate and their most recent refresher course completion certificate at the work site. Certification as a Certified Renovator lasts for 5 years. The Certified Renovator must take a refresher course every 5 years in order to maintain certification.

8. Must prepare required work documentation.

The EPA Renovation, Repair, and Painting Rule is found at 40 CFR 745.85 (a) and (b).

Role of Trained, Non-Certified Renovation Workers

- Trained, non-certified renovation workers are persons, working on renovation, repair and painting jobs who have had on-the-job training or similar classroom training from a Certified Renovator to perform tasks in conformance to the EPA RRP Rule.
- They must perform lead-safe work practices as described in the RRP rule:
  - Protect the home by "setting up" the work area.
  - Protect themselves.
  - Perform renovation work safely.
    - Prohibited Practices must not be used.
    - Control dust and debris.
  - Clean the work area.

United States
Environmental Protection
Agency

Feb 09

8-4

On-the-job training must be provided for each worker and for each job to the extent that each worker is adequately trained for the tasks he or she will be performing. This training may occur while the worker is engaged in productive work, which provides knowledge and skills essential to the full and adequate performance of the job. However, work conducted during training must be in full compliance with the RRP Rule.

Trainees will benefit by seeing the "Steps" to lead safety found in *Steps to LEAD SAFE Renovation, Repair and Painting* in Appendix 5 (this document is also referred to as the "*Steps Guide*"). It contains a seven step primer on lead safety and can be used as a field text to hand out to non-certified worker trainees in the field. In the "Steps Guide", steps 2 through 6 contain information specific to work performed by non-certified personnel, while step 1 and step 7 contain information on testing painted surfaces and cleaning verification which are Certified Renovator responsibilities. Step 7 also discusses clearance examination which is performed only by Certified Lead Inspectors, Certified Lead Risk Assessors, and Certified Dust Sampling Technicians.

The information in the "Steps Guide" can be covered in about 5 minutes per Step and then reinforced by on-the-job practical exercises such as setting up barriers and signs, demonstrations of cleaning procedures, etc. It is recommended that the material in the "Steps Guide" be covered in a toolbox (on-site) meeting format with handouts on the specific information to be covered.

It is very important that non-certified personnel be allowed to participate in hands-on learning as work progresses and that skill sets that are learned by each student are documented. Documentation is required by the RRP Rule to assure that non-certified workers are trained to perform renovation activities to which they are assigned. Remember that the RRP Rule requires all non-certified personnel on the job to be given skills training specific to the tasks that they will perform on the job and that each person's training must be documented by topic area covered in the on-the-job training that is performed. The required documentation will be discussed in more detail later.

Steps for Teaching Lead Safety During Renovations

- **Approach to training non-certified renovators**

United States
Environmental Protection
Agency

Feb 09   8-5

Training for non-certified renovation workers can be delivered in one session covering all 7 Steps or the information can be covered in a series of "toolbox" meetings over the course of several days. You should spend about 5-10 minutes on the information contained in each "Step" and then conduct on-the-job training to teach the skills needed to renovate lead safely.

If this training is offered in the classroom, Slides 8-6 through 8-15 could be used to teach the material found in the *Steps to LEAD SAFE Renovation, Repair, and Painting*. This document is included as Appendix 5 of your student manual. Use the *Steps to LEAD SAFE Renovation, Repair, and Painting* as a student handout for training non-certified renovation workers. The handout should also include write-ups of demonstrations and practical hands-on exercises, and a checklist of desired skills to reinforce the "toolbox" talks or classroom training. During either "toolbox" talks or classroom instruction, have non-certified renovator trainees refer to the training handout while you teach the information.

Use the "Steps" Guide

- *Steps to LEAD SAFE Renovation, Repair and Painting* covers basic lead safe practices and can be used as a training guide outside of the classroom in conjunction with on-the-job demonstrations and hands-on training.
- It is strongly recommended that you use this guide as a basis for training.

⬥EPA
United States
Environmental Protection
Agency

Feb 09

8-6

Before You Train: Print copies of *Steps to LEAD SAFE Renovation, Repair, and Painting* and give one copy to each non-certified renovator trainee.

Step 1: Determine If the Job Involves Lead-Based Paint

- Lead-based paint (LBP) is found many older homes:
  - 1960-1978 homes – 1 in 4 have LBP.
  - 1940-1960 homes – 7 in 10 have LBP.
  - Pre-1940 homes – 9 in 10 have LBP.
- Renovation, repair or painting that disturbs lead-based paint can create significant lead-based paint hazards in homes.
- Just a little lead-based paint dust can poison kids, their parents and pets, and can cause problems for pregnant women and their unborn children.
- The Certified Renovator will determine if lead-based paint is present on work surfaces.
- If information about lead-based paint is not available for a pre-1978 homes or a child-occupied facility, assume that lead-based paint is present and use lead-safe work practices.

EPA
United States
Environmental Protection
Agency

Feb 09   8-7

During Training:
Review the information on this slide with the non-certified renovator students as they follow along on pages 4 & 5 of the *Steps to LEAD SAFE Renovation, Repair, and Painting*.

Notes to the On-The-Job Instructor: This information is included in the on-the-job training so non-certified renovators will understand why they need to use lead-safe work practices. Non-certified renovators are not required to determine whether lead-based paint is present, but they should understand that when it is identified as present, generating dust can cause significant problems if not properly and safely controlled.

More information:
- Review pages 4 and 5 of the *Steps to LEAD SAFE Renovation, Repair and Painting*.

Step 2: Set It Up Safely

- **Containment is used to keep dust IN the work area and non-workers OUT!**
- **Signs and barriers are used to limit access.**
- **Inside versus outside jobs**
  - **Review all procedures and differences in setup.**

Feb 09

8-8

What To Do

To keep the dust in, and people out, of your work area, you will need to take slightly different steps for inside or outside jobs.

For Inside Jobs

- Place signs, barrier tape, and/or cones to keep all non-workers, especially children, out of the work area. Keep pets out of the work area for their safety and to prevent them from tracking dust and debris throughout the home.

- Remove furniture and belongings from the work area. If an item is too large or too heavy to move, cover it with heavy plastic sheeting and tape the sheeting securely in place.

- Use heavy plastic sheeting to cover floors in the work area to a minimum of 6 feet from the area of paint disturbance. Close and seal doors, close windows.

- Close and cover air vents in the work area. This will keep dust from getting into the system and moving through the home.

For Outside Jobs

- Keep non-workers away from the work area by marking it off with signs, tape and/or cones. Have owner keep pets out of the work area.

- Cover the ground and plants with heavy plastic sheeting to catch debris. The covering should extend at least 10 feet out from the building. Secure the covering to the exterior.

- Close windows and doors within 20 feet of the work area to keep dust and debris from going into the home.

- Move (if possible) or cover play areas and equipment within 20 feet of the work area.

Step 2: Set It Up Safely – Continued

Review special setup for "dustier" jobs, including:

- **Demolition.**
- **Opening up wall cavities.**
- **Removing old drop ceilings.**
- **Paint scraping/dry hand sanding.**

Feb 09   8-9

Some jobs create more dust than can be contained by the methods described on the previous page. Certified Renovators should exercise their judgment as to whether those methods provide sufficient containment or if additional precautions are necessary. Jobs that typically require additional precautions include:

- Demolition.
- Opening up wall cavities.
- Removing old drop ceilings.
- Paint scraping/dry hand sanding.

These jobs call for additional steps to contain dust inside the work area. In addition to the practices reviewed so far, consider the following:

- Turning off forced-air heating and air-conditioning systems. This will keep dust from circulating through the house.
- Interior vertical containment to limit the size of the work area.

Step 3: Protect Yourself

- **Without the right personal protective equipment (PPE) workers can swallow and inhale lead from the job, and can carry lead on their skin and work clothes home to their families.**
- **Review the "shopping list."**
- **Advise workers to:**
  - Protect eyes.
  - Keep clothes clean or use disposable clothing.
  - Wear a respirator. The appropriate respirator keeps lead out of the lungs and stomach.
  - Wash-up each time they leave the work area and especially at the end of the day. **EPA**
    United States
    Environmental Protection
    Agency

Feb 09   8-10

Protect your Eyes.
- Always wear safety goggles or safety glasses when scraping, hammering, etc.

Wear protective clothing and consider wearing gloves.
- Protective clothing and shoe covers are very important in preventing "take home" lead and to prevent you from tracking lead out of the work area. They can also help prevent contamination of areas that have already been cleaned during final cleanup.
- Keep clothes clean. At the end of the work day, vacuum off dust or change out of dusty clothes. Do not use compressed air to blow dust off clothing. Wash dirty work clothes separately from household laundry.
- Wear a painter's hat to protect your head from dust and debris.
- Gloves are not required by the RRP Rule, but they also help prevent ingestion exposures to lead.

Wear respiratory protection.
- When work creates dust or paint chips, employers should consider respiratory protection, such as a N-100 disposable respirator, to prevent workers from breathing leaded dust.

Post warning signs.
- Post a warning sign at each work area entrance.
- Signs should read: "Warning, Lead Work Area, Poison, No Smoking or Eating" to remind workers that eating, drinking and smoking in the work area is prohibited.

Wash up.
- Workers should wash their hands and faces each time they stop work. It is especially important to wash up before eating and at the end of the day.

Note: OSHA rules may require employers to take further steps to protect the health of workers on the job.

Step 4: Control the Spread of Dust

- The goal is to control the spread of dust that is created.
- Review the "shopping list."
- Use the right tools.
- Disposable plastic drop cloths control the spread of dust and debris.
- Avoid prohibited practices.

Feb 09
8-11

Control the spread of dust.
- Keep the work area closed off from the rest of the home.
- Don't track dust and debris out of the work area.
- Stay in the contained work area and on the contained paths.
- Vacuum off suits when exiting the work area so the dust stays inside containment.
- Remove disposable shoe covers and make sure your shoes are clean by using tack pads or damp paper towels to wipe off your shoes each time you step off the protective sheeting.
- Keep components in the work area until they are wrapped securely in heavy plastic sheeting or bagged in heavy duty plastic bags. Once wrapped or bagged, HEPA vacuum the exterior and remove them from the work area and store them in a safe area away from residents.
- Launder non-disposable protective clothing separate from family laundry.
- Do not use Prohibited Practices, including:
    - Open-flame burning or high heat removal of paint, and,
    - Power tools such as sanders without HEPA attachments.

 The HUD Rule also prohibits extensive dry scraping and sanding <u>by hand</u>, use of heat guns that char paint and paint stripping in a poorly ventilated space using a volatile paint stripper. States, localities or tribes may prohibit additional work practices.

Step 5: Leave the Work Area Clean

- The goal should be to leave the work area completely free of dust and debris.
- Review the "shopping list."
- Discuss daily cleaning procedures.
- Discuss end of job cleaning procedures.

United States
Environmental Protection
Agency

Feb 09

8-12

On a daily basis, pick up the work area (recommended).
- Pick up as you go. Put trash in heavy-duty plastic bags.
- Vacuum the work area with a HEPA vacuum several times during the day and for sure at the end of the day. <u>Do not clean with standard household or shop vacuum cleaners. Use only HEPA vacuums.</u>
- Clean tools at the end of the day.
- Wash your hands each time you leave the work area and especially well before you go home.
- Dispose of all disposable personal protective clothing daily.

When the job is complete, clean the work area (required).
- Carefully remove plastic sheeting on the floor, fold it with the dirty side in, tape the edges shut or seal it in a heavy duty plastic bag, and dispose of it. Keep plastic sheeting in doorways and openings that separate the work area from non-work areas in place until the work area is released as clean.
- Make sure all paint chips, dust, trash and debris, including building components, are removed from the area to be cleaned and disposed of properly.
- HEPA vacuum or wet wipe all wall surfaces. HEPA vacuum all other surfaces in the work area. Use a beater bar attachment on carpets.
- Wet wipe all remaining surfaces in the work area and wet mop all uncarpeted floors until dust and debris are removed.
- Visually inspect your work. Look around the work area and two feet beyond, and on paths where debris was carried. You should see no dust, paint chips or debris.
- Re-clean the area thoroughly if you find dust or debris.

Step 6: Control the Waste

- Discuss the waste bagging procedure.
- Demonstrate folding a small section of plastic with the dirty side turned in.
- Discuss temporary storage of waste.
- Discuss how to deal with waste water appropriately.
- Discuss waste disposal rules that apply to the specific job.

♺EPA
United States
Environmental Protection
Agency

Feb 09   8-13

Bag or wrap your waste at the work site and in the work area.

Collect and control all your waste. This includes dust, debris, paint chips, protective sheeting, HEPA filters, dirty water, clothes, mop heads, wipes, protective clothing, respirators, gloves, architectural components, and other waste. Use heavy plastic sheeting or bags to collect waste. Gooseneck seal the bag with duct tape. Consider double bagging waste to prevent tears. Large components should be wrapped in protective sheeting and sealed with tape. Bag and seal all waste before removing it from the work area. HEPA vacuum the exterior of waste bags and bundles before removing them from the work area. Store all waste in a secure container or dumpster until disposal. Limit on-site storage time. Avoid transporting waste in an open truck or a personal vehicle.

Dispose of waste water appropriately.

Water used in the work area to remove paint or to clean surfaces should be filtered through a 0.5 micron filter. Never dump this water down a sink or tub, in a storm drain, or on the ground. It may be dumped in a toilet if local rules allow. If local regulations do not allow this, you may be required to contain and test the water, and contact a waste disposal company to assist you with disposal. **Check with your local water treatment authority, and in Federal and state regulations for more information.**

Be aware of waste disposal rules.

EPA considers most residential renovation, repair and painting activities "routine residential maintenance." The waste generated by these activities is classified as solid, non-hazardous waste and can be disposed of in an ordinary waste landfill. Some states and localities have more stringent waste disposal requirements that must be followed.

Step 7: Cleaning Verification or Clearance Testing

- Cleaning verification will be performed by a Certified Renovator after most renovations.
- A clearance examination may be requested in place of cleaning verification by the owner, and is required in some cases.
- Discuss what happens when cleaning verification and/or clearance is not passed.

United States
Environmental Protection
Agency

Feb 09   8-14

When all the cleaning is complete, and before the space is reoccupied, a cleaning verification procedure or clearance examination must be conducted to make sure leaded dust is not left behind. If the HUD Rule applies, a clearance examination is required in place of the cleaning verification procedure. The first step to both cleaning verification and a clearance examination is a visual inspection of the work area to determine if dust or debris was left behind. If dust or debris are present in the work area, cleaning must be repeated and the visual inspection repeated until the work area is free of visible dust and debris. Once the visual inspection by the Certified Renovator is complete, either the cleaning verification procedure or clearance examination can proceed.

Training Documentation

- **The Certified Renovator assigned to the job must maintain at the job site the following records for on-the-job training :**
  - Written certification of worker training:
    - Must show which workers have what training;
    - Must list all training topics covered for each worker; and,
    - Must be signed by the Certified Renovator who did the training.
  - All training documentation must be kept for 3 years following completion of the renovation.

 United States Environmental Protection Agency

Feb 09

8-15

When you give this "toolbox training", use of a training guide, such as *Steps to LEAD SAFE Renovation, Repair and Painting*, will make documentation easier. You should keep a copy of the training guide used at the "toolbox" training you conduct on-site. Make a list of each lead safe practical skill covered for each individual non-certified worker. A list of the practical skills taught to each non-certified worker with the material covered in the toolbox meetings will provide adequate documentation to meet RRP Rule requirements.

Now You Know...

- That Certified Renovators are responsible for training non-certified renovation workers.
- The roles of Certified Renovators and trained, non-certified workers during conduct of a renovation.
- How to use *Steps to LEAD SAFE Renovation, Repair and Painting* to train non-certified renovation workers.

United States
Environmental Protection
Agency

Feb 09

8-16

Appendix 1:

EPA's Renovation, Repair, and Painting Program Final Rule (40 CFR Part 745)

Tuesday,
April 22, 2008

Part II

Environmental Protection Agency

40 CFR Part 745
Lead; Renovation, Repair, and Painting
Program; Lead Hazard Information
Pamphlet; Notice of Availability; Final
Rule

EPA will recognize those kits that meet certain performance standards for limited false positives and negatives. EPA will also recognize only those kits that have been properly validated by a laboratory independent of the kit manufacturer. For most kits, this will mean participating in EPA's Environmental Technology Verification (ETV) program. With stakeholder input, EPA is adapting a voluntary consensus standard, ASTM's "Standard Practice for Evaluating the Performance Characteristics of Qualitative Chemical Spot Test Kits for Lead in Paint" (Ref. 28), for use as a testing protocol to determine whether a particular kit has met the performance standards established in this final rule.

J. Environmental Justice

Executive Order 12898, entitled *Federal Actions to Address Environmental Justice in Minority Populations and Low-Income Populations* (59 FR 7629, February 16, 1994) establishes federal executive policy on environmental justice. Its main provision directs federal agencies, to the greatest extent practicable and permitted by law, to make environmental justice part of their mission by identifying and addressing, as appropriate, disproportionately high and adverse human health or environmental effects of their programs, policies, and activities on minority populations and low-income populations in the United States.

EPA has assessed the potential impact of this rule on minority and low-income populations. The results of this assessment are presented in the Economic Analysis, which is available in the public docket for this rulemaking (Ref. 24). As a result of this assessment, the Agency has determined that this final rule will not have disproportionately high and adverse human health or environmental effects on minority or low-income populations because it increases the level of environmental protection for all affected populations without having any disproportionately high and adverse human health or environmental effects on any population, including any minority or low-income population.

VI. Congressional Review Act

The Congressional Review Act, 5 U.S.C. 801 *et seq.*, as added by the Small Business Regulatory Enforcement Fairness Act of 1996, generally provides that before a rule may take effect, the agency promulgating the rule must submit a rule report, which includes a copy of the rule, to each House of the Congress and to the Comptroller General

of the United States. EPA will submit a report containing this rule and other required information to the U.S. Senate, the U.S. House of Representatives, and the Comptroller General of the United States prior to publication of the rule in the **Federal Register**. A major rule cannot take effect until 60 days after it is published in the **Federal Register**. This action is a "major rule" as defined by 5 U.S.C. 804(2). This rule is effective June 23, 2008.

List of Subjects in 40 CFR Part 745

Environmental protection, Child-occupied facility, Housing renovation, Lead, Lead-based paint, Renovation, Reporting and recordkeeping requirements.

Dated: March 31, 2008,

Steven L. Johnson,

Administrator.

■ Therefore, 40 CFR chapter I is amended as follows:

PART 745—[AMENDED]

■ 1. The authority citation for part 745 continues to read as follows:

Authority: 15 U.S.C. 2605, 2607, 2681-2692 and 42 U.S.C. 4852d.

■ 2. Section 745.80 is revised to read as follows:

§ 745.80 Purpose.

This subpart contains regulations developed under sections 402 and 406 of the Toxic Substances Control Act (15 U.S.C. 2682 and 2686) and applies to all renovations performed for compensation in target housing and child-occupied facilities. The purpose of this subpart is to ensure the following:

(a) Owners and occupants of target housing and child-occupied facilities receive information on lead-based paint hazards before these renovations begin; and

(b) Individuals performing renovations regulated in accordance with § 745.82 are properly trained; renovators and firms performing these renovations are certified; and the work practices in § 745.85 are followed during these renovations.

■ 3. Section 745.81 is revised to read as follows:

§ 745.81 Effective dates.

(a) *Training, certification and accreditation requirements and work practice standards.* The training, certification and accreditation requirements and work practice standards are applicable in any State or Indian Tribal area that does not have a renovation program that is authorized under subpart Q of this

part. The training, certification and accreditation requirements and work practice standards in this subpart will become effective as follows:

(1) *Training programs.* Effective June 23, 2008, no training program may provide, offer, or claim to provide training or refresher training for EPA certification as a renovator or a dust sampling technician without accreditation from EPA under § 745.225 Training programs may apply for accreditation under § 745.225 beginning April 22, 2009.

(2) *Firms.* (i) Firms may apply for certification under § 745.89 beginning October 22, 2009.

(ii) On or after April 22, 2010, no firm may perform, offer, or claim to perform renovations without certification from EPA under § 745.89 in target housing or child-occupied facilities, unless the renovation qualifies for one of the exceptions identified in § 745.82(a) or (c).

(3) *Individuals.* On or after April 22, 2010, all renovations must be directed by renovators certified in accordance with § 745.90(a) and performed by certified renovators or individuals trained in accordance with § 745.90(b)(2) in target housing or child-occupied facilities, unless the renovation qualifies for one of the exceptions identified in § 745.82(a) or (c).

(4) *Work practices.* On or after April 22, 2010, all renovations must be performed in accordance with the work practice standards in § 745.85 and the associated recordkeeping requirements in § 745.86(b)(6) and (b)(7) in target housing or child-occupied facilities, unless the renovation qualifies for one of the exceptions identified in § 745.82(a) or (c).

(5) The suspension and revocation provisions in § 745.91 are effective April 22, 2010.

(b) *Renovation-specific pamphlet.* Before December 22, 2008, renovators or firms performing renovations in States and Indian Tribal areas without an authorized program may provide owners and occupants with either of the following EPA pamphlets: *Protect Your Family From Lead in Your Home* or *Renovate Right: Important Lead Hazard Information for Families, Child Care Providers and Schools.* After that date, *Renovate Right: Important Lead Hazard Information for Families, Child Care Providers and Schools* must be used exclusively.

(c) *Pre-Renovation Education Rule.* With the exception of the requirement to use the pamphlet entitled *Renovate Right: Important Lead Hazard Information for Families, Child Care roviders and Schools*, the provisions of he Pre-Renovation Education Rule in his subpart have been in effect since une 1999.

4. Section 745.82 is revised to read as ollows:

745.82 Applicability.

(a) This subpart applies to all enovations performed for ompensation in target housing and hild-occupied facilities, except for the ollowing:

(1) Renovations in target housing or hild-occupied facilities in which a written determination has been made by an inspector or risk assessor (certified oursuant to either Federal regulations at 745.226 or a State or Tribal ertification program authorized oursuant to § 745.324) that the omponents affected by the renovation re free of paint or other surface oatings that contain lead equal to or in xcess of 1.0 milligrams/per square entimeter (mg/cm²) or 0.5% by weight, where the firm performing the enovation has obtained a copy of the etermination.

(2) Renovations in target housing or hild-occupied facilities in which a ertified renovator, using an EPA ertified renovator, using an EPA ecognized test kit as defined in § 745.83 nd following the kit manufacturer's nstructions, has tested each component ffected by the renovation and etermined that the components are free of paint or other surface coatings that ontain lead equal to or in excess of 1.0 ng/cm² or 0.5% by weight. If the omponents make up an integrated whole, such as the individual stair reads and risers of a single staircase, he renovator is required to test only one of the individual components, unless he individual components appear to ave been repainted or refinished eparately.

(b) The information distribution equirements in § 745.84 do not apply to mergency renovations, which are enovation activities that were not olanned but result from a sudden, unexpected event (such as non-routine ailures of equipment) that, if not mmediately attended to, presents a afety or public health hazard, or hreatens equipment and/or property with significant damage. Interim ontrols performed in response to an levated blood lead level in a resident hild are also emergency renovations. 'mergency renovations other than nterim controls are also exempt from he warning sign, containment, waste andling, training, and certification equirements in §§ 745.85, 745.89, and '45.90 to the extent necessary to espond to the emergency. Emergency

renovations are not exempt from the cleaning requirements of § 745.85(a)(5), which must be performed by certified renovators or individuals trained in accordance with § 745.90(b)(2), the cleaning verification requirements of § 745.85(b), which must be performed by certified renovators, and the recordkeeping requirements of § 745.86(b)(6) and (b)(7).

(c) The training requirements in § 745.90 and the work practice standards for renovation activities in § 745.85 apply to all renovations covered by this subpart, except for renovations in target housing for which the firm performing the renovation has obtained a statement signed by the owner that the renovation will occur in the owner's residence, no child under age 6 resides there, no pregnant woman resides there, the housing is not a child-occupied facility, and the owner acknowledges that the renovation firm will not be required to use the work practices contained in EPA's renovation, repair, and painting rule. For the purposes of this section, a child resides in the primary residence of his or her custodial parents, legal guardians, and foster parents. A child also resides in the primary residence of an informal caretaker if the child lives and sleeps most of the time at the caretaker's residence.

■ 5. Section 745.83 is amended as follows:

■ a. Remove the definitions of "Emergency renovation operations" and "Multi-family housing."

■ b. Revise the definitions of "Pamphlet," "Renovation," and "Renovator."

■ c. Add 13 definitions in alphabetical order.

§ 745.83 Definitions.

*   *   *   *   *

Child-occupied facility means a building, or portion of a building, constructed prior to 1978, visited regularly by the same child, under 6 years of age, on at least two different days within any week (Sunday through Saturday period), provided that each day's visit lasts at least 3 hours and the combined weekly visits last at least 6 hours, and the combined annual visits last at least 60 hours. Child-occupied facilities may include, but are not limited to, day care centers, preschools and kindergarten classrooms. Child-occupied facilities may be located in target housing or in public or commercial buildings. With respect to common areas in public or commercial buildings that contain child-occupied facilities, the child-occupied facility encompasses only those common areas

that are routinely used by children under age 6, such as restrooms and cafeterias. Common areas that children under age 6 only pass through, such as hallways, stairways, and garages are not included. In addition, with respect to exteriors of public or commercial buildings that contain child-occupied facilities, the child-occupied facility encompasses only the exterior sides of the building that are immediately adjacent to the child-occupied facility or the common areas routinely used by children under age 6.

Cleaning verification card means a card developed and distributed, or otherwise approved, by EPA for the purpose of determining, through comparison of wet and dry disposable cleaning cloths with the card, whether post-renovation cleaning has been properly completed.

Component or building component means specific design or structural elements or fixtures of a building or residential dwelling that are distinguished from each other by form, function, and location. These include, but are not limited to, interior components such as: Ceilings, crown molding, walls, chair rails, doors, door trim, floors, fireplaces, radiators and other heating units, shelves, shelf supports, stair treads, stair risers, stair stringers, newel posts, railing caps, balustrades, windows and trim (including sashes, window heads, jambs, sills or stools and troughs), built in cabinets, columns, beams, bathroom vanities, counter tops, and air conditioners; and exterior components such as: Painted roofing, chimneys, flashing, gutters and downspouts, ceilings, soffits, fascias, rake boards, cornerboards, bulkheads, doors and door trim, fences, floors, joists, lattice work, railings and railing caps, siding, handrails, stair risers and treads, stair stringers, columns, balustrades, windowsills or stools and troughs, casings, sashes and wells, and air conditioners.

Dry disposable cleaning cloth means a commercially available dry, electrostatically charged, white disposable cloth designed to be used for cleaning hard surfaces such as uncarpeted floors or counter tops.

Firm means a company, partnership, corporation, sole proprietorship or individual doing business, association, or other business entity; a Federal, State, Tribal, or local government agency; or a nonprofit organization.

HEPA vacuum means a vacuum cleaner which has been designed with a high-efficiency particulate air (HEPA) filter as the last filtration stage. A HEPA filter is a filter that is capable of capturing particles of 0.3 microns with 99.97% efficiency. The vacuum cleaner must be designed so that all the air drawn into the machine is expelled through the HEPA filter with none of the air leaking past it.

Interim controls means a set of measures designed to temporarily reduce human exposure or likely exposure to lead-based paint hazards, including specialized cleaning, repairs, maintenance, painting, temporary containment, ongoing monitoring of lead-based paint hazards or potential hazards, and the establishment and operation of management and resident education programs.

Minor repair and maintenance activities are activities, including minor heating, ventilation or air conditioning work, electrical work, and plumbing, that disrupt 6 square feet or less of painted surface per room for interior activities or 20 square feet or less of painted surface for exterior activities where none of the work practices prohibited or restricted by § 745.85(a)(3) are used and where the work does not involve window replacement or demolition of painted surface areas. When removing painted components, or portions of painted components, the entire surface area removed is the amount of painted surface disturbed. Jobs, other than emergency renovations, performed in the same room within the same 30 days must be considered the same job for the purpose of determining whether the job is a minor repair and maintenance activity.

Pamphlet means the EPA pamphlet titled *Renovate Right: Important Lead Hazard Information for Families, Child Care Providers and Schools* developed under section 406(a) of TSCA for use in complying with section 406(b) of TSCA, or any State or Tribal pamphlet approved by EPA pursuant to 40 CFR 745.326 that is developed for the same purpose. This includes reproductions of the pamphlet when copied in full and without revision or deletion of material from the pamphlet (except for the addition or revision of State or local sources of information). Before December 22, 2008, the term "pamphlet" also means any pamphlet developed by EPA under section 406(a) of TSCA or any State or Tribal pamphlet approved by EPA pursuant to § 745.326.

* * * * *

Recognized test kit means a commercially available kit recognized by EPA under § 745.88 as being capable of allowing a user to determine the presence of lead at levels equal to or in excess of 1.0 milligrams per square centimeter, or more than 0.5% lead by weight, in a paint chip, paint powder, or painted surface.

Renovation means the modification of any existing structure, or portion thereof, that results in the disturbance of painted surfaces, unless that activity is performed as part of an abatement as defined by this part (40 CFR 745.223). The term renovation includes (but is not limited to): The removal, modification or repair of painted surfaces or painted components (e.g., modification of painted doors, surface restoration, window repair, surface preparation activity (such as sanding, scraping, or other such activities that may generate paint dust)); the removal of building components (e.g., walls, ceilings, plumbing, windows); weatherization projects (e.g., cutting holes in painted surfaces to install blown-in insulation or to gain access to attics, planing thresholds to install weather-stripping), and interim controls that disturb painted surfaces. A renovation performed for the purpose of converting a building, or part of a building, into target housing or a child-occupied facility is a renovation under this subpart. The term renovation does not include minor repair and maintenance activities.

Renovator means an individual who either performs or directs workers who perform renovations. A certified renovator is a renovator who has successfully completed a renovator course accredited by EPA or an EPA-authorized State or Tribal program.

Training hour means at least 50 minutes of actual learning, including, but not limited to, time devoted to lecture, learning activities, small group activities, demonstrations, evaluations, and hands-on experience.

Wet disposable cleaning cloth means a commercially available, pre-moistened white disposable cloth designed to be used for cleaning hard surfaces such as uncarpeted floors or counter tops.

Wet mopping system means a device with the following characteristics: A long handle, a mop head designed to be used with disposable absorbent cleaning pads, a reservoir for cleaning solution, and a built-in mechanism for distributing or spraying the cleaning solution onto a floor, or a method of equivalent efficacy.

Work area means the area that the certified renovator establishes to contain the dust and debris generated by a renovation.

§ 745.84 [Removed]

■ 6. Section 745.84 is removed.

§ 745.85 [Redesignated as § 745.84]

■ 7. Section 745.85 is redesignated as § 745.84.

■ 8. Newly designated § 745.84 is amended as follows:

■ a. Revise the introductory text of paragraph (a) and revise paragraph (a)(2)(i).

■ b. Revise the introductory text of paragraph (b) and revise paragraphs (b)(2) and (b)(4).

■ c. Redesignate paragraph (c) as paragraph (d).

■ d. Add a new paragraph (c).

■ e. Revise the introductory text of newly designated paragraph (d).

§ 745.84 Information distribution requirements.

(a) *Renovations in dwelling units.* No more than 60 days before beginning renovation activities in any residential dwelling unit of target housing, the firm performing the renovation must:

* * * * *

(2) * * *

(i) Obtain, from the adult occupant, a written acknowledgment that the occupant has received the pamphlet; or certify in writing that a pamphlet has been delivered to the dwelling and that the firm performing the renovation has been unsuccessful in obtaining a written acknowledgment from an adult occupant. Such certification must include the address of the unit undergoing renovation, the date and method of delivery of the pamphlet, names of the persons delivering the pamphlet, reason for lack of acknowledgment (e.g., occupant refuses to sign, no adult occupant available), the signature of a representative of the firm performing the renovation, and the date of signature.

* * * * *

(b) *Renovations in common areas.* No more than 60 days before beginning renovation activities in common areas of multi-unit target housing, the firm performing the renovation must:

* * * * *

(2) *Comply with one of the following.* (i) Notify in writing, or ensure written notification of, each affected unit and make the pamphlet available upon request prior to the start of renovation. Such notification shall be accomplished by distributing written notice to each affected unit. The notice shall describe the general nature and locations of the planned renovation activities; the expected starting and ending dates; and a statement of how the occupant can obtain the pamphlet, at no charge, from the firm performing the renovation, or

(ii) While the renovation is ongoing, post informational signs describing the general nature and locations of the renovation and the anticipated completion date. These signs must be posted in areas where they are likely to be seen by the occupants of all of the affected units. The signs must be accompanied by a posted copy of the pamphlet or information on how interested occupants can review a copy of the pamphlet or obtain a copy from the renovation firm at no cost to occupants.

*   *   *   *   *

(4) If the scope, locations, or expected starting and ending dates of the planned renovation activities change after the initial notification, and the firm provided written initial notification to each affected unit, the firm performing the renovation must provide further written notification to the owners and occupants providing revised information on the ongoing or planned activities. This subsequent notification must be provided before the firm performing the renovation initiates work beyond that which was described in the original notice.

(c) *Renovations in child-occupied facilities.* No more than 60 days before beginning renovation activities in any child-occupied facility, the firm performing the renovation must:

(1)(i) Provide the owner of the building with the pamphlet, and comply with one of the following:

(A) Obtain, from the owner, a written acknowledgment that the owner has received the pamphlet.

(B) Obtain a certificate of mailing at least 7 days prior to the renovation.

(ii) If the child-occupied facility is not the owner of the building, provide an adult representative of the child-occupied facility with the pamphlet, and comply with one of the following:

(A) Obtain, from the adult representative, a written acknowledgment that the adult representative has received the pamphlet; or certify in writing that a pamphlet has been delivered to the facility and that the firm performing the renovation has been unsuccessful in obtaining a written acknowledgment from an adult representative. Such certification must include the address of the child-occupied facility undergoing renovation, the date and method of delivery of the pamphlet, names of the persons delivering the pamphlet, reason for lack of acknowledgment (e.g., representative refuses to sign), the signature of a representative of the firm performing the renovation, and the date of signature.

(B) Obtain a certificate of mailing at least 7 days prior to the renovation.

(2) Provide the parents and guardians of children using the child-occupied facility with the pamphlet and information describing the general nature and locations of the renovation and the anticipated completion date by complying with one of the following:

(i) Mail or hand-deliver the pamphlet and the renovation information to each parent or guardian of a child using the child-occupied facility.

(ii) While the renovation is ongoing, post informational signs describing the general nature and locations of the renovation and the anticipated completion date. These signs must be posted in areas where they can be seen by the parents or guardians of the children frequenting the child-occupied facility. The signs must be accompanied by a posted copy of the pamphlet or information on how interested parents or guardians can review a copy of the pamphlet or obtain a copy from the renovation firm at no cost to the parents or guardians.

(3) The renovation firm must prepare, sign, and date a statement describing the steps performed to notify all parents and guardians of the intended renovation activities and to provide the pamphlet.

(d) *Written acknowledgment.* The written acknowledgments required by paragraphs (a)(1)(i), (a)(2)(i), (b)(1)(i), (c)(1)(i)(A), and (c)(1)(ii)(A) of this section must:

*   *   *   *   *

■ 9. Section 745.85 is added to subpart E to read as follows:

§ 745.85   Work practice standards.

(a) *Standards for renovation activities.* Renovations must be performed by certified firms using certified renovators as directed in § 745.89. The responsibilities of certified firms are set forth in § 745.89(d) and the responsibilities of certified renovators are set forth in § 745.90(b).

(1) *Occupant protection.* Firms must post signs clearly defining the work area and warning occupants and other persons not involved in renovation activities to remain outside of the work area. To the extent practicable, these signs must be in the primary language of the occupants. These signs must be posted before beginning the renovation and must remain in place and readable until the renovation and the post-renovation cleaning verification have been completed. If warning signs have been posted in accordance with 24 CFR 35.1345(b)(2) or 29 CFR 1926.62(m), additional signs are not required by this section.

(2) *Containing the work area.* Before beginning the renovation, the firm must isolate the work area so that no dust or debris leaves the work area while the renovation is being performed. In addition, the firm must maintain the integrity of the containment by ensuring that any plastic or other impermeable materials are not torn or displaced, and taking any other steps necessary to ensure that no dust or debris leaves the work area while the renovation is being performed. The firm must also ensure that containment is installed in such a manner that it does not interfere with occupant and worker egress in an emergency.

(i) *Interior renovations.* The firm must:

(A) Remove all objects from the work area, including furniture, rugs, and window coverings, or cover them with plastic sheeting or other impermeable material with all seams and edges taped or otherwise sealed.

(B) Close and cover all ducts opening in the work area with taped-down plastic sheeting or other impermeable material.

(C) Close windows and doors in the work area. Doors must be covered with plastic sheeting or other impermeable material. Doors used as an entrance to the work area must be covered with plastic sheeting or other impermeable material in a manner that allows workers to pass through while confining dust and debris to the work area.

(D) Cover the floor surface, including installed carpet, with taped-down plastic sheeting or other impermeable material in the work area 6 feet beyond the perimeter of surfaces undergoing renovation or a sufficient distance to contain the dust, whichever is greater.

(E) Use precautions to ensure that all personnel, tools, and other items, including the exteriors of containers of waste, are free of dust and debris before leaving the work area.

(ii) *Exterior renovations.* The firm must:

(A) Close all doors and windows within 20 feet of the renovation. On multi-story buildings, close all doors and windows within 20 feet of the renovation on the same floor as the renovation, and close all doors and windows on all floors below that are the same horizontal distance from the renovation.

(B) Ensure that doors within the work area that will be used while the job is being performed are covered with plastic sheeting or other impermeable material in a manner that allows workers to pass through while confining dust and debris to the work area.

(C) Cover the ground with plastic sheeting or other disposable impermeable material extending 10 feet beyond the perimeter of surfaces undergoing renovation or a sufficient distance to collect falling paint debris, whichever is greater, unless the property line prevents 10 feet of such ground covering.

(D) In certain situations, the renovation firm must take extra precautions in containing the work area to ensure that dust and debris from the renovation does not contaminate other buildings or other areas of the property or migrate to adjacent properties.

(3) *Prohibited and restricted practices.* The work practices listed below shall be prohibited or restricted during a renovation as follows:

(i) Open-flame burning or torching of lead-based paint is prohibited.

(ii) The use of machines that remove lead-based paint through high speed operation such as sanding, grinding, power planing, needle gun, abrasive blasting, or sandblasting, is prohibited unless such machines are used with HEPA exhaust control.

(iii) Operating a heat gun on lead-based paint is permitted only at temperatures below 1100 degrees Fahrenheit.

(4) *Waste from renovations*—(i) Waste from renovation activities must be contained to prevent releases of dust and debris before the waste is removed from the work area for storage or disposal. If a chute is used to remove waste from the work area, it must be covered.

(ii) At the conclusion of each work day and at the conclusion of the renovation, waste that has been collected from renovation activities must be stored under containment, in an enclosure, or behind a barrier that prevents release of dust and debris out of the work area and prevents access to dust and debris.

(iii) When the firm transports waste from renovation activities, the firm must contain the waste to prevent release of dust and debris.

(5) *Cleaning the work area.* After the renovation has been completed, the firm must clean the work area until no dust, debris or residue remains.

(i) *Interior and exterior renovations.* The firm must:

(A) Collect all paint chips and debris and, without dispersing any of it, seal this material in a heavy-duty bag.

(B) Remove the protective sheeting. Mist the sheeting before folding it, fold the dirty side inward, and either tape shut to seal or seal in heavy-duty bags. Sheeting used to isolate contaminated rooms from non-contaminated rooms must remain in place until after the cleaning and removal of other sheeting. Dispose of the sheeting as waste.

(ii) *Additional cleaning for interior renovations.* The firm must clean all objects and surfaces in the work area and within 2 feet of the work area in the following manner, cleaning from higher to lower:

(A) *Walls.* Clean walls starting at the ceiling and working down to the floor by either vacuuming with a HEPA vacuum or wiping with a damp cloth.

(B) *Remaining surfaces.* Thoroughly vacuum all remaining surfaces and objects in the work area, including furniture and fixtures, with a HEPA vacuum. The HEPA vacuum must be equipped with a beater bar when vacuuming carpets and rugs.

(C) Wipe all remaining surfaces and objects in the work area, except for carpeted or upholstered surfaces, with a damp cloth. Mop uncarpeted floors thoroughly, using a mopping method that keeps the wash water separate from the rinse water, such as the 2-bucket mopping method, or using a wet mopping system.

(b) *Standards for post-renovation cleaning verification*—(1) *Interiors.* (i) A certified renovator must perform a visual inspection to determine whether dust, debris or residue is still present. If dust, debris or residue is present, these conditions must be removed by re-cleaning and another visual inspection must be performed.

(ii) After a successful visual inspection, a certified renovator must:

(A) Verify that each windowsill in the work area has been adequately cleaned, using the following procedure.

(*1*) Wipe the windowsill with a wet disposable cleaning cloth that is damp to the touch. If the cloth matches or is lighter than the cleaning verification card, the windowsill has been adequately cleaned.

(*2*) If the cloth does not match and is darker than the cleaning verification card, re-clean the windowsill as directed in paragraphs (a)(5)(ii)(B) and (a)(5)(ii)(C) of this section, then either use a new cloth or fold the used cloth in such a way that an unused surface is exposed, and wipe the surface again. If the cloth matches or is lighter than the cleaning verification card, that windowsill has been adequately cleaned.

(*3*) If the cloth does not match and is darker than the cleaning verification card, wait for 1 hour or until the surface has dried completely, whichever is longer.

(*4*)After waiting for the windowsill to dry, wipe the windowsill with a dry disposable cleaning cloth. After this wipe, the windowsill has been adequately cleaned.

(B) Wipe uncarpeted floors and countertops within the work area with a wet disposable cleaning cloth. Floors must be wiped using anapplication device with a long handle and a head to which the cloth is attached. The cloth must remain damp at all times while it is being used to wipe the surface for post-renovation cleaning verification. If the surface within the work area is greater than 40 square feet, the surface within the work area must be divided into roughly equal sections that are each less than 40 square feet. Wipe each such section separately with a new wet disposable cleaning cloth. If the cloth used to wipe each section of the surface within the work area matches the cleaning verification card, the surface has been adequately cleaned.

(*1*) If the cloth used to wipe a particular surface section does not match the cleaning verification card, re-clean that section of the surface as directed in paragraphs (a)(5)(ii)(B) and (a)(5)(ii)(C) of this section, then use a new wet disposable cleaning cloth to wipe that section again. If the cloth matches the cleaning verification card, that section of the surface has been adequately cleaned.

(*2*) If the cloth used to wipe a particular surface section does not match the cleaning verification card after the surface has been re-cleaned, wait for 1 hour or until the entire surface within the work area has dried completely, whichever is longer.

(*3*) After waiting for the entire surface within the work area to dry, wipe each section of the surface that has not yet achieved post-renovation cleaning verification with a dry disposable cleaning cloth. After this wipe, that section of the surface has been adequately cleaned.

(iii) When the work area passes the post-renovation cleaning verification, remove the warning signs.

(2) *Exteriors.* A certified renovator must perform a visual inspection to determine whether dust, debris or residue is still present on surfaces in and below the work area, including windowsills and the ground. If dust, debris or residue is present, these conditions must be eliminated and another visual inspection must be performed. When the area passes the visual inspection, remove the warning signs.

(c) *Optional dust clearance testing.* Cleaning verification need not be performed if the contract between the renovation firm and the person contracting for the renovation or another Federal, State, Territorial, Tribal, or local law or regulation requires:

(1) The renovation firm to perform dust clearance sampling at the conclusion of a renovation covered by this subpart.

(2) The dust clearance samples are required to be collected by a certified inspector, risk assessor or dust sampling technician.

(3) The renovation firm is required to re-clean the work area until the dust clearance sample results are below the clearance standards in § 745.227(e)(8) or any applicable State, Territorial, Tribal, or local standard.

(d) *Activities conducted after post-renovation cleaning verification.* Activities that do not disturb paint, such as applying paint to walls that have already been prepared, are not regulated by this subpart if they are conducted after post-renovation cleaning verification has been performed.

10. Section 745.86 is revised to read as follows:

§ 745.86 Recordkeeping and reporting requirements.

(a) Firms performing renovations must retain and, if requested, make available to EPA all records necessary to demonstrate compliance with this subpart for a period of 3 years following completion of the renovation. This 3–year retention requirement does not supersede longer obligations required by other provisions for retaining the same documentation, including any applicable State or Tribal laws or regulations.

(b) Records that must be retained pursuant to paragraph (a) of this section shall include (where applicable):

(1) Reports certifying that a determination had been made by an inspector (certified pursuant to either Federal regulations at § 745.226 or an EPA-authorized State or Tribal certification program) that lead-based paint is not present on the components affected by the renovation, as described in § 745.82(b)(1).

(2) Signed and dated acknowledgments of receipt as described in § 745.84(a)(1)(i), (a)(2)(i), (b)(1)(i), (c)(1)(i)(A), and (c)(1)(ii)(A).

(3) Certifications of attempted delivery as described in § 745.84(a)(2)(i) and (c)(1)(ii)(A).

(4) Certificates of mailing as described in § 745.84(a)(1)(ii), (a)(2)(ii), (b)(1)(ii), (c)(1)(i)(B), and (c)(1)(ii)(B).

(5) Records of notification activities performed regarding common area renovations, as described in § 745.84(b)(3) and (b)(4), and renovations in child-occupied facilities, as described in § 745.84(c)(2).

(6) Any signed and dated statements received from owner-occupants documenting that the requirements of § 745.85 do not apply. These statements must include a declaration that the renovation will occur in the owner's residence, a declaration that no children under age 6 reside there, a declaration that no pregnant woman resides there, a declaration that the housing is not a child-occupied facility, the address of the unit undergoing renovation, the owner's name, an acknowledgment by the owner that the work practices to be used during the renovation will not necessarily include all of the lead-safe work practices contained in EPA's renovation, repair, and painting rule, the signature of the owner, and the date of signature. These statements must be written in the same language as the text of the renovation contract, if any.

(7) Documentation of compliance with the requirements of § 745.85, including documentation that a certified renovator was assigned to the project, that the certified renovator provided on-the-job training for workers used on the project, that the certified renovator performed or directed workers who performed all of the tasks described in § 745.85(a), and that the certified renovator performed the post-renovation cleaning verification described in § 745.85(b). If the renovation firm was unable to comply with all of the requirements of this rule due to an emergency as defined in § 745.82, the firm must document the nature of the emergency and the provisions of the rule that were not followed. This documentation must include a copy of the certified renovator's training certificate, and a certification by the certified renovator assigned to the project that:

(i) Training was provided to workers (topics must be identified for each worker).

(ii) Warning signs were posted at the entrances to the work area.

(iii) If test kits were used, that the specified brand of kits was used at the specified locations and that the results were as specified.

(iv) The work area was contained by:

(A) Removing or covering all objects in the work area (interiors).

(B) Closing and covering all HVAC ducts in the work area (interiors).

(C) Closing all windows in the work area (interiors) or closing all windows in and within 20 feet of the work area (exteriors).

(D) Closing and sealing all doors in the work area (interiors) or closing and sealing all doors in and within 20 feet of the work area (exteriors).

(E) Covering doors in the work area that were being used to allow passage but prevent spread of dust.

(F) Covering the floor surface, including installed carpet, with taped-down plastic sheeting or other impermeable material in the work area 6 feet beyond the perimeter of surfaces undergoing renovation or a sufficient distance to contain the dust, whichever is greater (interiors) or covering the ground with plastic sheeting or other disposable impermeable material anchored to the building extending 10 feet beyond the perimeter of surfaces undergoing renovation or a sufficient distance to collect falling paint debris, whichever is greater, unless the property line prevents 10 feet of such ground covering, weighted down by heavy objects (exteriors).

(G) Installing (if necessary) vertical containment to prevent migration of dust and debris to adjacent property (exteriors).

(v) Waste was contained on-site and while being transported off-site.

(vi) The work area was properly cleaned after the renovation by:

(A) Picking up all chips and debris, misting protective sheeting, folding it dirty side inward, and taping it for removal.

(B) Cleaning the work area surfaces and objects using a HEPA vacuum and/or wet cloths or mops (interiors).

(vii) The certified renovator performed the post-renovation cleaning verification (the results of which must be briefly described, including the number of wet and dry cloths used).

(c) When test kits are used, the renovation firm must, within 30 days of the completion of the renovation, provide identifying information as to the manufacturer and model of the test kits used, a description of the components that were tested including their locations, and the test kit results to the person who contracted for the renovation.

(d) If dust clearance sampling is performed in lieu of cleaning verification as permitted by § 745.85(c), the renovation firm must provide, within 30 days of the completion of the renovation, a copy of the dust sampling report to the person who contracted for the renovation.

11. Section 745.87 is amended by revising paragraph (e) to read as follows:

§ 745.87 Enforcement and inspections.

* * * * *

(e) Lead-based paint is assumed to be present at renovations covered by this subpart. EPA may conduct inspections and issue subpoenas pursuant to the provisions of TSCA section 11 (15 U.S.C. 2610) to ensure compliance with this subpart.

■ 12. Section 745.88 is revised to read as follows:

§ 745.88 Recognized test kits.

(a) Effective June 23, 2008, EPA recognizes the test kits that have been determined by National Institute of Standards and Technology research to meet the negative response criteria described in paragraph (c)(1) of this section. This recognition will last until EPA publicizes its recognition of the first test kit that meets both the negative response and positive response criteria in paragraph (c) of this section.

(b) No other test kits will be recognized until they are tested through EPA's Environmental Technology Verification Program or other equivalent EPA approved testing program.

(1) Effective September 1, 2008, to initiate the testing process, a test kit manufacturer must submit a sufficient number of kits, along with the instructions for using the kits, to EPA. The test kit manufacturer should first visit the following website for information on where to apply:*http://www.epa.gov/etv/howtoapply.html*.

(2) After the kit has been tested through the Environmental Technology Verification Program or other equivalent approved EPA testing program, EPA will review the report to determine whether the required criteria have been met.

(3) Before September 1, 2010, test kits must meet only the negative response criteria in paragraph (c)(1) of this section. The recognition of kits that meet only this criteria will last until EPA publicizes its recognition of the first test kits that meets both of the criteria in paragraph (c) of this section.

(4) After September 1, 2010, test kits must meet both of the criteria in paragraph (c) of this section.

(5) If the report demonstrates that the kit meets the required criteria, EPA will issue a notice of recognition to the kit manufacturer, provide them with the report, and post the information on EPA's website.

(6) If the report demonstrates that the kit does not meet the required criteria, EPA will notify the kit manufacturer and provide them with the report.

(c) *Response criteria*—(1) *Negative response criteria.* For paint containing lead at or above the regulated level, 1.0 mg/cm^2 or 0.5% by weight, a demonstrated probability (with 95% confidence) of a negative response less than or equal to 5% of the time.

(2) *Positive response criteria.* For paint containing lead below the regulated level, 1.0 mg/cm^2 or 0.5% by weight, a demonstrated probability (with 95% confidence) of a positive

response less than or equal to 10% of the time.

■ 13. Section 745.89 is added to subpart E to read as follows:

§ 745.89 Firm certification.

(a) *Initial certification.* (1) Firms that perform renovations for compensation must apply to EPA for certification to perform renovations or dust sampling. To apply, a firm must submit to EPA a completed "Application for Firms," signed by an authorized agent of the firm, and pay at least the correct amount of fees. If a firm pays more than the correct amount of fees, EPA will reimburse the firm for the excess amount.

(2) After EPA receives a firm's application, EPA will take one of the following actions within 90 days of the date the application is received:

(i) EPA will approve a firm's application if EPA determines that it is complete and that the environmental compliance history of the firm, its principals, or its key employees does not show an unwillingness or inability to maintain compliance with environmental statutes or regulations. An application is complete if it contains all of the information requested on the form and includes at least the correct amount of fees. When EPA approves a firm's application, EPA will issue the firm a certificate with an expiration date not more than 5 years from the date the application is approved. EPA certification allows the firm to perform renovations covered by this section in any State or Indian Tribal area that does not have a renovation program that is authorized under subpart Q of this part.

(ii) EPA will request a firm to supplement its application if EPA determines that the application is incomplete. If EPA requests a firm to supplement its application, the firm must submit the requested information or pay the additional fees within 30 days of the date of the request.

(iii) EPA will not approve a firm's application if the firm does not supplement its application in accordance with paragraph (a)(2)(ii) of this section or if EPA determines that the environmental compliance history of the firm, its principals, or its key employees demonstrates an unwillingness or inability to maintain compliance with environmental statutes or regulations. EPA will send the firm a letter giving the reason for not approving the application. EPA will not refund the application fees. A firm may reapply for certification at any time by filing a new, complete application that includes the correct amount of fees.

(b) *Re-certification.* To maintain its certification, a firm must be re-certified by EPA every 5 years.

(1) *Timely and complete application.* To be re-certified, a firm must submit a complete application for re-certification. A complete application for re-certification includes a completed "Application for Firms" which contains all of the information requested by the form and is signed by an authorized agent of the firm, noting on the form that it is submitted as a re-certification. A complete application must also include at least the correct amount of fees. If a firm pays more than the correct amount of fees, EPA will reimburse the firm for the excess amount.

(i) An application for re-certification is timely if it is postmarked 90 days or more before the date the firm's current certification expires. If the firm's application is complete and timely, the firm's current certification will remain in effect until its expiration date or until EPA has made a final decision to approve or disapprove the re-certification application, whichever is later.

(ii) If the firm submits a complete re-certification application less than 90 days before its current certification expires, and EPA does not approve the application before the expiration date, the firm's current certification will expire and the firm will not be able to conduct renovations until EPA approves its re-certification application.

(iii) If the firm fails to obtain recertification before the firm's current certification expires, the firm must not perform renovations or dust sampling until it is certified anew pursuant to paragraph (a) of this section.

(2) *EPA action on an application.* After EPA receives a firm's application for re-certification, EPA will review the application and take one of the following actions within 90 days of receipt:

(i) EPA will approve a firm's application if EPA determines that it is timely and complete and that the environmental compliance history of the firm, its principals, or its key employees does not show an unwillingness or inability to maintain compliance with environmental statutes or regulations. When EPA approves a firm's application for re-certification, EPA will issue the firm a new certificate with an expiration date 5 years from the date that the firm's current certification expires. EPA certification allows the firm to perform renovations or dust sampling covered by this section in any State or Indian Tribal area that does not have a renovation program that is authorized under subpart Q of this part.

(ii) EPA will request a firm to supplement its application if EPA determines that the application is incomplete.

(iii) EPA will not approve a firm's application if it is not received or is not complete as of the date that the firm's current certification expires, or if EPA determines that the environmental compliance history of the firm, its principals, or its key employees demonstrates an unwillingness or inability to maintain compliance with environmental statutes or regulations. EPA will send the firm a letter giving the reason for not approving the application. EPA will not refund the application fees. A firm may reapply for certification at any time by filing a new application and paying the correct amount of fees.

(c) *Amendment of certification.* A firm must amend its certification within 90 days of the date a change occurs to information included in the firm's most recent application. If the firm fails to amend its certification within 90 days of the date the change occurs, the firm may not perform renovations or dust sampling until its certification is amended.

(1) To amend a certification, a firm must submit a completed "Application for Firms," signed by an authorized agent of the firm, noting on the form that it is submitted as an amendment and indicating the information that has changed. The firm must also pay at least the correct amount of fees.

(2) If additional information is needed to process the amendment, or the firm did not pay the correct amount of fees, EPA will request the firm to submit the necessary information or fees. The firm's certification is not amended until the firm complies with the request.

(3) Amending a certification does not affect the certification expiration date.

(d) *Firm responsibilities.* Firms performing renovations must ensure that:

(1) All individuals performing renovation activities on behalf of the firm are either certified renovators or have been trained by a certified renovator in accordance with § 745.90.

(2) A certified renovator is assigned to each renovation performed by the firm and discharges all of the certified renovator responsibilities identified in § 745.90.

(3) All renovations performed by the firm are performed in accordance with the work practice standards in § 745.85.

(4) The pre-renovation education requirements of § 745.84 have been performed.

(5) The recordkeeping requirements of § 745.86 are met.

■ 14. Section 745.90 is added to subpart E to read as follows:

§ 745.90 Renovator certification and dust sampling technician certification.

(a) *Renovator certification and dust sampling technician certification.* (1) To become a certified renovator or certified dust sampling technician, an individual must successfully complete the appropriate course accredited by EPA under § 745.225 or by a State or Tribal program that is authorized under subpart Q of this part. The course completion certificate serves as proof of certification. EPA renovator certification allows the certified individual to perform renovations covered by this section in any State or Indian Tribal area that does not have a renovation program that is authorized under subpart Q of this part. EPA dust sampling technician certification allows the certified individual to perform dust clearance sampling under § 745.85(c) in any State or Indian Tribal area that does not have a renovation program that is authorized under subpart Q of this part.

(2) Individuals who have successfully completed an accredited abatement worker or supervisor course, or individuals who have successfully completed an EPA, HUD, or EPA/HUD model renovation training course may take an accredited refresher renovator training course in lieu of the initial renovator training course to become a certified renovator.

(3) Individuals who have successfully completed an accredited lead-based paint inspector or risk assessor course may take an accredited refresher dust sampling technician course in lieu of the initial training to become a certified dust sampling technician.

(4) To maintain renovator certification or dust sampling technician certification, an individual must complete a renovator or dust sampling technician refresher course accredited by EPA under § 745.225 or by a State or Tribal program that is authorized under subpart Q of this part within 5 years of the date the individual completed the initial course described in paragraph (a)(1) of this section. If the individual does not complete a refresher course within this time, the individual must re-take the initial course to become certified again.

(b) *Renovator responsibilities.* Certified renovators are responsible for ensuring compliance with § 745.85 at all renovations to which they are assigned. A certified renovator:

(1) Must perform all of the tasks described in § 745.85(b) and must either perform or direct workers who perform all of the tasks described in § 745.85(a).

(2) Must provide training to workers on the work practices they will be using in performing their assigned tasks.

(3) Must be physically present at the work site when the signs required by § 745.85(a)(1) are posted, while the work area containment required by § 745.85(a)(2) is being established, and while the work area cleaning required by § 745.85(a)(5) is performed.

(4) Must regularly direct work being performed by other individuals to ensure that the work practices are being followed, including maintaining the integrity of the containment barriers and ensuring that dust or debris does not spread beyond the work area.

(5) Must be available, either on-site or by telephone, at all times that renovations are being conducted.

(6) When requested by the party contracting for renovation services, must use an acceptable test kit to determine whether components to be affected by the renovation contain lead-based paint.

(7) Must have with them at the work site copies of their initial course completion certificate and their most recent refresher course completion certificate.

(8) Must prepare the records required by § 745.86(b)(7).

(c) *Dust sampling technician responsibilities.* When performing optional dust clearance sampling under § 745.85(c), a certified dust sampling technician:

(1) Must collect dust samples in accordance with § 745.227(e)(8), must send the collected samples to a laboratory recognized by EPA under TSCA section 405(b), and must compare the results to the clearance levels in accordance with § 745.227(e)(8).

(2) Must have with them at the work site copies of their initial course completion certificate and their most recent refresher course completion certificate.

■ 15. Section 745.91 is added to subpart E to read as follows:

§ 745.91 Suspending, revoking, or modifying an individual's or firm's certification.

(a)(1) *Grounds for suspending, revoking, or modifying an individual's certification.* EPA may suspend, revoke, or modify an individual's certification if the individual fails to comply with Federal lead-based paint statutes or regulations. EPA may also suspend, revoke, or modify a certified renovator's certification if the renovator fails to ensure that all assigned renovations comply with § 745.85. In addition to an administrative or judicial finding of violation, execution of a consent agreement in settlement of an enforcement action constitutes, for purposes of this section, evidence of a failure to comply with relevant statutes or regulations.

(2) *Grounds for suspending, revoking, or modifying a firm's certification.* EPA may suspend, revoke, or modify a firm's certification if the firm:

(i) Submits false or misleading information to EPA in its application for certification or re-certification.

(ii) Fails to maintain or falsifies records required in § 745.86.

(iii) Fails to comply, or an individual performing a renovation on behalf of the firm fails to comply, with Federal lead-based paint statutes or regulations. In addition to an administrative or judicial finding of violation, execution of a consent agreement in settlement of an enforcement action constitutes, for purposes of this section, evidence of a failure to comply with relevant statutes or regulations.

(b) *Process for suspending, revoking, or modifying certification.* (1) Prior to taking action to suspend, revoke, or modify an individual's or firm's certification, EPA will notify the affected entity in writing of the following:

(i) The legal and factual basis for the proposed suspension, revocation, or modification.

(ii) The anticipated commencement date and duration of the suspension, revocation, or modification.

(iii) Actions, if any, which the affected entity may take to avoid suspension, revocation, or modification, or to receive certification in the future.

(iv) The opportunity and method for requesting a hearing prior to final suspension, revocation, or modification.

(2) If an individual or firm requests a hearing, EPA will:

(i) Provide the affected entity an opportunity to offer written statements in response to EPA's assertions of the legal and factual basis for its proposed action.

(ii) Appoint an impartial official of EPA as Presiding Officer to conduct the hearing.

(3) The Presiding Officer will:

(i) Conduct a fair, orderly, and impartial hearing within 90 days of the request for a hearing.

(ii) Consider all relevant evidence, explanation, comment, and argument submitted.

(iii) Notify the affected entity in writing within 90 days of completion of the hearing of his or her decision and order. Such an order is a final agency action which may be subject to judicial review. The order must contain the commencement date and duration of the suspension, revocation, or modification.

(4) If EPA determines that the public health, interest, or welfare warrants immediate action to suspend the certification of any individual or firm prior to the opportunity for a hearing, it will:

(i) Notify the affected entity in accordance with paragraph (b)(1)(i) through (b)(1)(iii) of this section, explaining why it is necessary to suspend the entity's certification before an opportunity for a hearing.

(ii) Notify the affected entity of its right to request a hearing on the immediate suspension within 15 days of the suspension taking place and the procedures for the conduct of such a hearing.

(5) Any notice, decision, or order issued by EPA under this section, any transcript or other verbatim record of oral testimony, and any documents filed by a certified individual or firm in a hearing under this section will be available to the public, except as otherwise provided by section 14 of TSCA or by part 2 of this title. Any such hearing at which oral testimony is presented will be open to the public, except that the Presiding Officer may exclude the public to the extent necessary to allow presentation of information which may be entitled to confidential treatment under section 14 of TSCA or part 2 of this title.

(6) EPA will maintain a publicly available list of entities whose certification has been suspended, revoked, modified, or reinstated.

(7) Unless the decision and order issued under paragraph (b)(3)(iii) of this section specify otherwise:

(i) An individual whose certification has been suspended must take a refresher training course (renovator or dust sampling technician) in order to make his or her certification current.

(ii) An individual whose certification has been revoked must take an initial renovator or dust sampling technician course in order to become certified again.

(iii) A firm whose certification has been revoked must reapply for certification after the revocation ends in order to become certified again. If the firm's certification has been suspended and the suspension ends less than 5 years after the firm was initially certified or re-certified, the firm does not need to do anything to re-activate its certification.

■ 16. Section 745.220 is amended by revising paragraph (a) to read as follows:

§ 745.220 Scope and applicability.

(a) This subpart contains procedures and requirements for the accreditation of training programs for lead-based paint activities and renovations, procedures and requirements for the certification of individuals and firms engaged in lead-based paint activities, and work practice standards for performing such activities. This subpart also requires that, except as discussed below, all lead-based paint activities, as defined in this subpart, be performed by certified individuals and firms.

* * * * *

■ 17. Section 745.225 is amended as follows:

■ a. Revise paragraph (a).

■ b. Revise the introductory text of paragraph (b), revise paragraph (b)(1)(ii), and add paragraph (b)(1)(iv)(C).

■ c. Revise the introductory text of paragraph (c), add paragraphs (c)(6)(vi), (c)(6)(vii), (c)(8)(vi), and (c)(8)(vii), and revise paragraphs (c)(8)(iv) and (c)(10).

■ d. Remove the phrase "lead-based paint activities" and add in its place the phrase "renovator, dust sampling technician, or lead-based paint activities" wherever it appears in paragraph (c)(13).

■ e. Add paragraph (c)(14)(ii)(D)(6).

■ f. Add paragraphs (d)(6) and (d)(7).

■ g. Revise the introductory text of paragraph (e).

■ h. Remove the word "activities" wherever it appears in paragraph (e)(1).

■ i. Revise paragraph (e)(2).

§ 745.225 Accreditation of training programs; target housing and child-occupied facilities.

(a) *Scope.* (1) A training program may seek accreditation to offer courses in any of the following disciplines: Inspector, risk assessor, supervisor, project designer, abatement worker, renovator, and dust sampling technician. A training program may also seek accreditation to offer refresher courses for each of the above listed disciplines.

(2) Training programs may first apply to EPA for accreditation of their lead-based paint activities courses or refresher courses pursuant to this section on or after August 31, 1998. Training programs may first apply to EPA for accreditation of their renovator or dust sampling technician courses or refresher courses pursuant to this section on or after April 22, 2009.

(3) A training program must not provide, offer, or claim to provide EPA-accredited lead-based paint activities courses without applying for and receiving accreditation from EPA as required under paragraph (b) of this section on or after March 1, 1999. A training program must not provide, offer, or claim to provide EPA-accredited renovator or dust sampling technician courses without applying for

and receiving accreditation from EPA as required under paragraph (b) of this section on or after June 23, 2008.

(b) *Application process.* The following are procedures a training program must follow to receive EPA accreditation to offer lead-based paint activities courses, renovator courses, or dust sampling technician courses:

(1) * * *

(ii) A list of courses for which it is applying for accreditation. For the purposes of this section, courses taught in different languages are considered different courses, and each must independently meet the accreditation requirements.

* * * * *

(iv) * * *

(C) When applying for accreditation of a course in a language other than English, a signed statement from a qualified, independent translator that they had compared the course to the English language version and found the translation to be accurate.

* * * * *

(c) *Requirements for the accreditation of training programs.* For a training program to obtain accreditation from EPA to offer lead-based paint activities courses, renovator courses, or dust sampling technician courses, the program must meet the following requirements:

* * * * *

(6) * * *

(vi) The renovator course must last a minimum of 8 training hours, with a minimum of 2 hours devoted to hands-on training activities. The minimum curriculum requirements for the renovator course are contained in paragraph (d)(6) of this section. Hands-on training activities must cover renovation methods that minimize the creation of dust and lead-based paint hazards, interior and exterior containment and cleanup methods, and post-renovation cleaning verification.

(vii) The dust sampling technician course must last a minimum of 8 training hours, with a minimum of 2 hours devoted to hands-on training activities. The minimum curriculum requirements for the dust sampling technician course are contained in paragraph (d)(7) of this section. Hands-on training activities must cover dust sampling methodologies.

* * * * *

(8) * * *

(iv) For initial inspector, risk assessor, project designer, supervisor, or abatement worker course completion certificates, the expiration date of

interim certification, which is 6 months from the date of course completion.

* * * * *

(vi) The language in which the course was taught.

(vii) For renovator and dust sampling technician course completion certificates, a photograph of the individual.

* * * * *

(10) Courses offered by the training program must teach the work practice standards contained in § 745.85 or § 745.227, as applicable, in such a manner that trainees are provided with the knowledge needed to perform the renovations or lead-based paint activities they will be responsible for conducting.

* * * * *

(14) * * *

(ii) * * *

(D) * * *

(6) A digital photograph of the student.

(d) * * *

(6) *Renovator.* (i) Role and responsibility of a renovator.

(ii) Background information on lead and its adverse health effects.

(iii) Background information on EPA, HUD, OSHA, and other Federal, State, and local regulations and guidance that pertains to lead-based paint and renovation activities.

(iv) Procedures for using acceptable test kits to determine whether paint is lead-based paint.

(v) Renovation methods to minimize the creation of dust and lead-based paint hazards.

(vi) Interior and exterior containment and cleanup methods.

(vii) Methods to ensure that the renovation has been properly completed, including cleaning verification, and clearance testing.

(viii) Waste handling and disposal.

(ix) Providing on-the-job training to other workers.

(x) Record preparation.

(7) *Dust sampling technician.* (i) Role and responsibility of a dust sampling technician.

(ii) Background information on lead and its adverse health effects.

(iii) Background information on Federal, State, and local regulations and guidance that pertains to lead-based paint and renovation activities.

(iv) Dust sampling methodologies.

(v) Clearance standards and testing.

(vi) Report preparation.

* * * * *

(e) *Requirements for the accreditation of refresher training programs.* A training program may seek accreditation to offer refresher training courses in any

of the following disciplines: Inspector, risk assessor, supervisor, project designer, abatement worker, renovator, and dust sampling technician. To obtain EPA accreditation to offer refresher training, a training program must meet the following minimum requirements:

* * * * *

(2) Refresher courses for inspector, risk assessor, supervisor, and abatement worker must last a minimum of 8 training hours. Refresher courses for project designer, renovator, and dust sampling technician must last a minimum of 4 training hours.

* * * * *

■ 18. Section 745.320 is amended by revising paragraph (c) to read as follows:

§ 745.320 Scope and purpose.

* * * * *

(c) A State or Indian Tribe may seek authorization to administer and enforce all of the provisions of subpart E of this part, just the pre-renovation education provisions of subpart E of this part, or just the training, certification, accreditation, and work practice provisions of subpart E of this part. The provisions of §§ 745.324 and 745.326 apply for the purposes of such program authorizations.

* * * * *

■ 19. Section 745.324 is amended as follows:

■ a. Revise paragraph (a)(1).

■ b. Remove the phrase "lead-based paint training accreditation and certification" from the second sentence of paragraph (b)(1)(iii).

■ c. Revise paragraph (b)(2)(ii).

■ d. Revise paragraphs (e)(2)(i) and (e)(4).

■ e. Revise paragraph (f)(2).

■ f. Revise paragraph (i)(8).

§ 745.324 Authorization of State or Tribal programs.

(a) *Application content and procedures.* (1) Any State or Indian Tribe that seeks authorization from EPA to administer and enforce the provisions of subpart E or subpart L of this part must submit an application to the Administrator in accordance with this paragraph.

* * * * *

(b) * * *

(2) * * *

(ii) An analysis of the State or Tribal program that compares the program to the Federal program in subpart E or subpart L of this part, or both. This analysis must demonstrate how the program is, in the State's or Indian Tribe's assessment, at least as protective as the elements in the Federal program at subpart E or subpart L of this part, or both. EPA will use this analysis to evaluate the protectiveness of the State or Tribal program in making its determination pursuant to paragraph (e)(2)(i) of this section.

* * * * *

(e) * * *

(2) * * *

(i) The State or Tribal program is at least as protective of human health and the environment as the corresponding Federal program under subpart E or subpart L of this part, or both; and

* * * * *

(4) If the State or Indian Tribe applies for authorization of State or Tribal programs under both subpart E and subpart L, EPA may, as appropriate, authorize one program and disapprove the other.

* * * * *

(f) * * *

(2) If a State or Indian Tribe does not have an authorized program to administer and enforce the pre-renovation education requirements of subpart E of this part by August 31, 1998, the Administrator will, by such date, enforce those provisions of subpart E of this part as the Federal program for that State or Indian Country. If a State or Indian Tribe does not have an authorized program to administer and enforce the training, certification and accreditation requirements and work practice standards of subpart E of this part by April 22, 2009, the Administrator will, by such date, enforce those provisions of subpart E of this part as the Federal program for that State or Indian Country.

* * * * *

(i) * * *

(8) By the date of such order, the Administrator will establish and enforce the provisions of subpart E or subpart L of this part, or both, as the Federal program for that State or Indian Country.

■ 20. Section 745.326 is revised to read as follows:

§ 745.326 Renovation: State and Tribal program requirements.

(a) *Program elements.* To receive authorization from EPA, a State or Tribal program must contain the following program elements:

(1) For pre-renovation education programs, procedures and requirements for the distribution of lead hazard information to owners and occupants of target housing and child-occupied facilities before renovations for compensation.

(2) For renovation training, certification, accreditation, and work practice standards programs:

(i) Procedures and requirements for the accreditation of renovation and dust sampling technician training programs.

(ii) Procedures and requirements for the certification of renovators and dust sampling technicians.

(iii) Procedures and requirements for the certification of individuals and/or firms.

(iv) Requirements that all renovations be conducted by appropriately certified individuals and/or firms.

(v) Work practice standards for the conduct of renovations.

(3) For all renovation programs, development of the appropriate infrastructure or government capacity to effectively carry out a State or Tribal program.

(b) *Pre-renovation education.* To be considered at least as protective as the Federal program, the State or Tribal program must:

(1) Establish clear standards for identifying renovation activities that trigger the information distribution requirements.

(2) Establish procedures for distributing the lead hazard information to owners and occupants of housing and child-occupied facilities prior to renovation activities.

(3) Require that the information to be distributed include either the pamphlet titled *Renovate Right: Important Lead Hazard Information for Families, Child Care Providers and Schools,* developed by EPA under section 406(a) of TSCA, or an alternate pamphlet or package of lead hazard information that has been submitted by the State or Tribe, reviewed by EPA, and approved by EPA for that State or Tribe. Such information must contain renovation-specific information similar to that in *Renovate Right: Important Lead Hazard Information for Families, Child Care Providers and Schools,* must meet the content requirements prescribed by section 406(a) of TSCA, and must be in a format that is readable to the diverse audience of housing and child-occupied facility owners and occupants in that State or Tribe.

(i) A State or Tribe with a pre-renovation education program approved before June 23, 2008, must demonstrate that it meets the requirements of this section no later than the first report that it submits pursuant to § 745.324(h) on or after April 22, 2009.

(ii) A State or Tribe with an application for approval of a pre-renovation education program submitted but not approved before June 23, 2008, must demonstrate that it meets the requirements of this section either by amending its application or in the first report that it submits pursuant

to § 745.324(h) of this part on or after April 22, 2009.

(iii) A State or Indian Tribe submitting its application for approval of a pre-renovation education program on or after June 23, 2008, must demonstrate in its application that it meets the requirements of this section.

(c) *Accreditation of training programs.* To be considered at least as protective as the Federal program, the State or Tribal program must meet the requirements of either paragraph (c)(1) or (c)(2) of this section:

(1) The State or Tribal program must establish accreditation procedures and requirements, including:

(i) Procedures and requirements for the accreditation of training programs, including, but not limited to:

(A) Training curriculum requirements.

(B) Training hour requirements.

(C) Hands-on training requirements.

(D) Trainee competency and proficiency requirements.

(E) Requirements for training program quality control.

(ii) Procedures and requirements for the re-accreditation of training programs.

(iii) Procedures for the oversight of training programs.

(iv) Procedures and standards for the suspension, revocation, or modification of training program accreditations; or

(2) The State or Tribal program must establish procedures and requirements for the acceptance of renovation training offered by training providers accredited by EPA or a State or Tribal program authorized by EPA under this subpart.

(d) *Certification of renovators.* To be considered at least as protective as the Federal program, the State or Tribal program must:

(1) Establish procedures and requirements for individual certification that ensure that certified renovators are trained by an accredited training program.

(2) Establish procedures and requirements for re-certification.

(3) Establish procedures for the suspension, revocation, or modification of certifications.

(e) *Work practice standards for renovations.* To be considered at least as protective as the Federal program, the State or Tribal program must establish standards that ensure that renovations are conducted reliably, effectively, and safely. At a minimum, the State or Tribal program must contain the following requirements:

(1) Renovations must be conducted only by certified contractors.

(2) Renovations are conducted using lead-safe work practices that are at least

s protective to occupants as the equirements in § 745.85.

(3) Certified contractors must retain ppropriate records.

21. Section 745.327 is amended by evising paragraphs (b)(1)(iv) and b)(2)(ii) to read as follows:

745.327　State or Indian Tribal lead-based aint compliance and enforcement rograms.

*　　*　　*　　*　　*

(b) *　*　*

(1) *　*　*

(iv) Requirements that regulate the onduct of renovation activities as escribed at § 745.326.

(2) *　*　*

(ii) For the purposes of enforcing a enovation program, State or Tribal fficials must be able to enter a firm's lace of business or work site.

*　　*　　*　　*　　*

22. Section 745.339 is revised to read s follows:

745.339　Effective date.

States and Indian Tribes may seek uthorization to administer and enforce ubpart L of this part pursuant to this ubpart at any time. States and Indian ribes may seek authorization to dminister and enforce the pre-enovation education provisions of ubpart E of this part pursuant to this ubpart at any time. States and Indian ribes may seek authorization to dminister and enforce all of subpart E f this part pursuant to this subpart ffective June 23, 2008.

FR Doc. E8–8141 Filed 4–21–08; 8:45 am]

ILLING CODE 6560-50-S

NVIRONMENTAL PROTECTION GENCY

0 CFR Part 745

EPA–HQ–OPPT–2004–0126; FRL–8358–6]

ead Hazard Information Pamphlet; lotice of Availability

GENCY: Environmental Protection gency (EPA).

CTION: Notice of availability.

UMMARY: This notice announces the vailability of EPA's new lead hazard nformation pamphlet for renovation ctivities, *Renovate Right: Lead Hazard nformation for Families, Child Care roviders and Schools (Renovate Right).* here is an increased risk of exposure lead-based paint hazards during enovation activities, particularly for hildren under 6 years of age. To better nform families, child care providers, nd schools about the risks and to

encourage greater public health and safety during renovation activities in target housing and child-occupied facilities, EPA has developed a renovation-specific information pamphlet. This new pamphlet gives information on lead-based paint hazards, lead testing, how to select a contractor, what precautions to take during the renovation, and proper cleanup activities.

DATES: After June 23, 2008, the new pamphlet or *Protect Your Family From Lead in Your Home* may be used for compliance with the Pre-Renovation Education Rule under TSCA section 406(b). After December 22, 2008, the new pamphlet must be used exclusively.

FOR FURTHER INFORMATION CONTACT: *For general information contact*: Colby Lintner, Regulatory Coordinator, Environmental Assistance Division (7408M), Office of Pollution Prevention and Toxics, Environmental Protection Agency, 1200 Pennsylvania Ave., NW., Washington, DC 20460–0001; telephone number: (202) 554–1404; e-mail address: *TSCA-Hotline@epa.gov.*

For technical information contact: Mike Wilson, National Program Chemicals Division, Office of Pollution Prevention and Toxics, Environmental Protection Agency, 1200 Pennsylvania Ave., NW., Washington, DC 20460–0001; telephone number (201) 566–0521; e-mail address: *wilson.mike@epa.gov.*

SUPPLEMENTARY INFORMATION:

I. General Information

A. Does this Action Apply to Me?

You may be potentially affected by this action if you perform renovations of target housing or child-occupied facilities for compensation. "Target housing" is defined in section 401 of TSCA as any housing constructed prior to 1978, except housing for the elderly or persons with disabilities (unless any child under age 6 resides or is expected to reside in such housing) or any 0-bedroom dwelling. EPA's Renovation, Repair, and Painting rule defines a child-occupied facility as a building, or a portion of a building, constructed prior to 1978, visited regularly by the same child, under 6 years of age, on at least 2 different days within any week (Sunday through Saturday period), provided that each day's visit lasts at least 3 hours and the combined weekly visits last at least 6 hours, and the combined annual visits last at least 60 hours. Child-occupied facilities may be located in public or commercial buildings or in target housing.

Potentially affected entities may include, but are not limited to:

• Building construction (NAICS code 236), e.g., single family housing construction, multi-family housing construction, residential remodelers.

• Specialty trade contractors (NAICS code 238), e.g., plumbing, heating, and air-conditioning contractors, painting and wall covering contractors, electrical contractors, finish carpentry contractors, drywall and insulation contractors, siding contractors, tile and terrazzo contractors, glass and glazing contractors.

• Real estate (NAICS code 531), e.g., lessors of residential buildings and dwellings, residential property managers.

• Child day care services (NAICS code 624410).

• Elementary and secondary schools (NAICS code 611110), e.g., elementary schools with kindergarten classrooms.

This listing is not intended to be exhaustive, but rather provides a guide for readers regarding entities likely to be affected by this action. Other types of entities not listed in this unit could also be affected. The North American Industrial Classification System (NAICS) codes have been provided to assist you and others in determining whether this action might apply to certain entities. To determine whether you or your business may be affected by this action, you should carefully examine the applicability provisions in 40 CFR 745.82. If you have any questions regarding the applicability of this action to a particular entity, consult the technical person listed under **FOR FURTHER INFORMATION CONTACT.**

B. How Can I Get Copies of the Pamphlet and Other Related Information?

1. *The pamphlet.* Single copies of the pamphlet may be obtained by calling the National Lead Information Clearinghouse (NLIC) at 1–800–424–LEAD or TDD: 1–800–526–5456, or the EPA Public Information Center at (202) 260–2080. Multiple copies are available through the Government Printing Office (GPO). The public may order by calling the GPO Order Desk at (202) 512–1800, faxing (202) 512–2233, or writing to Superintendent of Documents, P.O. Box 371954, Pittsburgh, PA 15250–7954. Request the publication by title, *Renovate Right: Lead Hazard Information for Families, Child Care Providers and Schools.* The pamphlet is also available on EPA's website at *http://www.epa.gov/lead.* The pamphlet may be reproduced by an individual or corporation without permission from EPA.

Appendix 2:

U.S. Department of Housing and Urban Development (HUD) Requirements

EPA Certified Renovation Firms and Certified Renovators
Additional Requirements of HUD's Lead Safe Housing Rule

The U.S. Department of Housing and Urban Development's Lead Safe Housing Rule (HUD's Lead Safe Housing Rule (LSHR), which is found in HUD's regulations at 24 CFR Part 35, Subparts B through M), generally applies to work performed in target housing units receiving HUD housing assistance, such as rehabilitation or acquisition assistance.

Under the LSHR, the program participant (governmental jurisdiction, non-profit, community organization or the property owner who accepts HUD funds) becomes responsible for compliance with the LSHR and is referred to as the designated party (or DP). Renovation firms may include, for example, for-profit contractors, non-profit organizations, or a designated party using its own employees for renovation. In the spirit of maintaining good customer relations, certified renovation firms should ask their client if:

1) The work involves lead hazard control (including abatement, interim control of lead hazards or ongoing lead-based paint maintenance); and

2) The housing receives financial assistance. If so, the renovator should ask the client to find out if the assistance is federal assistance.

Most clients would appreciate these questions so they may avoid violating HUD or EPA rules. See www.hud.gov/offices/lead/enforcement/lshr.cfm for more information.

The information below and in the table explain the basic requirements of HUD's regulation for renovators who have not yet had experience with HUD-funded work. The term "rehabilitation" is used by HUD to describe residential renovation work. When HUD funds pay for this work, funding often flows from HUD through cities, states or other program participants, and addressing lead-based painted surfaces becomes a routine part of the job. HUD's specific requirements depend on the amount of Federal rehabilitation assistance the project is receiving:

1) Up to $5,000 per unit: "Do no harm" approach. Lead safety requirements cover only the surfaces being disturbed. Program participants can either test these surfaces to determine if they contain lead-based paint or presume they contain lead-based paint. Work which disturbs painted surfaces known or presumed to contain lead-based paint is done using lead safe work practices, and clearance of the worksite is performed at the end of the job (unless it is a very small "de minimis" scale project) to ensure that no lead dust hazards remain in the work area. Training that meets the EPA's RRP Rule requirements is sufficient for this work.

2) Greater than $5,000 and up to $25,000 per unit: Identify and control lead hazards. Identify all lead hazards at the affected units and common areas servicing those units by performing a lead-based paint risk assessment. Control the hazards using interim controls. Participants may skip the risk assessment and presume that all potential lead hazards are present, and then must use standard treatments to address them. In addition to training that meets the EPA's RRP Rule requirements, HUD-approved interim control training (such as the HUD-EPA RRP curriculum) is required for renovators and workers.

3) Greater than $25,000 per unit: Identify and abate lead hazards. Identify all lead hazards at the property by performing a risk assessment and then abate all the hazards. Participants may skip the risk assessment and presume that all potential lead hazards are present and abate them. This approach requires certified abatement contractors perform the abatement part of the job.

EPA Certified Renovation Firms and Certified Renovators
Additional Requirements of HUD's Lead Safe Housing Rule

These approaches also include all the basic HUD requirements describe in the slide presentations in Module 2. They clearly demonstrate the importance to the renovator of asking the client whether federal housing assistance is provided for the project.

The differences between HUD's LSHR and the Environmental Protection Agency's (EPA's) Renovation, Repair and Painting (RRP) regulation, part of EPA's regulations at 40 CFR Part 745, and the changes for HUD LSHR projects, are summarized in the following table and explained in the narrative after the table:

Differences between HUD LSHR and EPA RRP regulations

Stage of Job	Requirement	HUD LSHR	EPA RRP	Changes to LSHR Projects to Comply with RRP.
Planning and Set-Up	Determination that lead-based paint (LBP) is present.	EPA-recognized test kits cannot be used to say paint is not LBP. Only a certified LBP inspector or risk assessor may determine whether LBP is present.	Certified renovators use an EPA-recognized test kit to determine if RRP rule applies or not.	None.
	Training	HUD does not certify renovators or firms. All workers and supervisors must complete a HUD-approved curriculum in lead safe work practices, except that non-certified renovation workers need only on-the-job training if they are supervised by a certified LBP abatement supervisor who is also a certified renovator.	EPA or EPA-authorized States certify renovation firms and accredit training providers that certify renovators. Only the certified renovator is required to have classroom training. Workers must receive on-the-job training from the certified renovator.	Renovation firms must be certified. At least one certified renovator must be at the job or available when work is being done. (The certified renovator may be a certified LBP abatement supervisor who has completed the 4-hour RRP refresher course.)

EPA Certified Renovation Firms and Certified Renovators
Additional Requirements of HUD's Lead Safe Housing Rule

Stage of Job	Requirement	HUD LSHR	EPA RRP	Changes to LSHR Projects to Comply with RRP.
	Pre-Renovation Education	HUD requires conformance with EPA regulations, including EPA's Pre-Renovation Education Rule. EPA had required renovators to hand out the EPA / HUD / CPSC *Protect Your Family from Lead in Your Home* (Lead Disclosure Rule) pamphlet.	Renovators must hand out the EPA / HUD *Renovate Right: Important Lead Hazard Information for Families, Child Care Providers and Schools* pamphlet. (This requirement went into effect on December 22, 2008.)	None.
During the Job	Treating LBP hazards	Depending on type and amount of HUD assistance, HUD requires that lead hazards be treated using "interim controls" or "ongoing lead-based paint maintenance."	EPA generally requires that renovations in target housing be performed using lead-safe work practices.	None.
	Prohibited Work Practices	HUD prohibits 6 work practices. These include EPA's 3 prohibited work practices plus: heat guns that char paint, dry scraping or sanding farther than 1 ft. of electrical outlets, and use of a volatile stripper in poorly ventilated space.	EPA prohibits 3 work practices (open flame burning or torching, heat guns above 1100 degrees F, machine removal without HEPA vacuum attachment).	None.

EPA Certified Renovation Firms and Certified Renovators
Additional Requirements of HUD's Lead Safe Housing Rule

Stage of Job	Requirement	HUD LSHR	EPA RRP	Changes to LSHR Projects to Comply with RRP.
	Threshold minimum amounts of interior paint disturbance which trigger lead activities.	HUD has a lower interior "*de minimis*" threshold (2 sq. ft. per room, or 10% of a small component type) than EPA for lead-safe work practices. HUD also uses this lower threshold for clearance and occupant notification.	EPA's interior threshold (6 sq. ft. per room) for minor repair and maintenance activities is higher than HUD's *de minimis* threshold.	None.
End of Job	Confirmatory Testing	HUD requires a clearance examination done by an independent party instead of the certified renovator's cleaning verification procedure.	EPA allows cleaning verification by the renovator or clearance examination. The cleaning verification does not involve sampling and laboratory analysis of the dust.	None.
	Notification to Occupants	HUD requires the designated party to distribute notices to occupants within 15 days after lead hazard evaluation and control activities in their unit (and common areas, if applicable).	EPA has no requirement to notify residents who are not the owners after the renovation.	None.

EPA Certified Renovation Firms and Certified Renovators
Additional Requirements of HUD's Lead Safe Housing Rule

A. Responsibilities Shifted from the Renovator to the Designated Party under HUD's LSHR:

1. Under the LSHR, the designated party is generally responsible to either have the paint tested by a certified lead inspector or risk assessor or presume the presence of lead-based paint. Therefore, when HUD's rule applies, the Certified Renovator may <u>not</u> use a paint test kit to determine that the paint is <u>not</u> lead-based paint. Note: Some states may have conflict-of-interest regulations prohibiting renovators from testing paint on which they will be working.

2. When the HUD LSHR applies, the designated party must have a qualified person, independent of the renovation firm, conduct a lead clearance examination. The Certified Renovator does not conduct a cleaning verification. See below for more information on clearance testing.

B. Additional HUD Requirements for the Renovator:

1. **Training requirements for workers and supervisors performing interim controls.** To meet the requirements of both rules:
   a. If the supervisor (in HUD terms) or Certified Renovator (in EPA terms) is certified as a lead-based paint abatement supervisor or has successfully completed an accredited abatement supervision or abatement worker course, that person must complete a 4-hour RRP refresher course.
   b. For workers who are not themselves supervisors / Certified Renovators:
      - If their supervisor on this project is a certified lead-based paint abatement supervisor who has completed a 4-hour RRP refresher course, the workers must obtain on-the-job training in lead-safe work practices from the supervisor.
      - Otherwise, the workers must successfully complete either a one-day RRP course, or another lead-safe work practices course approved by HUD for this purpose after consultation with the EPA. HUD has approved the one-day RRP course, the previously-published HUD/EPA one-day Renovation, Remodeling and Repair course, and other one-day courses listed on HUD's website, at www.hud.gov/offices/lead.
   c. Where the work is being done in a State or Tribal jurisdiction that has been authorized by the EPA to operate an RRP training and certification program, the one-day RRP course and half-day RRP refresher course must be accredited by the State or Tribe. HUD will approve all one-day RRP courses accredited by EPA-authorized States or Tribes.
   d. The 4-hour RRP refresher course is not sufficient on its own to meet either the EPA or HUD training requirements.

2. **The certified renovation firm and the certified renovator must take additional precautions to protect residents from lead poisoning beyond those in EPA's RRP Rule.**
   a. **Renovators must use lead-safe work practices in work exempt from the RRP Rule that:**
      - Disturbs between 2 and 6 ft^2 of paint per room, the LSHR's *de minimis* threshold and the RRP's minor repair and maintenance activities threshold, respectively. *Note:* Window replacement, window sash replacement, and demolition of painted surface areas disturb more paint than the LSHR's *de minimis* threshold.

- Disturbs more than 10% of a component type with a small surface area (such as window sills, baseboards, and trim).
  Note: The square foot and percent thresholds above apply to all work performed within a thirty day period.
- Is in target housing where the owner-occupant signs a statement under the RRP Rule that lead safe work practices are not required.
  Note: HUD does not allow any owner, whether an owner-occupant or landlord, to opt out of the use of lead safe work practices at any time, even though the EPA allows an owner-occupant to sign a statement that lead safe work practices are not required.

b. **Not using HUD's 3 additional prohibited work practices:**
- Heat guns that char the paint even if operating at below 1100 degrees F.
- Dry sanding or dry scraping, except dry scraping in conjunction with heat guns or within 1 ft of electrical outlets.
- Paint stripping using a volatile stripper in a poorly ventilated space.

c. **Taking additional measures to protect occupants** during longer interior hazard reduction activities: Temporarily relocating the occupant before and during longer interior hazard reduction activities to a suitable, decent, safe, and similarly accessible dwelling unit that does not have lead-based paint hazards. Temporary relocation is not required for shorter projects, where:
- The work is contained, completed in one period of 8-daytime hours, and does not create other safety, health or environmental hazards; or
- The work is completed within 5 calendar days, after each work day, the worksite and the area within 10 feet of the containment area are cleaned of visible dust and debris, and occupants have safe access to sleeping areas, and bathroom and kitchen facilities.

C.   Additional Designated Party Responsibilities that may Affect the Renovator

On jobs covered by the HUD LSHR, the certified renovation firm and the certified renovator should know other requirements for the designated party that may affect their role on the project.

1. **Designated party must provide occupants with two notices, if the amount of work is above HUD's *de minimis* threshold:**
   a. NOTICE OF EVALUATION OR PRESUMPTION: This notice informs the occupants that paint has been evaluated to determine if it is LBP or that paint has been presumed to be LBP. The designated party must notify the occupants within 15 calendar days of receiving the evaluation report or making the presumption. The renovator should ask the client if he/she has made this notice. The owner may provide a copy of this notice to the renovator so the renovator knows where LBP is located.
   b. NOTICE OF HAZARD REDUCTION ACTIVITY: This notice describes the hazard reduction work that was completed and gives the contact for occupants to get more information. The designated party must notify the occupants within 15 calendar days of completion the hazard reduction work. The renovator may be given a copy of this notice, or may be asked to prepare or distribute the notice for the owner at part of the renovator's work for the owner.

EPA Certified Renovation Firms and Certified Renovators
Additional Requirements of HUD's Lead Safe Housing Rule

2. **Depending on the type and amount of housing assistance provided, HUD generally requires that identified LBP hazards be treated.** Treatments may include LBP hazard abatement, interim controls or ongoing LBP maintenance. Renovators should inquire if their contract with the owner requires them to perform lead hazard treatment tasks listed below. If so, all workers and supervisors must have the proper training and qualifications. Generally, interim controls include the following activities, which are required if the amount of work is above HUD's *de minimis* threshold; for work below the *de minimis* threshold, any deteriorated paint must be repaired, but the work need not be done using lead-safe work practices, although HUD strongly encourages their use:

   a. Deteriorated LBP must be stabilized. This means that physical defects in the substrate of a paint surface or component that is causing the deterioration of the surface or component must also be repaired.

   b. Friction surfaces that are abraded must be treated if there are lead dust hazards nearby.

   c. Friction points must be either eliminated or treated so the LBP is not subject to abrasion.

   d. Impact surfaces must be treated if the paint on an impact surface is damaged or otherwise deteriorated and the damage is caused by impact from a related building component (such as a door knob that knocks the wall or a door that rubs against its door frame).

   e. LBP must be protected from impact.

   f. Chewable LBP surfaces must be made inaccessible for chewing by children of less than six years of age if there is evidence that such a child has chewed on the painted surface.

   g. Horizontal surfaces that are rough, pitted, or porous must be covered with a smooth, cleanable covering or coating.

3. **For certain types of HUD assistance, when a child known to have an environmental intervention blood lead level is present, the designated party must take additional steps to assess the situation and respond to potential lead hazards.** An environmental intervention blood lead level is a reading in a child under 6 years old of 20 micrograms per deciliter of blood (20 µg/dL), or two readings of 15 to 19 µg/dL at least 3 months apart. For certain types of HUD assistance (tenant-based rental assistance, project-based rental assistance, public housing, and HUD-owned multifamily housing), the owner or designated party may ask the renovator to perform work in the unit to address specific lead hazards identified by an environmental investigation risk assessment. All persons participating in such work should have appropriate training and qualifications.

4. **The designated party must arrange for a party independent of the renovator to conduct a clearance examination, if the amount of work is above HUD's *de minimis* threshold:**

   a. A clearance examination includes a visual assessment at the end of the renovation work for deteriorated paint, dust, debris, paint chips or other residue; sampling of dust on interior floors, window sills and window troughs; submitting the dust samples to a laboratory for analysis for lead; interpreting the lab results, and preparing a clearance report. EPA also allows a clearance examination to be used instead of the post-cleaning verification, if the clearance examination is required by federal, state or local regulations or by the contract. The unit – or, where work is contained, just the work area and an area just outside the containment – must pass clearance, and must not have any remaining lead hazards. If clearance fails at either the visual assessment step or the dust testing step, cleaning has to be redone in the failed part of the work area. The failed part of the work area is the specific area that was tested, as well as any areas that were not tested, and any other areas that are being represented by the sampled area. For example:

- Just one bedroom was tested, because it was to represent all bedrooms in the housing unit; it failed. Therefore, all of the bedrooms in the unit have to be re-cleaned and re-cleared.
- In a large multifamily apartment building, if a percentage of units are tested in accordance with the HUD Guidelines, if any fail, all of the units except those that passed clearance have to be re-cleaned and re-cleared. (If there are patterns of just certain component types failing, just those component types need to be re-cleaned and re-cleared in the failed and untested units.)

b. The person conducting the clearance examination must be both:
- A certified lead-based paint inspector, risk assessor, clearance examiner, or dust sampling technician, depending on the type of activity being performed. (Either the State or the EPA certifies this person, depending on whether or not the State the housing is in is authorized by EPA to certify people in the lead discipline.)
- Independent of the organization performing hazard reduction or maintenance activities. There is one exception, which is that designated party may use a qualified in-house employee to conduct clearance even if other in-house employees did the renovation work, but an in-house employee may not do both renovation and clearance.

D. How to Find Out About Lead-Based Paint Requirements that Apply to Planned Work in Properties Receiving HUD Housing Assistance, such as Rehabilitation or Acquisition Assistance:

Finding out whether the work is receiving federal housing assistance is important because failing to meet lead-based paint requirements could affect the continuation of the assistance. For each job, the renovation firm should find out whether:

- The housing receives financial assistance; and
- Any lead-based paint requirements apply to the work because of the assistance provided.

The renovation firm should take the following steps:

1. Ask the property owner if the property or the family receives any type of housing assistance, including low-interest loans, from a local, State, or Federal agency. If so:
   a. Find out the name of the agency, contact person, address and phone number. (See the list of types of agencies below.)
   b. Get a basic description of the type of assistance the property receives.

EPA Certified Renovation Firms and Certified Renovators
Additional Requirements of HUD's Lead Safe Housing Rule

Note: You should be able to explain to the owner that there will be information about the work that you will need, and that you also need to check if there are any special requirements.

2. If you have any questions about the Federal or State lead-based paint requirements that apply to the work, contact the public agency administering the assistance and discuss the project with the program specialist or rehabilitation specialist working with the property. For example:
   a. Is the project considered lead abatement? If so, what are the agency's abatement requirements?
   b. If the project is not abatement, what are the agency's lead-based paint requirements for the project, and how should they be incorporated into the work write-up?

Some types of public agencies administering housing assistance, such as rehabilitation or acquisition assistance, include:

- State Housing Agency, Corporation or Authority
- State Community Development Agency, Corporation or Authority
- State Housing Finance Agency

- City or County Housing Authority, Corporation or Authority
- City or County Community Development Agency, Corporation or Authority

- USDA Service Center - Rural Housing Programs

Appendix 3:

Renovate Right: Important Lead Hazard Information for Families, Child Care Providers and Schools

Renovate Right

Important Lead Hazard Information for Families, Child Care Providers and Schools

It's the Law!

Federal law requires that individuals receive certain information before renovating six square feet or more of painted surfaces in a room for interior projects or more than twenty square feet of painted surfaces for exterior projects in housing, child care facilities and schools built before 1978.

■ Homeowners and tenants: renovators must give you this pamphlet before starting work.

■ Child care facilities, including preschools and kindergarten classrooms, and the families of children under the age of six that attend those facilities: renovators must provide a copy of this pamphlet to child-care facilities and general renovation information to families whose children attend those facilities.

Also, beginning April 2010, federal law will require contractors that disturb lead-based paint in homes, child care facilities and schools, built before 1978 to be certified and follow specific work practices to prevent lead contamination. Therefore beginning in April 2010, ask to see your contractor's certification.

Renovating, Repairing, or Painting?

■ Is your home, your building, or the child care facility or school your children attend, being renovated, repaired, or painted?

■ Was your home, your building, or the child care facility or school your children under age 6 attend, built before 1978?

If the answer to these questions is YES, there are a few important things you need to know about lead-based paint.

This pamphlet provides basic facts about lead and information about lead safety when work is being done in your home, your building or the childcare facility or school your children attend.

The Facts About Lead

■ Lead can affect children's brains and developing nervous systems, causing reduced IQ, learning disabilities, and behavioral problems. Lead is also harmful to adults.

■ Lead in dust is the most common way people are exposed to lead. People can also get lead in their bodies from lead in soil or paint chips. Lead dust is often invisible.

■ Lead-based paint was used in more than 38 million homes until it was banned for residential use in 1978.

■ Projects that disturb lead-based paint can create dust and endanger you and your family. Don't let this happen to you. Follow the practices described in this pamphlet to protect you and your family.

Who Should Read This Pamphlet?

This pamphlet is for you if you:
- Reside in a home built before 1978,
- Own or operate a child care facility, including preschools and kindergarten classrooms, built before 1978, or
- Have a child under six who attends a child care facility built before 1978.

You will learn:
- Basic facts about lead and your health,
- How to choose a contractor, if you are a property owner,
- What tenants, and parents/guardians of a child in a child care facility or school should consider,
- How to prepare for the renovation or repair job,
- What to look for during the job and after the job is done,
- Where to get more information about lead.

This pamphlet is not for:
- **Abatement projects.** Abatement is a set of activities aimed specifically at eliminating lead or lead hazards. EPA has regulations for certification and training of abatement professionals. If your goal is to eliminate lead or lead hazards, contact the National Lead Information Center at **1-800-424-LEAD (5323)** for more information.
- **"Do-it-yourself" projects.** If you plan to do renovation work yourself, this document is a good start, but you will need more information to complete the work safely. Call the National Lead Information Center at **1-800-424-LEAD (5323)** and ask for more information on how to work safely in a home with lead-based paint.
- **Contractor education.** Contractors who want information about working safely with lead should contact the National Lead Information Center at **1-800-424-LEAD (5323)** for information about courses and resources on lead-safe work practices.

Lead and Your Health

Lead is especially dangerous to children under six years of age.

Lead can affect children's brains and developing nervous systems, causing:

- Reduced IQ and learning disabilities.
- Behavior problems.

Even children who appear healthy can have dangerous levels of lead in their bodies.

Lead is also harmful to adults. In adults, low levels of lead can pose many dangers, including:

- High blood pressure and hypertension.
- Pregnant women exposed to lead can transfer lead to their fetus.

Lead gets into the body when it is swallowed or inhaled.

- People, especially children, can swallow lead dust as they eat, play, and do other normal hand-to-mouth activities.
- People may also breathe in lead dust or fumes if they disturb lead-based paint. People who sand, scrape, burn, brush or blast or otherwise disturb lead-based paint risk unsafe exposure to lead.

What should I do if I am concerned about my family's exposure to lead?

- Call your local health department for advice on reducing and eliminating exposures to lead inside and outside your home, child care facility or school.
- Always use lead-safe work practices when renovation or repair will disturb lead-based paint.
- A blood test is the only way to find out if you or a family member already has lead poisoning. Call your doctor or local health department to arrange for a blood test.

For more information about the health effects of exposure to lead, visit the EPA lead website at www.epa.gov/lead/pubs/leadinfo.htm or call 1-800-424-LEAD (5323).

There are other things you can do to protect your family everyday.

- Regularly clean floors, window sills, and other surfaces.
- Wash children's hands, bottles, pacifiers, and toys often.
- Make sure children eat a healthy, nutritious diet consistent with the USDA's dietary guidelines, that helps protect children from the effects of lead.
- Wipe off shoes before entering house.

Where Does the Lead Come From?

Dust is the main problem. The most common way to get lead in the body is from dust. Lead dust comes from deteriorating lead-based paint and lead-contaminated soil that gets tracked into your home. This dust may accumulate to unsafe levels. Then, normal hand to-mouth activities, like playing and eating (especially in young children), move that dust from surfaces like floors and windowsills into the body.

Home renovation creates dust. Common renovation activities like sanding, cutting, and demolition can create hazardous lead dust and chips.

Proper work practices protect you from the dust. The key to protecting yourself and your family during a renovation, repair or painting job is to use lead-safe work practices such as containing dust inside the work area, using dust-minimizing work methods, and conducting a careful cleanup, as described in this pamphlet.

Other sources of lead. Remember, lead can also come from outside soil, your water, or household items (such as lead-glazed pottery and lead crystal). Contact the National Lead Information Center at **1-800-424-LEAD (5323)** for more information on these sources.

Checking Your Home for Lead-Based Paint

Percentage of Homes Likely to Contain Lead

Older homes, child care facilities, and schools are more likely to contain lead-based paint. Homes may be single-family homes or apartments. They may be private, government-assisted, or public housing. Schools are preschools and kindergarten classrooms. They may be urban, suburban, or rural.

You have the following options:

You may decide to assume your home, child care facility, or school contains lead. Especially in older homes and buildings, you may simply want to assume lead-based paint is present and follow the lead-safe work practices described in this brochure during the renovation, repair, or painting job.

You or your contractor may also test for lead using a lead test kit. Test kits must be EPA-approved and are available at hardware stores. They include detailed instructions for their use.

You can hire a certified professional to check for lead-based paint. These professionals are certified risk assessors or inspectors, and can determine if your home has lead or lead hazards.

- A certified inspector or risk assessor can conduct an inspection telling you whether your home, or a portion of your home, has lead-based paint and where it is located. This will tell you the areas in your home where lead-safe work practices are needed.

- A certified risk assessor can conduct a risk assessment telling you if your home currently has any lead hazards from lead in paint, dust, or soil. The risk assessor can also tell you what actions to take to address any hazards.

- For help finding a certified risk assessor or inspector, call the National Lead Information Center at **1-800-424-LEAD (5323)**.

For Property Owners

You have the ultimate responsibility for the safety of your family, tenants, or children in your care. This means properly preparing for the renovation and keeping persons out of the work area (see p. 8). It also means ensuring the contractor uses lead-safe work practices.

Beginning April 2010, federal law will require that contractors performing renovation, repair and painting projects that disturb lead-based paint in homes, child care facilities, and schools built before 1978 to be certified and follow specific work practices to prevent lead contamination.

Until contractors are required to be certified, make sure your contractor can explain clearly the details of the job and how the contractor will minimize lead hazards during the work.

- Ask if the contractor is trained to perform lead-safe work practices and to see a copy of their training certificate.
- Ask them what lead-safe methods they will use to set up and perform the job in your home, child care facility or school.
- Ask if the contractor is aware of the lead renovation rules. For example, contractors are required to provide you with a copy of this pamphlet before beginning work. A sample pre-renovation disclosure form is provided at the back of this pamphlet. Contractors may use this form to make documentation of compliance easier.
- Ask for references from at least three recent jobs involving homes built before 1978, and speak to each personally.

Always make sure the contract is clear about how the work will be set up, performed, and cleaned.

- Share the results of any previous lead tests with the contractor.
- Even before contractors are required to be certified you should specify in the contract that they follow the work practices described on pages 9 and 10 of this brochure.
- The contract should specify which parts of your home are part of the work area and specify which lead-safe work practices should be used in those areas. Remember, your contractor should confine dust and debris to the work area and should minimize spreading that dust to other areas of the home.
- The contract should also specify that the contractor clean the work area, verify that it was cleaned adequately, and re-clean it if necessary.

Once these practices are required, if you think a worker is failing to do what they are supposed to do or is doing something that is unsafe, you should:

- Direct the contractor to comply with the contract requirements,
- Call your local health or building department, or
- Call EPA's hotline 1-800-424-LEAD (5323).

For Tenants, and Families of Children Under Age Six in Child Care Facilities and Schools

You play an important role ensuring the ultimate safety of your family.

This means properly preparing for the renovation and staying out of the work area (see p. 8).

Beginning April 2010, federal law will require that contractors performing renovation, repair and painting projects that disturb lead-based paint in homes, child care facilities and schools built before 1978 that a child under age six visits regularly to be certified and follow specific work practices to prevent lead contamination.

The law will require anyone hired to renovate, repair, or do painting preparation work on a property built before 1978 to follow the steps described on pages 9 and 10 unless the area where the work will be done contains no lead-based paint.

Once these practices are required, if you think a worker is failing to do what they are supposed to do or is doing something that is unsafe, you should:

- Contact your landlord,
- Call your local health or building department, or
- Call EPA's hotline **1-800-424-LEAD (5323)**.

If you are concerned about lead hazards left behind after the job is over, you can check the work yourself (see page 10).

If your property receives housing assistance from HUD (or a state or local agency that uses HUD funds), you must follow the more stringent requirements of HUD's Lead-safe Housing Rule and the ones described in this pamphlet.

Preparing for a Renovation

The work areas should not be accessible to occupants while the work occurs. The rooms or areas where work is being done may be blocked off or sealed with plastic sheeting to contain any dust that is generated. The contained area will not be available to you until the work in that room or area is complete, cleaned thoroughly, and the containment has been removed. You will not have access to some areas and should plan accordingly.

You may need:

- Alternative bedroom, bathroom, and kitchen arrangements if work is occurring in those areas of your home.
- A safe place for pets because they, too, can be poisoned by lead and can track lead dust into other areas of the home.
- A separate pathway for the contractor from the work area to the outside, in order to bring materials in and out of the home. Ideally, it should not be through the same entrance that your family uses.
- A place to store your furniture. All furniture and belongings may have to be moved from the work area while the work is done. Items that can't be moved, such as cabinets, should be wrapped in heavy duty plastic.
- To turn off forced-air heating and air conditioning systems while work is done. This prevents dust from spreading through vents from the work area to the rest of your home. Consider how this may affect your living arrangements.

You may even want to move out of your home temporarily while all or parts of the work are being done.

Child care facilities and schools may want to consider alternative accommodations for children and access to necessary facilities.

During the Work

Beginning April 2010, federal law will require contractors that are hired to perform renovation, repair and painting projects in homes, child care facilities, and schools built before 1978 that disturb lead-based paint to be certified and follow specific work practices to prevent lead contamination.

Even before contractors are required to be certified and follow specific work practices, the contractor should follow these three simple procedures, described below:

1. **Contain the work area.** The area should be contained so that dust and debris do not escape from that area. Warning signs should be put up and heavy-duty plastic and tape should be used as appropriate to:
   - Cover the floors and any furniture that cannot be moved.
   - Seal off doors and heating and cooling system vents.

These will help prevent dust or debris from getting outside the work area.

2. **Minimize dust.** There is no way to eliminate dust, but some methods make less dust than others. For example, using water to mist areas before sanding or scraping; scoring paint before separating components; and prying and pulling apart components instead of breaking them are techniques that generate less dust than alternatives. Some methods generate large amounts of lead-contaminated dust and should not be used. They are:
   - Open flame burning or torching.
   - Sanding, grinding, planing, needle gunning, or blasting with power tools and equipment not equipped with a shroud and HEPA vacuum attachment.
   - Using a heat gun at temperatures greater than 1100°F.

3. **Clean up thoroughly.** The work area should be cleaned up daily to keep it as clean as possible. When all the work is done, the area should be cleaned up using special cleaning methods before taking down any plastic that isolates the work area from the rest of the home. The special cleaning methods should include:
   - Using a HEPA vacuum to clean up dust and debris on all surfaces, followed by
   - Wet mopping with plenty of rinse water.

When the final cleaning is done, look around. There should be no dust, paint chips, or debris in the work area. If you see any dust, paint chips, or debris, the area should be re-cleaned.

For Property Owners:
After the Work is Done

When all the work is finished, you will want to know if your home, child care facility, or school has been cleaned up properly. Here are some ways to check.

Even before contractors are required to be certified and follow specific work practices, you should:

Ask about your contractor's final cleanup check. Remember, lead dust is often invisible to the naked eye. It may still be present even if you cannot see it. The contractor should use disposable cleaning cloths to wipe the floor of the work area and compare them to a cleaning verification card to determine if the work area was adequately cleaned.

To order a cleaning verification card and detailed instructions visit the EPA lead website at **www.epa.gov/lead** or contact the National Lead Information Center at **1-800-424-LEAD (5323)** or visit their website at **www.epa.gov/lead/nlic.htm.**

You also may choose to have a lead-dust test. Lead-dust tests are wipe samples sent to a laboratory for analysis.

- You can specify in your contract that a lead-dust test will be done. In this case, make it clear who will do the testing.
- Testing should be done by a lead professional.

If you choose to do the testing, some EPA-recognized lead laboratories will send you a kit that allows you to collect samples and send them back to the lab for analysis.

Contact the National Lead Information Center at **1-800-424-LEAD (5323)** for lists of qualified professionals and EPA-recognized lead labs.

If your home, child care facility, or school fails the dust test, the area should be re-cleaned and tested again.

Where the project is done by contract, it is a good idea to specify in the contract that the contractor is responsible for re-cleaning if the home, child care facility, or school fails the test.

For Additional Information

You may need additional information on how to protect yourself and your children while a job is going on in your home, your building, or childcare facility.

■ The **National Lead Information Center** at 1-800-424-LEAD (5323) or www.epa.gov/lead/nlic.htm can tell you how to contact your state, local, and/or tribal programs or get general information about lead poisoning prevention.

  • State and tribal lead poisoning prevention or environmental protection programs can provide information about lead regulations and potential sources of financial aid for reducing lead hazards. If your State or local government has requirements more stringent than those described in this pamphlet, you must follow those requirements.

  • Local building code officials can tell you the regulations that apply to the renovation work that you are planning.

  • State, county, and local health departments can provide information about local programs, including assistance for lead-poisoned children and advice on ways to get your home checked for lead.

■ The **National Lead Information Center** can also provide a variety of resource materials, including the following guides to lead-safe work practices. Many of these materials are also available at www.epa.gov/lead/pubs/brochure.htm.

  • Lead Paint Safety, a Field Guide for Painting, Home Maintenance, and Renovation Work

  • Protect Your Family from Lead in Your Home

  • Lead in Your Home: A Parent's Reference Guide

For the hearing impaired, call the Federal Information Relay Service at 1-800-877-8339 to access any of the phone numbers in this brochure.

EPA Contacts

EPA Regional Offices

EPA addresses residential lead hazards through several different regulations. EPA requires training and certification for conducting abatement, education about hazards associated with renovations, disclosure about known lead paint and lead hazards in housing, and sets lead-paint hazard standards.

Your Regional EPA Office can provide further information regarding lead safety and lead protection programs at **www.epa.gov/lead.**

Region 1
(Connecticut,
Massachusetts, Maine,
New Hampshire, Rhode
Island, Vermont)
Regional Lead Contact
U.S. EPA Region 1
Suite 1100
One Congress Street
Boston, MA 02114-2023
(888) 372-7341

Region 2
(New Jersey, New York,
Puerto Rico, Virgin Islands)
Regional Lead Contact
U.S. EPA Region 2
2890 Woodbridge Avenue
Building 205, Mail Stop 225
Edison, NJ 08837-3679
(732) 321-6771

Region 3
(Delaware, Maryland,
Pennsylvania, Virginia,
Washington, DC,
West Virginia)
Regional Lead Contact
U.S. EPA Region 3
1650 Arch Street
Philadelphia, PA
19103-2029
(215) 814-5000

Region 4
(Alabama, Florida,
Georgia, Kentucky,
Mississippi, North Carolina,
South Carolina, Tennessee)
Regional Lead Contact
U.S. EPA Region 4
61 Forsyth Street, SW
Atlanta, GA 30303-8960
(404) 562-9900

Region 5
(Illinois, Indiana,
Michigan, Minnesota,
Ohio, Wisconsin)
Regional Lead Contact
U.S. EPA Region 5
77 West Jackson Boulevard
Chicago, IL 60604-3507
(312) 886-6003

Region 6
(Arkansas, Louisiana,
New Mexico, Oklahoma,
Texas)
Regional Lead Contact
U.S. EPA Region 6
1445 Ross Avenue,
12th Floor
Dallas, TX 75202-2733
(214) 665-6444

Region 7
(Iowa, Kansas,
Missouri, Nebraska)
Regional Lead Contact
U.S. EPA Region 7
901 N. 5th Street
Kansas City, KS 66101
(913) 551-7003

Region 8
(Colorado, Montana,
North Dakota, South
Dakota, Utah, Wyoming)
Regional Lead Contact
U.S. EPA Region 8
1595 Wynkoop Street
Denver, CO 80202
(303) 312-6312

Region 9
(Arizona, California,
Hawaii, Nevada)
Regional Lead Contact
U.S. Region 9
75 Hawthorne Street
San Francisco, CA 94105
(415) 947-8021

Region 10
(Alaska, Idaho,
Oregon, Washington)
Regional Lead Contact
U.S. EPA Region 10
1200 Sixth Avenue
Seattle, WA 98101-1128
(206) 553-1200

Other Federal Agencies

CPSC

The Consumer Product Safety Commission (CPSC) protects the public from the unreasonable risk of injury or death from 15,000 types of consumer products under the agency's jurisdiction. CPSC warns the public and private sectors to reduce exposure to lead and increase consumer awareness. Contact CPSC for further information regarding regulations and consumer product safety.

CPSC
4330 East West Highway
Bethesda, MD 20814
Hotline 1-(800) 638-2772
www.cpsc.gov

CDC Childhood Lead Poisoning Prevention Branch

The Centers for Disease Control and Prevention (CDC) assists state and local childhood lead poisoning prevention programs to provide a scientific basis for policy decisions, and to ensure that health issues are addressed in decisions about housing and the environment. Contact CDC Childhood Lead Poisoning Prevention Program for additional materials and links on the topic of lead.

CDC Childhood Lead Poisoning Prevention Branch
4770 Buford Highway, MS F-40
Atlanta, GA 30341
(770) 488-3300
www.cdc.gov/nceh/lead

HUD Office of Healthy Homes and Lead Hazard Control

The Department of Housing and Urban Development (HUD) provides funds to state and local governments to develop cost-effective ways to reduce lead-based paint hazards in America's privately-owned low-income housing. In addition, the office enforces the rule on disclosure of known lead paint and lead hazards in housing, and HUD's lead safety regulations in HUD-assisted housing, provides public outreach and technical assistance, and conducts technical studies to help protect children and their families from health and safety hazards in the home. Contact the HUD Office of Healthy Homes and Lead Hazard Control for information on lead regulations, outreach efforts, and lead hazard control research and outreach grant programs.

U.S. Department of Housing and Urban Development
Office of Healthy Homes and Lead Hazard Control
451 Seventh Street, SW, Room 8236
Washington, DC 20410-3000
HUD's Lead Regulations Hotline
(202) 402-7698
www.hud.gov/offices/lead/

Current Sample Pre-Renovation Form

Effective until April 2010.

Confirmation of Receipt of Lead Pamphlet

❏ I have received a copy of the pamphlet, *Renovate Right: Important Lead Hazard Information for Families, Child Care Providers and Schools* informing me of the potential risk of the lead hazard exposure from renovation activity to be performed in my dwelling unit. I received this pamphlet before the work began.

_____   _____

Printed name of recipient   Date

_____

Signature of recipient

Self-Certification Option (for tenant-occupied dwellings only) —
If the lead pamphlet was delivered but a tenant signature was not obtainable, you may check the appropriate box below.

❏ **Refusal to sign** — I certify that I have made a good faith effort to deliver the pamphlet, *Renovate Right: Important Lead Hazard Information for Families, Child Care Providers and Schools*, to the rental dwelling unit listed below at the date and time indicated and that the occupant refused to sign the confirmation of receipt. I further certify that I have left a copy of the pamphlet at the unit with the occupant.

❏ **Unavailable for signature** — I certify that I have made a good faith effort to deliver the pamphlet, *Renovate Right: Important Lead Hazard Information for Families, Child Care providers and Schools*, to the rental dwelling unit listed below and that the occupant was unavailable to sign the confirmation of receipt. I further certify that I have left a copy of the pamphlet at the unit by sliding it under the door.

_____   _____

Printed name of person certifying   Attempted delivery
                                                                        date and time
                                                                        lead pamphlet delivery

_____

Signature of person certifying lead pamphlet delivery

_____

_____

Unit Address

Note Regarding Mailing Option — As an alternative to delivery in person, you may mail the lead pamphlet to the owner and/or tenant. Pamphlet must be mailed at least 7 days before renovation (Document with a certificate of mailing from the post office).

Future Sample Pre-Renovation Form

This sample form may be used by renovation firms to document compliance with the Federal pre-renovation education and renovation, repair, and painting regulations.

Occupant Confirmation

Pamphlet Receipt

❏ I have received a copy of the lead hazard information pamphlet informing me of the potential risk of the lead hazard exposure from renovation activity to be performed in my dwelling unit. I received this pamphlet before the work began.

Owner-occupant Opt-out Acknowledgment

❏ (A) I confirm that I own and live in this property, that no child under the age of 6 resides here, that no pregnant woman resides here, and that this property is not a child-occupied facility.

Note: A child resides in the primary residence of his or her custodial parents, legal guardians, foster parents, or informal caretaker if the child lives and sleeps most of the time at the caretaker's residence.

Note: A child-occupied facility is a pre-1978 building visited regularly by the same child, under 6 years of age, on at least two different days within any week, for at least 3 hours each day, provided that the visits total at least 60 hours annually.

If Box A is checked, check either Box B or Box C, but not both.

❏ (B) I request that the renovation firm use the lead-safe work practices required by EPA's Renovation, Repair, and Painting Rule; or

❏ (C) I understand that the firm performing the renovation will not be required to use the lead-safe work practices required by EPA's Renovation, Repair, and Painting Rule.

Printed Name of Owner-occupant

Signature of Owner-occupant   Signature Date

Renovator's Self Certification Option (for tenant-occupied dwellings only)

Instructions to Renovator: If the lead hazard information pamphlet was delivered but a tenant signature was not obtainable, you may check the appropriate box below.

❏ **Declined** – I certify that I have made a good faith effort to deliver the lead hazard information pamphlet to the rental dwelling unit listed below at the date and time indicated and that the occupant declined to sign the confirmation of receipt. I further certify that I have left a copy of the pamphlet at the unit with the occupant.

❏ **Unavailable for signature** – I certify that I have made a good faith effort to deliver the lead hazard information pamphlet to the rental dwelling unit listed below and that the occupant was unavailable to sign the confirmation of receipt. I further certify that I have left a copy of the pamphlet at the unit by sliding it under the door or by (fill in how pamphlet was left). _____

Printed Name of Person Certifying Delivery   Attempted Delivery Date

---

Signature of Person Certifying Lead Pamphlet Delivery

Unit Address

Note Regarding Mailing Option — As an alternative to delivery in person, you may mail the lead hazard information pamphlet to the owner and/or tenant. Pamphlet must be mailed at least seven days before renovation. Mailing must be documented by a certificate of mailing from the post office.

Note: This form is not effective until April 2010.

1-800-424-LEAD (5323)
www.epa.gov/lead

EPA-740-F-08-002
March 2008

Appendix 4:

Small Entity Compliance Guide to Renovate Right

United States
Environmental
Protection Agency
Office of Pollution Prevention and Toxics

EPA-740-F-08-003
December 2008

mall Entity Compliance uide to Renovate Right PA's Lead-Based Paint enovation, Repair, and ainting Program

A handbook for contractors, property managers and maintenance personnel working in homes, child care facilities and schools built before 1978

Appx 5

LEAD
Awareness
Program

Who Should Read this Handbook?

- Anyone who owns or manages housing or child-occupied facilities built before 1978.

- Contractors who perform activities that disturb painted surfaces in homes and child-occupied facilities built before 1978 (including certain repairs and maintenance, and painting preparation activities).

About this Handbook

This handbook summarizes requirements of EPA's Lead-Based Paint Renovation, Repair and Painting Program Rule, aimed at protecting against lead-based paint hazards associated with renovation, repair and painting activities. The rule requires workers to be trained to use lead-safe work practices and requires renovation firms to be EPA-certified; these requirements will become effective April 22, 2010.

To ensure compliance, you should also read the complete rule on which the program is based. While EPA has summarized the provisions of the rule in this guide, the legal requirements that apply to renovation work are governed by EPA's 2008 Lead Rule. A copy of the rule is available on EPA's website at www.epa.gov/lead/pubs/renovation.

A companion pamphlet, entitled *Renovate Right: Important Lead Hazard Information for Families, Child Care Providers, and Schools* (EPA-740-F-08-002), has been prepared in conjunction with the rule for distribution to persons affected by work that disturbs lead-based paint. (See page 17 for information on how to get copies of the rule, the *Renovate Right* pamphlet, and other related materials).

Other state or local requirements that are different from or more stringent than the federal requirements may apply in your state. For example, federal law allows EPA to authorize states to administer their own program in lieu of the federal lead program. Even in states without an authorized lead program, a state may promulgate its own rules that may be different or go beyond the federal requirements. For more information on the rules that apply in your state, please contact the National Lead Information Center at 1-800-424-LEAD (5323).

Your feedback is important. Please review this guide and contact the National Lead Information Center at 1-800-424-LEAD (5323) with any comments regarding its usefulness and readability, and improvements you think are needed.

What Is the Lead-Based Paint Renovation, Repair and Painting Program (RRP)?

- The Lead-Based Paint Renovation, Repair and Painting Program is a federal regulatory program affecting contractors, property managers, and others who disturb painted surfaces.

- It applies to residential houses, apartments, and child-occupied facilities such as schools and day-care centers built before 1978.

- It includes pre-renovation education requirements as well as training, certification, and work practice requirements.

    - Pre-renovation education requirements are effective now:

        - Contractors, property managers, and others who perform renovations for compensation in residential houses, apartments, and child-occupied facilities built before 1978 are required to distribute a lead pamphlet before starting renovation work.

    - Training, certification, and work practice requirements become effective April 22, 2010:

        - Firms are required to be certified, their employees must be trained in use of lead-safe work practices, and lead-safe work practices that minimize occupants' exposure to lead hazards must be followed.

- Renovation is broadly defined as any activity that disturbs painted surfaces and includes most repair, remodeling, and maintenance activities, including window replacement.

- The program includes requirements implementing both Section 402(c) and 406(b) of the Toxic Substances Control Act (TSCA). (www.epa.gov/lead/pubs/titleten.html)

- EPA's lead regulations can be found at 40 CFR Part 745, Subpart E.

How Can this Handbook Help Me?

- Understanding the lead program's requirements can help you protect your customers from the hazards of lead and can, therefore, mean more business for you.

- This handbook presents simple steps to follow to comply with the EPA's lead program. It also lists ways these steps can be easily incorporated into your work.

- Distributing the lead pamphlet and incorporating required work practices into your job site will help protect your customers and occupants from the hazards of lead-based paint.

Who Must Follow the 2008 Lead Rule's Requirements?

In general, anyone who is paid to perform work that disturbs paint in housing and child-occupied facilities built before 1978, this may include, but is not limited to:

– Residential rental property owners/managers

– General contractors

– Special trade contractors, including

• Painters

• Plumbers

• Carpenters

• Electricians

What Activities Are Subject to the Lead Renovation, Repair and Painting Program?

In general, any activity that disturbs paint in pre-1978 housing and child-occupied facilities, including:

• Remodeling and repair/maintenance

• Electrical work

• Plumbing

• Painting

• Carpentry

• Window replacement

What Housing or Activities Are Excluded and Not Subject to the Rule?

• Housing built in 1978 or later.

• Housing for elderly or disabled persons, unless children under 6 reside or are expected to reside there.

• Zero-bedroom dwellings (studio apartments, dormitories, etc.).

• Housing or components declared lead-free by a certified inspector or risk assessor.

• Minor repair and maintenance activities that disturb 6 square feet or less of paint per room inside, or 20 square feet or less on the exterior of a home or building.

• Note: minor repair and maintenance activities do not include window replacement and projects involving demolition or prohibited practices.

What Does the Program Require Me To Do?

Pre-renovation education requirements - Effective now.

- In housing, you must:
  - Distribute EPA's lead pamphlet to the owner and occupants before renovation starts.
- In a child-occupied facility, you must:
  - Distribute the lead pamphlet to the owner of the building or an adult representative of the child-occupied facility before the renovation starts.
- For work in common areas of multi-family housing or child-occupied facilities, you must:
  - Distribute renovation notices to tenants or parents/guardians of the children attending the child-occupied facility. Or you must post informational signs about the renovation or repair job.
- Informational signs must:
  - Be posted where they will be seen;
  - Describe the nature, locations, and dates of the renovation; and
  - Be accompanied by the lead pamphlet or by information on how parents and guardians can get a free copy (see page 31 for information on obtaining copies).
- Obtain confirmation of receipt of the lead pamphlet (see page 23) from the owner, adult representative, or occupants (as applicable), or a certificate of mailing from the post office.
- Retain records for three years.
- *Note:* Pre-renovation education requirements do not apply to emergency renovations. Emergency renovations include interim controls performed in response to a resident child with an elevated blood-lead level.

Training, Certification, and Work Practice Requirements– Effective after April 22, 2010.

- Firms must be certified.
- Renovators must be trained.
- Lead-safe work practices must be followed. Examples of these practices include:
  - Work-area containment to prevent dust and debris from leaving the work area.
  - Prohibition of certain work practices like open-flame burning and the use of power tools without HEPA exhaust control.
  - Thorough clean up followed by a verification procedure to minimize exposure to lead-based paint hazards.
- The training, certification, and work practice requirements do not apply where the firm obtained a signed statement from the owner that all of the following are met:
  - The renovation will occur in the owner's residence;
  - No child under age 6 resides there;
  - No woman who is pregnant resides there;
  - The housing is not a child-occupied facility; and
  - The owner acknowledges that the renovation firm will not be required to use the work practices contained in the rule.

When Do These Requirements Become Fully Applicable to Me?

– April 2009:

- Training providers may begin applying for accreditation.

- Once training providers are accredited, they may offer training courses that will allow renovators to become certified.

– October 2009 - Renovation firms may begin applying to EPA for certification.

– April 2010 - Program fully effective. Work practices must be followed.

How Will a Firm Become Certified?

Beginning in October 2009, firms may apply to EPA for certification to perform renovations or dust sampling. To apply, a firm must submit to EPA a completed "Application for Firms," signed by an authorized agent of the firm, and pay the correct amount of fees. To obtain a copy of the "Application for Firms" contact the NLIC at 1-800-424-LEAD (5323) or visit www.epa.gov/lead/pubs/renovation.htm.

What Are the Responsibilities of a Certified Firm?

Firms performing renovations must ensure that:

1. All individuals performing activities that disturb painted surfaces on behalf of the firm are either certified renovators or have been trained by a certified renovator.

2. A certified renovator is assigned to each renovation and performs all of the certified renovator responsibilities.

3. All renovations performed by the firm are performed in accordance with the work practice standards of the Lead-Based Paint Renovation, Repair, and Painting Program (see the flowchart on page 9 for details about the work practice standards).

4. Pre-renovation education requirements of the Lead-Based Paint Renovation, Repair, and Painting Program are performed.

5. The program's recordkeeping requirements are met.

How Will a Renovator Become Certified?

To become a certified renovator an individual must successfully complete an eight-hour initial renovator training course offered by an accredited training provider (training providers are accredited by EPA, or by an authorized state or tribal program). The course completion certificate serves as proof of certification. Training providers can apply for accreditation for renovator and dust sampling technician training beginning in April 2009. Once accredited, trainers can begin to provide certification training.

Are There Streamlined Requirements for Contractors with Previous Lead Training?

Yes. Individuals who have successfully completed an accredited lead abatement worker or supervisor course, or individuals who have successfully completed an EPA, Department of Housing and Urban Development (HUD), or EPA/HUD model renovation training course, need only take a four-hour refresher renovator training course instead of the eight-hour initial renovator training course to become certified.

What Are the Responsibilities of a Certified Renovator?

Certified renovators are responsible for ensuring overall compliance with the Lead-Based Paint Renovation, Repair, and Painting Program's requirements for lead-safe work practices at renovations they are assigned. A certified renovator (see the flowchart on page 9 for details about the work practice standards):

1. Must use a test kit acceptable to EPA, when requested by the party contracting for renovation services, to determine whether components to be affected by the renovation contain lead-based paint (EPA will announce which test kits are acceptable prior to April 2010. Please check our Web site at www.epa.gov/lead).

2. Must provide on-the-job training to workers on the work practices they will be using in performing their assigned tasks.

3. Must be physically present at the work site when warning signs are posted, while the work-area containment is being established, and while the work-area cleaning is performed.

4. Must regularly direct work being performed by other individuals to ensure that the work practices are being followed, including maintaining the integrity of the containment barriers and ensuring that dust or debris does not spread beyond the work area.

5. Must be available, either on-site or by telephone, at all times renovations are being conducted.

6. Must perform project cleaning verification.

7. Must have with them at the work site copies of their initial course completion certificate and their most recent refresher course completion certificate.

8. Must prepare required records.

How Long Will Firm and Renovator Certifications Last?

To maintain their certification, renovators and firms must be re-certified by EPA every five years. A firm must submit to EPA a completed "Application for Firms," signed by an authorized agent of the firm, and pay the correct amount of fees. Renovators must successfully complete a refresher training course provided by an accredited training provider.

What Are the Recordkeeping Requirements?

- All documents must be retained for three years following the completion of a renovation.

- Records that must be retained include:

  - Reports certifying that lead-based paint is not present.

  - Records relating to the distribution of the lead pamphlet.

  - Any signed and dated statements received from owner-occupants documenting that the requirements do not apply (i.e., there is no child under age 6 or no pregnant woman who resides at the home, and it is not a child-occupied facility).

  - Documentation of compliance with the requirements of the Lead-Based Paint Renovation, Repair, and Painting Program (EPA has prepared a sample form that is available at www.epa.gov/lead/pubs/samplechecklist.pdf).

What Are the Required Work Practices?

The flow charts on the following pages will help determine if your project is subject to the Lead-Based Paint Renovation, Repair and Painting Program's requirements and, if so, the specific requirements for your particular project. The flowcharts, and other information included in this guide, are not intended to be a replacement for official training.

EPA's Lead Program Rule At-A-Glance

Do the Requirements Apply to the Renovation?

If you will be getting paid to do work that disturbs painted surfaces in a pre-1978 home, apartment building, or child-occupied facility, answer the questions below to determine if the EPA lead program requires you to distribute the lead pamphlet and/or if you will need to comply with training, certification, and work practice requirements when conducting the work.

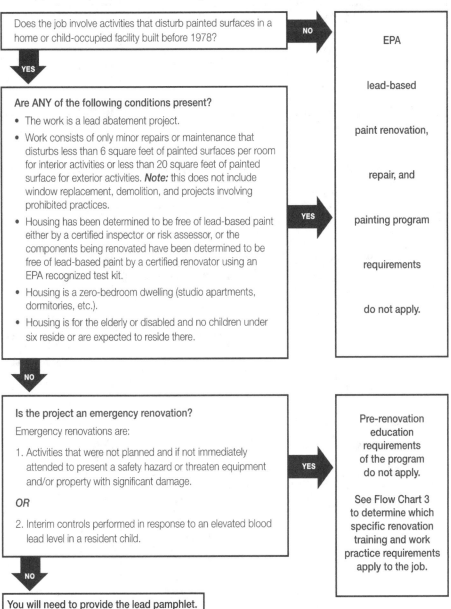

Does the job involve activities that disturb painted surfaces in a home or child-occupied facility built before 1978?

NO → EPA lead-based paint renovation, repair, and painting program requirements do not apply.

YES ↓

Are ANY of the following conditions present?

- The work is a lead abatement project.
- Work consists of only minor repairs or maintenance that disturbs less than 6 square feet of painted surfaces per room for interior activities or less than 20 square feet of painted surface for exterior activities. *Note:* this does not include window replacement, demolition, and projects involving prohibited practices.
- Housing has been determined to be free of lead-based paint either by a certified inspector or risk assessor, or the components being renovated have been determined to be free of lead-based paint by a certified renovator using an EPA recognized test kit.
- Housing is a zero-bedroom dwelling (studio apartments, dormitories, etc.).
- Housing is for the elderly or disabled and no children under six reside or are expected to reside there.

YES → (same as above)

NO ↓

Is the project an emergency renovation?

Emergency renovations are:

1. Activities that were not planned and if not immediately attended to present a safety hazard or threaten equipment and/or property with significant damage.

OR

2. Interim controls performed in response to an elevated blood lead level in a resident child.

YES → Pre-renovation education requirements of the program do not apply.

See Flow Chart 3 to determine which specific renovation training and work practice requirements apply to the job.

NO ↓

You will need to provide the lead pamphlet. See Flow Chart 2 for specific requirements.

How Do I Comply with the Pre-Renovation Education Requirements?

Requirements to distribute pre-renovation educational materials vary based on the location of the renovation. Select the location below that best describes the location of your project, and follow the applicable procedure on the right.

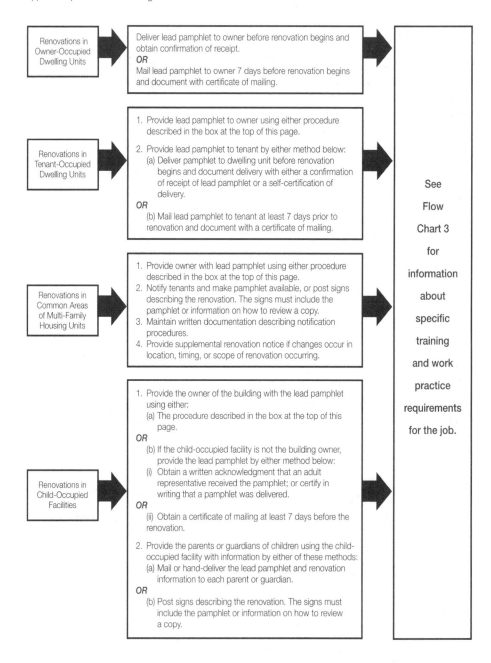

Renovations in Owner-Occupied Dwelling Units

Deliver lead pamphlet to owner before renovation begins and obtain confirmation of receipt.
OR
Mail lead pamphlet to owner 7 days before renovation begins and document with certificate of mailing.

Renovations in Tenant-Occupied Dwelling Units

1. Provide lead pamphlet to owner using either procedure described in the box at the top of this page.
2. Provide lead pamphlet to tenant by either method below:
   (a) Deliver pamphlet to dwelling unit before renovation begins and document delivery with either a confirmation of receipt of lead pamphlet or a self-certification of delivery.
   OR
   (b) Mail lead pamphlet to tenant at least 7 days prior to renovation and document with a certificate of mailing.

Renovations in Common Areas of Multi-Family Housing Units

1. Provide owner with lead pamphlet using either procedure described in the box at the top of this page.
2. Notify tenants and make pamphlet available, or post signs describing the renovation. The signs must include the pamphlet or information on how to review a copy.
3. Maintain written documentation describing notification procedures.
4. Provide supplemental renovation notice if changes occur in location, timing, or scope of renovation occurring.

Renovations in Child-Occupied Facilities

1. Provide the owner of the building with the lead pamphlet using either:
   (a) The procedure described in the box at the top of this page.
   OR
   (b) If the child-occupied facility is not the building owner, provide the lead pamphlet by either method below:
   (i) Obtain a written acknowledgment that an adult representative received the pamphlet; or certify in writing that a pamphlet was delivered.
   OR
   (ii) Obtain a certificate of mailing at least 7 days before the renovation.
2. Provide the parents or guardians of children using the child-occupied facility with information by either of these methods:
   (a) Mail or hand-deliver the lead pamphlet and renovation information to each parent or guardian.
   OR
   (b) Post signs describing the renovation. The signs must include the pamphlet or information on how to review a copy.

See Flow Chart 3 for information about specific training and work practice requirements for the job.

Do the Renovation Training and Work Practices Apply?

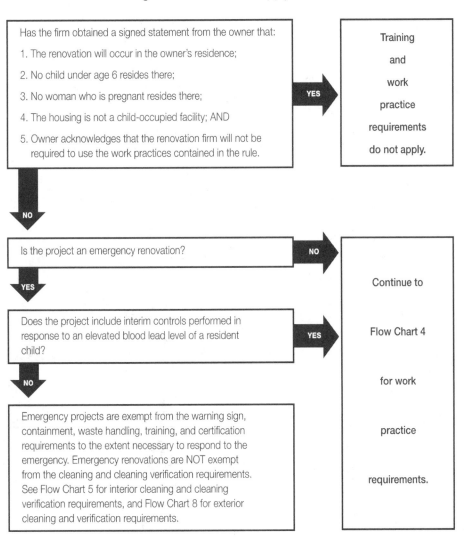

Has the firm obtained a signed statement from the owner that:

1. The renovation will occur in the owner's residence;

2. No child under age 6 resides there;

3. No woman who is pregnant resides there;

4. The housing is not a child-occupied facility; AND

5. Owner acknowledges that the renovation firm will not be required to use the work practices contained in the rule.

YES

Training and work practice requirements do not apply.

NO

Is the project an emergency renovation?

NO

YES

Does the project include interim controls performed in response to an elevated blood lead level of a resident child?

YES

Continue to Flow Chart 4 for work practice requirements.

NO

Emergency projects are exempt from the warning sign, containment, waste handling, training, and certification requirements to the extent necessary to respond to the emergency. Emergency renovations are NOT exempt from the cleaning and cleaning verification requirements. See Flow Chart 5 for interior cleaning and cleaning verification requirements, and Flow Chart 8 for exterior cleaning and verification requirements.

Work Practice Requirements

General

(A) Renovations must be performed by certified firms using certified renovators.

(B) Firms must post signs clearly defining the work area and warning occupants and other persons not involved in renovation activities to remain outside of the work area. These signs should be in the language of the occupants.

(C) Prior to the renovation, the firm must contain the work area so that no dust or debris leaves the work area while the renovation is being performed.

(D) Work practices listed below are prohibited during a renovation:

    1. Open-flame burning or torching of lead-based paint;

    2. Use of machines that remove lead-based paint through high speed operation such as sanding, grinding, power planing, needle gun, abrasive blasting, or sandblasting, unless such machines are used with HEPA exhaust control; and

    3. Operating a heat gun on lead-based paint at temperatures of 1100 degrees Fahrenheit or higher.

(E) Waste from renovations:

    1. Waste from renovation activities must be contained to prevent releases of dust and debris before the waste is removed from the work area for storage or disposal.

    2. At the conclusion of each work day and at the conclusion of the renovation, waste that has been collected from renovation activities must be stored to prevent access to and the release of dust and debris.

    3. Waste transported from renovation activities must be contained to prevent release of dust and debris.

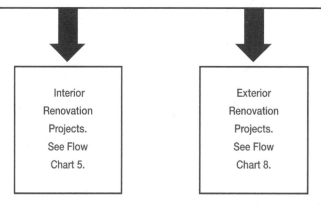

Interior Renovation Projects. See Flow Chart 5.

Exterior Renovation Projects. See Flow Chart 8.

Work Practice Requirements Specific to Interior Renovations

The firm must:

(A) Remove all objects from the work area or cover them with plastic sheeting with all seams and edges sealed.

(B) Close and cover all ducts opening in the work area with taped-down plastic sheeting.

(C) Close windows and doors in the work area. Doors must be covered with plastic sheeting.

(D) Cover the floor surface with taped-down plastic sheeting in the work area a minimum of six feet beyond the perimeter of surfaces undergoing renovation or a sufficient distance to contain the dust, whichever is greater.

(E) Use precautions to ensure that all personnel, tools, and other items, including the exteriors of containers of waste, are free of dust and debris when leaving the work area.

(F) After the renovation has been completed, the firm must clean the work area until no dust, debris or residue remains. The firm must:

    1. Collect all paint chips and debris, and seal it in a heavy-duty bag.

    2. Remove and dispose of protective sheeting as waste.

    3. Clean all objects and surfaces in the work area and within two feet of the work area in the following manner:

        a. Clean walls starting at the ceiling and working down to the floor by either vacuuming with a HEPA vacuum or wiping with a damp cloth.

        b. Thoroughly vacuum all remaining surfaces and objects in the work area, including furniture and fixtures, with a HEPA vacuum.

        c. Wipe all remaining surfaces and objects in the work area, except for carpeted or upholstered surfaces, with a damp cloth. Mop uncarpeted floors thoroughly using a mopping method that keeps the wash water separate from the rinse water, or using a wet mopping system.

Cleaning verification is required to ensure the work area
is adequately cleaned and ready for re-occupancy.
See Flow Chart 6 for instructions on performing cleaning
verification for interior projects.

Interior Cleaning Verification: Visual Inspection and Optional Clearance Testing

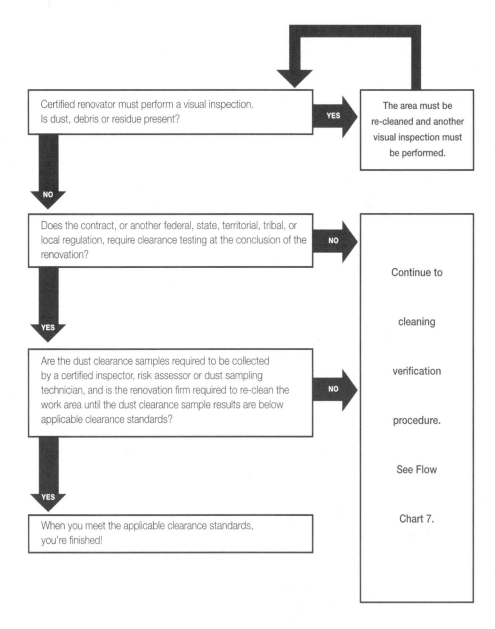

Certified renovator must perform a visual inspection.
Is dust, debris or residue present?

YES → The area must be re-cleaned and another visual inspection must be performed.

NO ↓

Does the contract, or another federal, state, territorial, tribal, or local regulation, require clearance testing at the conclusion of the renovation?

NO →

YES ↓

Are the dust clearance samples required to be collected by a certified inspector, risk assessor or dust sampling technician, and is the renovation firm required to re-clean the work area until the dust clearance sample results are below applicable clearance standards?

NO →

YES ↓

When you meet the applicable clearance standards, you're finished!

Continue to cleaning verification procedure. See Flow Chart 7.

Interior Cleaning Verification: Floors, Countertops, and Window Sills

Note: For areas greater than 40 square feet, separate the area into sections and use a new disposable cleaning cloth for each section.

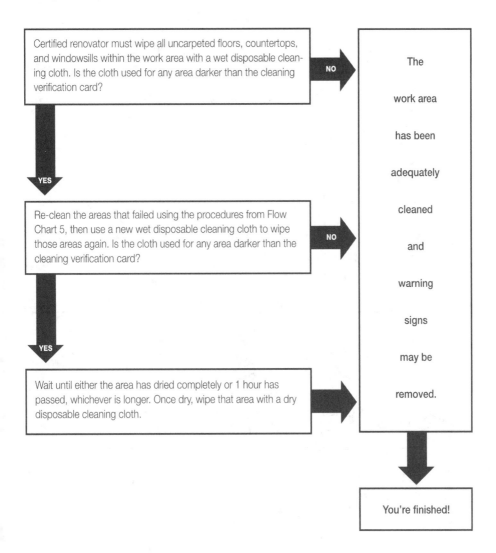

Certified renovator must wipe all uncarpeted floors, countertops, and windowsills within the work area with a wet disposable cleaning cloth. Is the cloth used for any area darker than the cleaning verification card?

NO

YES

Re-clean the areas that failed using the procedures from Flow Chart 5, then use a new wet disposable cleaning cloth to wipe those areas again. Is the cloth used for any area darker than the cleaning verification card?

NO

YES

Wait until either the area has dried completely or 1 hour has passed, whichever is longer. Once dry, wipe that area with a dry disposable cleaning cloth.

The work area has been adequately cleaned and warning signs may be removed.

You're finished!

Work Practice Requirements Specific to Exterior Renovations

The firm must:

(A) Close all doors and windows within 20 feet of the renovation.

(B) Ensure that doors within the work area that will be used while the job is being performed are covered with plastic sheeting in a manner that allows workers to pass through while confining dust and debris.

(C) Cover the ground with plastic sheeting or other disposable impermeable material extending a minimum of 10 feet beyond the perimeter or a sufficient distance to collect falling paint debris, whichever is greater.

(D) In situations such as where work areas are in close proximity to other buildings, windy conditions, etc., the renovation firm must take extra precautions in containing the work area, like vertical containment.

(E) After the renovation has been completed, the firm must clean the work area until no dust, debris or residue remains. The firm must:

1. Collect all paint chips and debris, and seal it in a heavy-duty bag.

2. Remove and dispose of protective sheeting as waste.

3. Waste transported from renovation activities must be contained to prevent release of dust and debris.

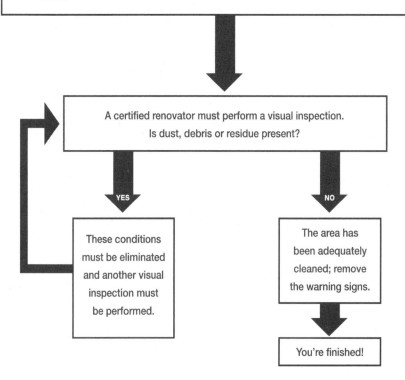

A certified renovator must perform a visual inspection.
Is dust, debris or residue present?

YES

These conditions must be eliminated and another visual inspection must be performed.

NO

The area has been adequately cleaned; remove the warning signs.

You're finished!

How Is My Compliance Determined, and What Happens if the Agency Discovers a Violation?

To maximize compliance, EPA implements a balanced program of compliance assistance, compliance incentives, and traditional law enforcement. EPA knows that small businesses that must comply with complicated new statutes or rules often want to do the right thing, but may lack the requisite knowledge, resources, or skills. Compliance assistance information and technical advice helps small businesses to understand and meet their environmental obligations. Compliance incentives, such as EPA's Small Business Policy, apply to businesses with 100 or fewer employees and encourage persons to voluntarily discover, disclose, and correct violations before they are identified by the government (more information about EPA's Small Business Policy is available at www.epa.gov/compliance/incentives/smallbusiness/index.html). EPA's enforcement program is aimed at protecting the public by targeting persons or entities who neither comply nor cooperate to address their legal obligations.

EPA uses a variety of methods to determine whether businesses are complying, including inspecting work sites, reviewing records and reports, and responding to citizen tips and complaints. Under TSCA, EPA (or a state, if this program has been delegated to it) may file an enforcement action against violators seeking penalties of up to $32,500 per violation, per day. The proposed penalty in a given case will depend on many factors, including the number, length, and severity of the violations, the economic benefit obtained by the violator, and its ability to pay. EPA has policies in place to ensure penalties are calculated fairly. These policies are available to the public. In addition, any company charged with a violation has the right to contest EPA's allegations and proposed penalty before an impartial judge or jury.

EPA encourages small businesses to work with the Agency to discover, disclose, and correct violations. The Agency has developed self-disclosure, small business, and small community policies to modify penalties for small and large entities that cooperate with EPA to address compliance problems. In addition, EPA has established compliance assistance centers to serve over one million small businesses (see Construction Industry Compliance Assistance Center for information regarding this rule at www.cicacenter.org). For more information on compliance assistance and other EPA programs for small businesses, please contact EPA's Small Business Ombudsman at 202-566-2075.

Frequent Questions

What is the legal status of this guide?

This guide was prepared pursuant to section 212 of SBREFA. EPA has tried to help explain in this guide what you must do to comply with the Toxic Substances Control Act (TSCA) and EPA's lead regulations. However, this guide has no legal effect and does not create any legal rights. Compliance with the procedures described in this guide does not establish compliance with the rule or establish a presumption or inference of compliance. The legal requirements that apply to renovation work are governed by EPA's 2008 Lead Rule, which controls if there is any inconsistency between the rule and the information in this guide.

Is painting considered renovation if no surface preparation activity occurs?

No. If the surface to be painted is not disturbed by sanding, scraping, or other activities that may cause dust, the work is not considered renovation and EPA's lead program requirements do not apply. However, painting projects that involve surface preparation that disturbs paint, such as sanding and scraping, would be covered.

What if I renovate my own home?

EPA's lead program rules apply only to renovations performed for compensation; therefore, if you work on your own home, the rules do not apply. EPA encourages homeowners to use lead-safe work practices, nonetheless, in order to protect themselves, their families, and the value of their homes.

Is a renovation performed by a landlord or employees of a property management firm considered a compensated renovation under EPA's lead program rules?

Yes. The receipt of rent payments or salaries derived from rent payments is considered compensation under EPA's lead program. Therefore, renovation activities performed by landlords or employees of landlords are covered.

Do I have to give out the lead pamphlet seven days prior to beginning renovation activities?

The 7-day advance delivery requirement applies only when you deliver the lead pamphlet by mail; otherwise, you may deliver the pamphlet anytime before the renovation begins so long as the renovation begins within 60 days of the date that the pamphlet is delivered. For example, if your renovation is to begin May 30, you may deliver the pamphlet in person anytime between April 1 and start of the project on May 30, or you may deliver the pamphlet by mail anytime between April 1 and May 23.

Tips for Easy Compliance

1. For your convenience the sample forms on pages 23 and 25 of this handbook are included in the *Renovate Right* pamphlet (see page 31 for information on how to get copies). Attach the forms to the back of your customer renovation or repair contracts. The completed forms can be filed along with your regular paperwork.

2. Plan ahead to obtain enough copies of the lead pamphlet (see page 31 for information on how to get copies of the pamphlet).

Where Can I Get More Information?

Further information is available from the National Lead Information Center (800-424-LEAD) and on the Internet at www.epa.gov/lead. Available resources include:

* Full text version of the Lead-Based Paint Renovation, Repair, and Painting Program regulation.

* Interpretive guidance which provides more detailed information on the rule's requirements.

* A downloadable version of the lead pamphlet.

Why Is Lead Paint Dangerous?

Lead gets into the body when it is swallowed or inhaled. People, especially children, can swallow lead dust as they eat, play, and do other normal hand-to-mouth activities. People may also breathe in lead dust or fumes if they disturb lead-based paint. People who sand, scrape, burn, brush, blast or otherwise disturb lead-based paint risk unsafe exposure to lead.

Lead is especially dangerous to children under 6 years of age.

Lead can affect children's brains and developing nervous systems, causing:

* Reduced IQ and learning disabilities.

* Behavioral problems.

Even children who appear healthy can have dangerous levels of lead in their bodies.

Lead is also harmful to adults. In adults, low levels of lead can pose many dangers, including:

* High blood pressure and hypertension.

* Pregnant women exposed to lead can transfer lead to their fetus.

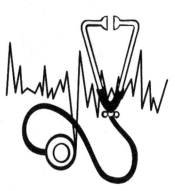

Other Resources

For additional information on how to protect yourself and your customers from lead paint hazards, visit www.epa.gov/lead or call the National Lead Information Center at 1-800-424-LEAD (5323). Available documents include:

- *Renovate Right: Important Lead Hazard Information for Families, Child Care Providers and Schools*
- *Joint EPA-HUD Curriculum: Lead Safety for Remodeling, Repair, and Painting*
- *Lead Paint Safety: A Field Guide for Painting, Home Maintenance, and Renovation Work*
- *Testing Your Home for Lead in Paint, Dust, and Soil*
- *Fight Lead Poisoning with a Healthy Diet*
- *Protect Your Family From Lead in Your Home*
- *Lead in Your Home: A Parent's Reference Guide*

Key Terms

Certificate of Mailing — A written verification from the Postal Service that you mailed the lead pamphlet to an owner or a tenant. This is less expensive than certified mail, which is also acceptable for meeting the Lead-Based Paint Renovation, Repair, and Painting Program requirements. (*Note: If using this delivery option, you must mail the pamphlet at least seven days prior to the start of renovation.*)

Certified Inspector or Risk Assessor — An individual who has been trained and is certified by EPA or an authorized state or Indian Tribe to conduct lead-based paint inspections or risk assessments.

Child-occupied Facility — May include, but is not limited to, day care centers, pre-schools and kindergarten classrooms. Child-occupied facilities may be located in target housing or in public or commercial buildings. The regulation defines a "child-occupied facility" as a building, or portion of a building, constructed prior to 1978, visited regularly by the same child, under 6 years of age, on at least two different days within any week (Sunday through Saturday period), provided that each day's visit lasts at least three hours and the combined weekly visits last at least six hours, and the combined annual visits last at least 60 hours.

Cleaning Verification Card — a card developed and distributed, or otherwise approved, by EPA for the purpose of determining, through comparison of wet and dry disposable cleaning cloths with the card, whether post-renovation cleaning has been properly completed.

Common Area — A portion of a building that is generally accessible to all residents or users. Common areas include (but are not limited to) hallways, stairways, laundry rooms, recreational rooms, playgrounds, community centers, and fenced areas. The term applies to both interiors and exteriors of the building. (*Note: Lead-Based Paint Renovation, Repair, and Painting Program requirements related to common areas apply only to multi-family housing.*)

Component — A specific design or structural element or fixture distinguished by its form, function, and location. A component can be located inside or outside the dwelling.

Examples

Interior	*Exterior*
Ceilings	Painted roofing
Crown molding	Chimneys
Walls	Flashing
Doors and trim	Gutters and downspouts
Floors	Ceilings
Fireplaces	Soffits
Radiators	Doors and trim
Shelves	Fences
Stair treads	Floors
Windows and trim	Joists
Built-in cabinets	Handrails
Beams	Window sills and sashes
Bathroom vanities	Air conditioners
Counter tops	
Air conditioners	

Confirmation of Receipt of Lead Hazard Information Pamphlet — A form that is signed by the owner or tenant of the housing confirming that they received a copy of the lead pamphlet before the renovation began. (See sample on page 23.)

Emergency Renovation — Unplanned renovation activities done in response to a sudden, unexpected event which, if not immediately attended to, presents a safety or public health hazard or threatens property with significant damage.

Examples
- *Renovation to repair damage from a tree that fell on a house.*
- *Renovation to repair a burst water pipe in an apartment complex.*
- *Interim controls performed in response to an elevated blood lead level in a resident child.*

Firm — A company, partnership, corporation, sole proprietorship or individual doing business, association, or other business entity; a Federal, State, Tribal, or local government agency; or a nonprofit organization.

General Contractor — One who contracts for the construction of an entire building or project, rather than for a portion of the work. The general contractor hires subcontractors (e.g. plumbing, electrical, etc.), coordinates all work, and is responsible for payment to subcontractors.

Housing for the Elderly — Retirement communities or similar types of housing specifically reserved for households of one or more persons 62 years of age or older at the time the unit is first occupied.

Interim Controls — Interim controls means a set of measures designed to temporarily reduce human exposure or likely exposure to lead-based paint hazards, including specialized cleaning, repairs, maintenance, painting, temporary containment, ongoing monitoring of lead-based paint hazards or potential hazards, and the establishment and operation of management and resident education programs.

Lead Abatement — Work designed to permanently eliminate lead-based paint hazards. If you are hired to do lead-abatement work only, the Lead-Based Paint Renovation, Repair, and Painting Program does not apply. Abatement does not include renovation, remodeling, or other activities done to repair, restore, or redesign a given building — even if such renovation activities incidentally eliminate lead-based paint hazards. (**Note:** *Some states define this term differently than described above. Consult your state officials if you are not sure how "lead abatement" is defined in your state.*)

Lead Pamphlet — The lead hazard information pamphlet for the purpose of pre-renovation education is *Renovate Right: Important Lead Hazard Information for Families, Child Care Facilities and Schools*, or an EPA-approved alternative pamphlet. (See page 31 for information on obtaining copies.)

Minor Repair and Maintenance — Activities that disrupt 6 square feet or less of painted surface per room for interior activities or 20 square feet or less of painted surface for exterior activities where none of the prohibited work practices is used and where the work does not involve window replacement or demolition of painted surface areas. When removing painted components, or portions of painted components, the entire surface area removed is the amount of painted surface disturbed. Jobs, other than emergency renovations, performed in the same room within the same 30 days must be considered the same job for the purpose of determining whether the job is a minor repair and maintenance activity.

Owner — Any person or entity that has legal title to housing, including individuals, partnerships, corporations, government agencies, Indian Tribes, and nonprofit organizations.

Prohibited Practices — Work practices listed below are prohibited during a renovation:

- Open-flame burning or torching of lead-based paint;
- Use of machines that remove lead-based paint through high speed operation such as sanding, grinding, power planing, needle gun, abrasive blasting, or sandblasting, unless such machines are used with HEPA exhaust control; and
- Operating a heat gun on lead-based paint at temperatures above 1100 degrees Fahrenheit.

Record of Notification — A written statement documenting the steps taken to notify occupants of renovation activities in common areas of multi-family housing. (See page 27 for sample.)

Renovation — Modification of all or part of any existing structure that disturbs a painted surface, except for some specifically exempted activities (e.g., minor repair and maintenance). Includes:

- Removal/modification of painted surfaces, components, or structures
- Surface preparation activities (sanding/scraping/other activities that may create paint dust)
- Window replacement

Examples

1. Demolition of painted walls or ceilings

2. Replastering

3. Plumbing repairs or improvements

4. Any other activities which disturb painted surfaces

Renovation Notice — Notice to tenants of renovations in common areas of multi-family housing. (See sample form on page 27.) Notice must describe nature, location, and expected timing of renovation activity; and must explain how the lead pamphlet may be obtained free of charge.

Renovator — A person who either performs or directs workers who perform renovation. A certified renovator is a renovator who has successfully completed a renovator course accredited by EPA or an EPA authorized State or Tribal program. (**Note:** *Because the term "renovation" is defined broadly by the Lead-Based Paint Renovation, Repair, and Painting Program, many contractors who are not generally considered "renovators", as that term is commonly used, are considered to be "renovators" under the program and must follow the rule's requirements.*)

Self-Certification of Delivery — An alternative method of documenting delivery of the lead hazard information pamphlet to a tenant. This method may be used whenever the tenant is unavailable or unwilling to sign a confirmation of receipt of lead pamphlet. (See sample form on page 23.) (**Note:** *This method is not a permissible substitute for delivery of the lead pamphlet to an owner.*)

Supplemental Renovation Notice — additional notification that is required when the scope, location, or timing of project changes.

Zero-Bedroom Dwelling — Any residential dwelling where the living area is not separated from the sleeping area. This term includes efficiency and studio apartments, dormitory housing, and military barracks.

Current Sample Pre-Renovation Form

For use until April 2010.

Confirmation of Receipt of Lead Pamphlet

___ I have received a copy of the lead pamphlet informing me of the potential risk of the lead hazard exposure from renovation activity to be performed in my dwelling unit. I received this pamphlet before the work began.

_____

Printed name of recipient   Date

_____

Signature of recipient

Self-Certification Option (for tenant-occupied dwellings only) — If the lead pamphlet was delivered but a tenant signature was not obtainable, you may check the appropriate box below.

___ **Refusal to sign** — I certify that I have made a good faith effort to deliver the lead pamphlet to the rental dwelling unit listed below at the date and time indicated and that the occupant refused to sign the confirmation of receipt. I further certify that I have left a copy of the pamphlet at the unit with the occupant.

___ **Unavailable for signature** — I certify that I have made a good faith effort to deliver the lead pamphlet to the rental dwelling unit listed below and that the occupant was unavailable to sign the confirmation of receipt. I further certify that I have left a copy of the pamphlet at the unit by sliding it under the door.

_____

Printed name of person certifying attempted delivery

_____

Date and time lead pamphlet delivery

_____

Signature of person certifying lead pamphlet delivery

_____

_____

Unit Address

Note Regarding Mailing Option — As an alternative to delivery in person, you may mail the lead pamphlet to the owner and/or tenant. Pamphlet must be mailed at least 7 days before renovation (Document with a certificate of mailing from the post office).

Future Sample Pre-Renovation Form

This sample form may be used by firms to document compliance with the requirements of the Federal Lead-Based Paint Renovation, Repair, and Painting Program after April 2010.

Occupant Confirmation

Pamphlet Receipt

___ I have received a copy of the lead hazard information pamphlet informing me of the potential risk of the lead hazard exposure from renovation activity to be performed in my dwelling unit. I received this pamphlet before the work began.

Owner-occupant Opt-out Acknowledgment

___ (A) I confirm that I own and live in this property, that no child under the age of 6 resides here, that no pregnant woman resides here, and that this property is not a child-occupied facility.

Note: A child resides in the primary residence of his or her custodial parents, legal guardians, foster parents, or informal caretaker if the child lives and sleeps most of the time at the caretaker's residence.

Note: A child-occupied facility is a pre-1978 building visited regularly by the same child, under 6 years of age, on at least two different days within any week, for at least 3 hours each day, provided that the visits total at least 60 hours annually.

If Box A is checked, check either Box B or Box C, but not both.

___ (B) I request that the renovation firm use the lead-safe work practices required by EPA's Lead-Based Paint Renovation, Repair, and Painting Rule; or

___ (C) I understand that the firm performing the renovation will not be required to use the lead-safe work practices required by EPA's Lead-Based Paint Renovation, Repair, and Painting Rule.

_____

Printed Name of Owner-occupant

_____   _____

Signature of Owner-occupant   Signature Date

Renovator's Self Certification Option (for tenant-occupied dwellings only)

Instructions to Renovator: If the lead hazard information pamphlet was delivered but a tenant signature was not obtainable, you may check the appropriate box below.

___ **Declined** – I certify that I have made a good faith effort to deliver the lead hazard information pamphlet to the rental dwelling unit listed below at the date and time indicated and that the occupant declined to sign the confirmation of receipt. I further certify that I have left a copy of the pamphlet at the unit with the occupant.

___ **Unavailable for signature** – I certify that I have made a good faith effort to deliver the lead hazard information pamphlet to the rental dwelling unit listed below and that the occupant was unavailable to sign the confirmation of receipt. I further certify that I have left a copy of the pamphlet at the unit by sliding it under the door or by (fill in how pamphlet was left)._____

_____   _____

Printed Name of Person Certifying Delivery   Attempted Delivery Date

_____

Signature of Person Certifying Lead Pamphlet Delivery

_____

_____

Unit Address

Note Regarding Mailing Option — As an alternative to delivery in person, you may mail the lead hazard information pamphlet to the owner and/or tenant. Pamphlet must be mailed at least 7 days before renovation. Mailing must be documented by a certificate of mailing from the post office.

Sample Forms (continued)

Renovation Notice — *For use in notifying tenants of renovations in common areas of multi-family housing.*

The following renovation activities will take place in the following locations:

_____

Activity *(e.g., sanding, window replacement)*

_____

Location *(e.g., lobby, recreation center)*

The expected starting date is_____and the expected ending date is_____.
Because this is an older building built before 1978, some of the paint disturbed during the renovation may contain lead. You may obtain a copy of the pamphlet, *Renovate Right*, by telephoning me at_____. Please leave a message and be sure to include your name, phone number and address. I will either mail you a pamphlet or slide one under your door.

_____   _____
Date   Printed name of renovator

_____
Signature of renovator

Record of Tenant Notification Procedures — *Future Sample Renovation Recordkeeping Checklist*

Project Address_____

Street (apt. #)_____

City_____ State_____ Zip Code_____

_____   _____
Owner of multi-family housing   Number of dwelling units

_____
Method of delivering notice forms *(e.g. delivery to units, delivery to mailboxes of units)*

_____
Name of person delivering notices

_____   _____
Signature of person delivering notices   Date of Delivery

Future Sample Renovation Recordkeeping Checklist
(effective April 2010)

Name of Firm: _____

Date and Location of Renovation: _____

Brief Description of Renovation: _____

Name of Assigned Renovator: _____

Name(s) of Trained Worker(s), if used: _____

Name of Dust Sampling Technician,
Inspector, or Risk Assessor, if used: _____

___ Copies of renovator and dust sampling technician qualifications (training certificates, certifications) on file.

___ Certified renovator provided training to workers on (check all that apply):

   ___ Posting warning signs   ___ Setting up plastic containment barriers

   ___ Maintaining containment   ___ Avoiding spread of dust to adjacent areas

   ___ Waste handling   ___ Post-renovation cleaning

   ___Test kits used by certified renovator to determine whether lead was present on components affected by renovation (identify kits used and describe sampling locations and results):

_____

___ Warning signs posted at entrance to work area.

___ Work area contained to prevent spread of dust and debris

   ___All objects in the work area removed or covered (interiors)

   ___HVAC ducts in the work area closed and covered (interiors)

   ___Windows in the work area closed (interiors)

   ___Windows in and within 20 feet of the work area closed (exteriors)

   ___Doors in the work area closed and sealed (interiors)

   ___Doors in and within 20 feet of the work area closed and sealed (exteriors)

   ___Doors that must be used in the work area covered to allow passage but prevent spread of dust

   ___Floors in the work area covered with taped-down plastic (interiors)

   ___Ground covered by plastic extending 10 feet from work area—plastic anchored to building and weighed down by heavy objects (exteriors)

   ___If necessary, vertical containment installed to prevent migration of dust and debris to adjacent property (exteriors)

___ Waste contained on-site and while being transported off-site.

___ Work site properly cleaned after renovation

   ___All chips and debris picked up, protective sheeting misted, folded dirty side inward, and taped for removal

   ___Work area surfaces and objects cleaned using HEPA vacuum and/or wet cloths or mops (interiors)

___ Certified renovator performed post-renovation cleaning verification (describe results, including the number of wet and dry cloths used): _____

_____

   ___If dust clearance testing was performed instead, attach a copy of report

___ I certify under penalty of law that the above information is true and complete.

_____   _____
Name and title   Date

Where Can I Get Copies of the Lead Pamphlet?

For single copies, in Spanish or English, of *Renovate Right: Important Lead Hazard Information for Families, Child Care Facilities and Schools* (EPA-740-F-08-002), call the National Lead Information Center (NLIC) at 1-800-424-LEAD. For any orders, be sure to use the appropriate stock reference number listed above.

There are four ways to get multiple copies:

1. Call the Government Printing Office order desk at (202) 512-1800.

2. Send fax requests to (202) 512-2233.

3. Request copies in writing from:
   Superintendent of Documents
   P.O. Box 371954
   Pittsburgh, PA 15250-7954

4. Obtain copies via the Internet at www.epa.gov/lead/pubs/brochure.htm

For single copies, in Spanish or English, of *Renovate Right: Important Lead Hazard Information for Families, Child Care Facilities and Schools* (EPA-740-F-08-002), call the National Lead Information Center (NLIC) at 1-800-424-LEAD. For any orders, be sure to use the appropriate stock reference number listed above.

The pamphlet may be photocopied for distribution as long as the text and graphics are readable.

Paperwork Reduction Act Notice: The incremental public burden for the collection of information contained in the Lead Renovation, Painting and Repair Program, which are approved under OMB Control No. 2070-0155 and identified under EPA ICR No. 1715, is estimated to average approximately 54 hours per year for training providers. For firms engaged in regulated renovation, repair, and painting activities, the average incremental burden is estimated to be about 6.5 hours per year. Comments regarding this burden estimate or any other aspect of this collection of information, including suggestions for reducing the burden, may be sent to: Director, Collection Strategies Division, Office of Environmental Information, U.S. Environmental Protection Agency (Mail Code 2822T), 1200 Pennsylvania Avenue, N.W., Washington, D.C. 20460. Include the OMB number identified above in any correspondence. Do not send any completed form(s) to this address. The actual information or form(s) should be submitted in accordance with the instructions accompanying the form(s), or as specified in the corresponding regulations.

1-800-424-LEAD (5323)
www.epa.gov/lead

Appendix 5:

Steps to LEAD SAFE
Renovation, Repair and Painting

Steps to
LEAD SAFE
Renovation, Repair
and Painting

United States
Environmental Protection
Agency

1-800-424-LEAD

www.epa.gov/lead

Renovating, Repairing or Painting?

Are you working on a home renovation, repair or painting project?

Does the project involve a home built before 1978?

If so, you need to know how to work safely with lead-based paint. This guide is designed to help contractors and homeowners plan for and complete a home renovation, repair or painting project using lead safe work practices. Lead safe work practices are a group of techniques that reduce the amount of dust produced by renovation activities. When used correctly, they make the work area safer for workers and the home safe for residents when renovation is complete. Following lead safe work practices will allow you to:

- Set up the job safely;

- Minimize the creation of dangerous lead dust; and

- Leave the work area clean and safe for residents after completing the job.

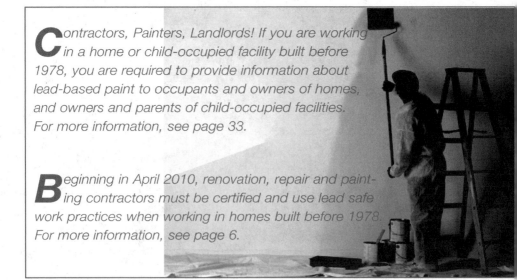

Contractors, Painters, Landlords! If you are working in a home or child-occupied facility built before 1978, you are required to provide information about lead-based paint to occupants and owners of homes, and owners and parents of child-occupied facilities. For more information, see page 33.

Beginning in April 2010, renovation, repair and painting contractors must be certified and use lead safe work practices when working in homes built before 1978. For more information, see page 6.

Table of Contents

Learn the Facts about Lead-Based Paint

About half of homes built before 1978 have lead-based paint. The likelihood of finding lead-based paint increases with the age of the home:

- Two out of three of homes built between 1940 and 1960 have lead-based paint.
- Nine out of ten homes built before 1940 have lead-based paint.

Older Homes are More Likely to Contain Lead-Based Paint

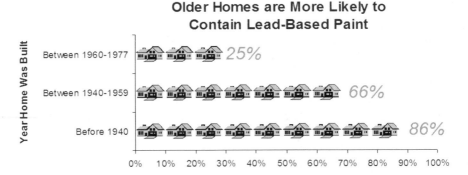

Percentage of Homes Containing Lead-Based Paint

Source: American Healthy Homes Survey: Draft Final Report for Peer Review: Lead and Arsenic Findings. October 7, 2008.

Lead-based paint may be found on any surface in the home—inside or outside. When lead-based paint is disturbed during renovation, repair or painting activities, dangerous amounts of lead dust can be created. Jobs such as demolition, window replacement, opening up walls, etc., can also release accumulated lead dust into the home. Even after a typical renovation cleanup, dangerous levels of lead dust can remain.

Lead gets into the body when it is swallowed or breathed.

- People, especially children, can swallow lead dust as they eat, play, and perform other ordinary hand-to-mouth activities.

- People may also breathe in lead dust or fumes while they work on jobs that sand, scrape, burn, brush, blast or otherwise disturb painted surfaces that contain lead paint.

- Additionally, pets may be poisoned by the same types of exposure to lead.

Once in the body, lead can have significant effects on human health.

- In children, lead poisoning damages the nervous system and causes developmental and behavioral problems that can affect them for their lifetime.

- In adults, lead poisoning causes health and reproductive problems. Pregnant women are especially vulnerable to the effects of lead.

Research has shown that general residential renovation activities are associated with an increased risk of elevated lead levels in children.

By working safely you can help prevent lead exposure and poisoning. This guide tells you how.

The Renovation, Repair and Painting Program Rule

&EPA
United States
Environmental Protection
Agency

This section summarizes requirements of EPA's Lead-Based Paint Renovation, Repair and Painting (RRP) Program Rule for contractors, and provides guidance to homeowners/occupants, so that each may learn to properly address lead-based paint hazards associated with renovation, repair and painting activities.

The RRP rule affects contractors, property managers and others who disturb known or presumed lead-based paint during renovation. The term renovation covers all activities done for compensation that disturb painted surfaces including most repair, remodeling and maintenance activities, such as window replacement, weatherization and demolition. The RRP rule applies to all renovation work performed in residential houses, apartments and child-occupied facilities such as schools and day-care centers built before 1978. Those affected by the RRP rule should read the complete rule, which is available on EPA's Web site at: **http://www.epa.gov/lead/pubs/renovation.htm**.

Training, certification, and work practice requirements in the Renovation, Repair and Painting Rule are effective April 22, 2010. Pre-renovation education requirements are effective now.

Requirements for Renovation Contractors Include:
Certification and Training Requirements

- All firms performing renovation, repair or painting work must become certified. This can be accomplished by applying to EPA or to the State, if it has an EPA-authorized renovation program, and paying a fee.

- Firms must have one or more "Certified Renovators" assigned to jobs where lead-based paint is disturbed. To become certified, a renovator must successfully complete an EPA or State-approved training course conducted by an EPA or State-accredited training provider.

- All renovation workers must be trained. Renovation workers can be trained on-the-job by a Certified Renovator to use lead safe work practices, or they can become Certified Renovators themselves.

Pre-Renovation Education Requirements

- Contractors, property managers and others who perform renovations for compensation in residential houses, apartments, and child-occupied facilities built before 1978 are required to distribute EPA's *Renovate Right* lead hazard information pamphlet before starting renovation work to occupants and owners of homes, and owners and parents of child-occupied facilities. More information about pre-renovation education requirements can be found on page 33.

Work Practice Requirements

- Renovators must use work-area containment to prevent dust and debris from leaving the work area.

- Certain work practices are prohibited. Open-flame burning, using heat guns at greater than 1,100 degrees Fahrenheit and the use of power tools without high-efficiency particulate air (HEPA) exhaust control (to collect dust generated) are prohibited.

- Thorough cleaning followed by a cleaning verification procedure to minimize exposure to lead-based paint hazards are required.

- Generally, minor repair and maintenance activities (less than 6 square feet per interior room or 20 square feet per exterior project) are exempt from the work practices requirements. However, this exemption does not apply to jobs involving window replacement or demolition, or that involve the use of any of the prohibited practices listed above.

Exemption from the RRP Rule

The training, certification and work practice requirements do not apply where the firm obtains a signed statement from the owner that all of the following conditions are met:

- The renovation will occur in the owner's residence;
- No child under age 6 resides there;
- No woman who is pregnant resides there;
- The housing is not a child-occupied facility; and,
- The owner acknowledges that the renovation firm will not be required to use the work practices contained in the rule.

Homeowners Working in Their Own Homes

The RRP rule applies only to renovations performed for compensation. If you work on your own home, the rules do not apply. Even so, EPA encourages homeowners to use lead safe work practices, in order to protect themselves, their families, and the value of their homes.

Landlords Working in Their Own Property

Landlords receive rental payments and maintenance personnel in rental property or child-occupied facilities receive wages or salaries derived from rent payments. This is considered compensation under the RRP rule. Therefore, renovation and repair activities performed by landlords or employees of landlords are covered by the rule. Work performed by landlords or their employees in pre-1978 housing and child-occupied facilities must be performed using lead safe work practices, if lead-based paint or presumed lead-based paint is disturbed.

Other Federal and State Regulations

The U.S. Department of Housing and Urban Development (HUD) Lead Safe Housing Rule

HUD's Lead Safe Housing Rule (24 CFR Part 35) covers pre-1978 federally-owned or assisted housing and federally-owned housing that is being sold. It does not cover child-occupied facilities outside of residential housing. The requirements of HUD's rule are similar to EPA's RRP rule, but there are some differences in the details, including:

- **Exemptions.** HUD's rule does not allow owners of federally-assisted housing to opt out of its requirements.

- **Training Requirements.** HUD does not recognize on-the-job training. To conduct lead hazard control in federally-assisted housing, either all workers must have completed a HUD-approved course, or the crew must be supervised by a Certified Renovator who is also a Certified Lead Abatement Supervisor.

- **Minor Repair and Maintenance.** HUD's definition of minor repair and maintenance that is exempt from its rule is different than EPA's (2 square feet interior and 20 square feet exterior or 10 percent of the surface area of a small building component type).

Other differences between the EPA and HUD rules (concerning paint testing, prohibited practices, clearance testing and waste disposal) are pointed out in the appropriate places.

State and Local Regulations

Other state or local requirements that are different from or more stringent than the federal requirements may apply. For example, federal law allows EPA to authorize states to administer their own lead renovation program in place of the federal lead program. Even in states without an authorized lead renovation program, a state may promulgate its own rules that may be different or go beyond the federal requirements.

For more information on the rules that apply in your state, please contact the National Lead Information Center at **1-800-424-LEAD (5323) or www.epa.gov/lead/nlic.htm**.

Step 1

Determine If the Job Involves Lead-Based Paint

Before you begin a job, consider whether lead-based paint will be an issue.

Find Out the Age of the Home or Child-Occupied Facility.
The age of a home can tell you a lot about whether lead-based paint is likely to be present.

- If it was built before 1978, it may have lead-based paint.

- The older the home, the greater the likelihood that lead is present in the paint and accumulated dust.

- Consider when additions were built. Some parts of the home may have been built later than others. Later additions are less likely to contain lead-based paint and contaminated dust.

- Lead-based paint may be found either inside or outside the home and is most common in kitchens or bathrooms and in high gloss paint on trim, such as on window sills, door frames, and railings.

Look for Information About Lead.
Information about lead-based paint in your home may be readily available. Under a federal disclosure law, when a pre-1978 home is sold or leased, the seller/landlord must provide information to the buyer/tenant about any known lead-based paint. Homeowners should check their records to see if they have information about lead-based paint and share this information with anyone performing work on the home.

Consider Lead Testing.

If a home was built before 1978, you must either assume that lead-based paint is present or have the work area tested for lead-based paint before starting the job. There are two options for testing paint in a home under the Renovation, Repair and Painting Rule:

1. Paint testing by a certified lead-based paint inspector or lead-based paint risk assessor — These licensed professionals conduct a surface-by-surface investigation for lead-based paint by collecting paint chips for laboratory analysis or by testing painted surfaces with an machine called an X-Ray Fluorescence Analyzer (XRF) which measures the amount of lead in the paint.

2. Paint testing by a Certified Renovator — Certified Renovators, at the request of the homeowner, can use EPA-recognized chemical spot test kits to test all painted surfaces affected by the renovation.

Note: HUD does not recognize testing by a Certified Renovator using spot test kits. In housing covered by the HUD Lead Safe Housing Rule, only the first option is allowed.

All surfaces affected by a renovation covered by the Renovation, Repair and Painting Rule must either be tested for lead-based paint or presumed to contain lead-based paint. Testing must include all affected surfaces coated with paint, shellac, varnish, stain, coating or even paint covered by wallpaper, if it will be disturbed during the renovation work. A report documenting the testing must list the surfaces tested and the surfaces which contain lead-based paint. If lead-based paint is present on an affected surface, then the lead safe work practices described in this pamphlet must be used on the job.

For a list of certified lead testing professionals in your area, contact the **National Lead Information Center** at **1-800-424-LEAD (5323)** or visit **http://cfpub.epa.gov/flpp.**

Remember, if the home was built before 1978 and there is no information available about the paint, renovators must presume lead-based paint is present and use the lead safe work practices described in this pamphlet. Make sure everyone involved on the job, including workers, supervisors and residents, uses proper safety precautions.

CAUTION

Set It Up Safely

When you work on a job with lead-based paint, you should separate the work area from the rest of the home. The goal of proper setup of the work area is to keep dust in the work area and non-workers out.

The work area is the area that may become contaminated during the work. The size of the work area may vary depending on the method used to disturb lead-based paint and the amount of dust and debris that is generated as a result. Whenever lead-based paint is disturbed, the work area must be protected by plastic sheeting applied to the floor, ground or other applicable surfaces to prevent contamination of the home or exterior, from dust generated by the work.

The Renovation, Repair and Painting Rule requires that the work area be protected by plastic sheeting that extends a minimum of 6 feet in all directions from the location where paint will be disturbed. The Rule further requires that protective plastic sheeting extend far enough from the location of paint disturbance so that all dust or debris generated by the work remains within the area protected by the plastic. The entire portion of the home or exterior that is protected by plastic sheeting, however large, is the work area.

Unauthorized persons and pets must be prevented from entering the work area. This can be accomplished by posting warning signs and by establishing barriers around the work area such as barrier tape, fencing, plastic barriers in doorways, etc.

Shopping List

Here is a list of supplies and tools you will need to set up the work area safely. These items are available in hardware, paint or garden supply stores.

Materials to Restrict Access and Cover the Floor/Ground

- ❑ Signs

- ❑ Barrier tape, rope or fencing

- ❑ Cones

- ❑ Heavy duty plastic sheeting

- ❑ Tape (masking, duct or painter's)

- ❑ Stapler

- ❑ Utility knife or scissors

What To Do

To keep the dust in and people out of your work area, you will need to take the steps below for inside or outside jobs. Some jobs create more dust than others and, therefore, call for additional precautions.

For Inside Jobs

- Have occupants leave the room where the work will be done and have them stay outside of the work area until after the final cleanup.

- Place signs, barrier tape and/or cones to keep all non-workers, especially children, out of the work area. Keep pets out of the work area for their safety and to prevent them from tracking dust and debris throughout the home. Signs should be in the primary language of the occupants and should say "Do Not Enter – Authorized Personnel Only" and "No Eating, Drinking, or Smoking."

- Remove furniture and belongings from the work area. These items may include: drapes, curtains, furniture, rugs, etc. If an item is too large to move, cover it with heavy plastic sheeting and tape the sheeting securely in place.

- Use heavy plastic sheeting to cover floors in the work area, to a minimum of 6 feet from the area of paint disturbance. Secure with tape.

- Close all doors in the work area, including closet and cabinet doors, and cover with plastic sheeting. When the work area boundary includes a door used to access the work area, cover the door with two layers of protective sheeting as described here:

  - Cut and secure one layer of sheeting to the perimeter of the doorframe. Do not pull the sheeting taut. Rather, create a few folds to leave slack at the top and bottom of the door before taping or stapling.

  - Cut a vertical slit in the middle of the sheeting leaving 6" uncut at the top and bottom. Reinforce with tape.

  - Cut and secure a second, overlapping layer of sheeting to the top of the door.

- Close and cover air vents in the work area. This will keep dust from getting into vents and moving through the home. You may need to turn off your HVAC system to prevent damage to the system.

- Put all necessary tools and supplies on the protective sheeting before you begin work to avoid stepping off the protective sheeting before the work is complete.

For Outside Jobs

- Keep non-workers away from the work area by marking it off with signs, tape and/or cones.

- Cover the ground and plants with heavy plastic sheeting to catch debris. The covering should extend at least 10 feet out from the building. Secure the covering to the exterior wall with a wood strip and staples, or tape.

- Close windows and doors within 20 feet of the work area to keep dust and debris from getting into the home.

- Move or cover any play areas that are within 20 feet of the work area.

- When working on the 2nd story or above, extend the sheeting farther out from the base of the home and to each side of the area where paint is being disturbed.

- Vertical shrouding on scaffolding should be used if work is close to a sidewalk, street, or property boundary, or the building is more than three stories high.

- Avoid working in high winds if possible. The EPA Renovation, Repair and Painting Rule does not specifically address wind speed, but when the wind is strong enough to move dust and debris, special precautions need to be taken to keep the work area contained. That may mean creating a wind screen of plastic at the edge of the ground-cover plastic to keep dust and debris from migrating. Ultimately, you are responsible for preventing dust and debris from leaving the work area, so take appropriate precautions when wind is a factor.

- Put all necessary tools and supplies on the protective sheeting before you begin work to avoid stepping off the protective sheeting before the work is complete.

Step 3

Protect Yourself

Workers should protect themselves.
Without the right personal protective equipment, workers may ingest or inhale lead from the job and may risk bringing lead from the worksite home to their families. The following items are available through hardware, paint, garden supply stores or other specialty suppliers.

Shopping List

❑ Protective eye wear

❑ Painter's hat

❑ Disposable coveralls

❑ Disposable N-100 rated respirator

❑ Disposable latex/rubber gloves

❑ Disposable shoe covers

What to Do

Protect your eyes.

- Always wear safety goggles or safety glasses when scraping, hammering, etc.

Keep clothes clean.

- Wear disposable protective clothing covers. Disposable protective clothing covers can be stored in a plastic bag and reused if they are fairly clean and are not torn. Small tears can be repaired with duct tape.

- At the end of the work period, vacuum off dust, and remove disposable protective clothing covers. Do not use compressed air to blow dust off disposable protective clothing covers or clothing.

- Do not hug other people until you have taken off your work clothes. Then, wash your work clothes separately from family laundry.

- Wear disposable shoe covers to prevent the tracking of dust from the work area and to protect your shoes from exposure to dust.

- Wear gloves to protect your hands and prevent exposure to dust.

- Wear a painter's hat to protect your head from dust and debris. These are easy to dispose of at the end of the day.

Wear respiratory protection.

When work creates dust or paint chips, workers should wear respiratory protection, such as an N-100 disposable respirator, to prevent them from breathing leaded dust.

Post a warning sign.

Post a sign at the work entrance reminding workers to avoid eating, drinking and smoking in the work area.

Your sign should say:
- Warning

- Lead Work Area

- Poison

- No Smoking, Drinking or Eating

Wash up.

Workers should wash their hands and faces each time they stop working. It is especially important to wash up before eating and at the end of the day.

Note: OSHA rules may require employers to take further steps to protect the health of workers on the job.
See **www.osha.gov/SLTC/lead/index.html.**

Step 4

Minimize the Dust

As you work, your goal is to keep down the dust.
Remember that as you scrape, drill, cut, open walls, etc., you are creating dust. You can keep dust down by using the right tools and following some simple practices that minimize and control the spread of dust. The following items are available through hardware, paint, garden supply stores or other specialty suppliers.

Shopping List

Materials for all jobs:

❏ Wet-dry sandpaper, sanding sponge

❏ Misting bottle or pump sprayer

❏ Heavy plastic sheeting

❏ Utility knife or scissors

❏ Masking tape, duct tape, or painters' tape

❏ High Efficiency Particulate Air (HEPA) vacuum cleaner (a special vacuum cleaner that can remove very small particles from floors, window sills, and carpets and not return them to the air)

❏ Heavy duty plastic bags

❏ Tack pads (large, sticky pads that help remove dust), paper towels, or disposable wipes

Other tools that may be needed:

❏ Low-temperature heat gun (under 1,100 degrees Fahrenheit)

❏ Chemical strippers without methylene chloride

❏ Power tools with HEPA filter equipped vacuum attachments

What To Do

Use the right tools.

- Use wet sanders and misters to keep down the dust created during sanding, drilling and cutting.

- Use HEPA vacuum attachments on power sanders and grinders to contain the dust created by these tools.

- When a heat gun is needed to remove paint, use a temperature setting below 1,100 degrees Fahrenheit.

Use work practices that minimize dust.

- Mist areas before sanding, scraping, drilling and cutting to keep the dust down (except within 1 foot of live electrical outlets).

- Score paint with a utility knife before separating components.

- Pry and pull apart components instead of pounding and hammering.

- Keep components that are being disposed of in the work area until they are wrapped securely in heavy plastic sheeting or bagged in heavy duty plastic bags. Once wrapped or bagged, remove them from the work area and store them in a safe area away from residents.

Control the spread of dust.

- Keep the work area closed off from the rest of the home.

- Don't track dust out of the work area:

  - Stay in the contained work area and on the contained paths.

  - Vacuum off suits when exiting the work area so the dust stays inside the work area.

  - Every time you leave the plastic sheeting, remove your disposable shoe covers, and wipe or vacuum your shoes, especially, the soles, before you step off the plastic sheeting. A large disposable tack pad on the floor can help to clean the soles of your shoes.

- Launder non-disposable protective clothing separately from family laundry.

Do Not Use Prohibited Practices.
The Renovation, Repair and Painting Rule prohibits the use of some dangerous work practices by contractors. These "Prohibited Practices" are:

- Open-flame burning or torching of lead-based paint.

- The use of machines that remove lead-based paint through high-speed operation such as sanding, grinding, power planing, abrasive blasting or sandblasting, unless such machines are used with a HEPA exhaust control.

- Operating a heat gun on lead-based paint at temperatures greater than 1,100 degrees Fahrenheit.

In federally-assisted housing, HUD's rule prohibits additional work practices:

- Extensive dry scraping and sanding by hand.

- Heat guns that char paint.

- Paint stripping in a poorly ventilated space using a volatile paint stripper.

Note: The EPA Renovation, Repair and Painting Rule does not apply to homeowners who renovate their own property. However, because the practices prohibited under the rules generate significant amounts of dust, EPA recommends that they be avoided by the do-it-yourself homeowner also.

Step 5

Leave the Work Area Clean

The work area should be left clean at the end of every day and especially at the end of the job. The area should be completely free of dust and debris. The following cleaning supplies, tools, and equipment are available in hardware, paint or garden supply stores.

Shopping List

- ❏ Heavy-duty plastic bags
- ❏ HEPA vacuum with attachments and a powered beater bar
- ❏ Masking tape, duct tape, or painters tape
- ❏ Misting bottle or pump sprayer
- ❏ Disposable wet-cleaning wipes or hand towels
- ❏ Detergent or general-purpose cleaner
- ❏ Mop and disposable mop heads
- ❏ Two buckets or one two-sided bucket with a wringer
- ❏ Shovel and rake
- ❏ Wet Mopping System
- ❏ Electrostatically charged dry cleaning cloths

What To Do

On a daily basis, renovators and do-it-yourself homeowners should:

- Pick up as you go. Put trash in heavy-duty plastic bags.

- Vacuum the work area with a HEPA vacuum cleaner frequently during the day and at the end of the day.

- Clean tools at the end of the day.

- Wash up each time you take a break and before you go home.

- Dispose of or clean off your personal protective equipment.

- Continue to separate the work area from the rest of the home and remind residents to stay out of the area.

When the job is complete, renovators and do-it-yourself homeowners should:

- Remove plastic sheeting carefully, fold it with the dirty side in, tape it shut, and dispose of it.

- Make sure all trash and debris, including building components, are disposed of properly.

- Vacuum all surfaces, including walls, with a HEPA vacuum cleaner.

- Mist and scrub the work area with a general-purpose cleaner on a wet rag or mop, changing the rinse water often until dust and debris are removed.

- Vacuum all surfaces again once they are dry.

- Visually inspect your work. Look around the home, both inside and out. You should not be able to see any dust, paint chips or debris.

- Re-clean the area thoroughly if you find dust or debris.

Step 6

Control the Waste

What to Do

Bag or wrap your waste at the work site and in the work area.

- Collect and control all your waste. This includes dust, debris, paint chips, protective sheeting, HEPA filters, dirty water, clothes, mop heads, wipes, protective clothing, respirators, gloves, architectural components and other waste.

- Use heavy plastic sheeting or bags to collect waste. Seal the bag securely with duct tape. Consider double bagging waste to prevent tears. Large components should be wrapped in protective sheeting and sealed with tape.

- Bag and seal all waste before removing it from the work area.

- Store all waste in a secure container or dumpster until disposal.

- Limit on-site storage time.

- Avoid transporting waste in an open truck or personal vehicle.

Dispose of waste water appropriately.

- Water used for cleanup should be filtered and dumped in a toilet if local rules allow. If not, collect it in a drum and take it with you. Never dump this water down a sink or tub, down a storm drain, or on the ground. Always dispose of waste water in accordance with federal, state and local regulations.

- EPA's Web site has state information on solid and hazardous waste disposal. See the following link for futher information: **http://www.epa.gov/epawaste/wyl/stateprograms.htm**.

Be aware of waste disposal rules.

- Because EPA considers most residential renovation and remodeling as "routine residential maintenance," most waste generated during these activities is classified as solid, non-hazardous waste, and should be taken to a licensed solid waste landfill. This is not the case for work done in commercial, public or other nonresidential child-occupied facilities, where waste may be considered hazardous and require special disposal methods. See the following link for futher information: **www.epa.gov/lead/pubs/fslbp.htm**.

- Always check state and local requirements before disposing of waste. Some are more stringent than federal regulations.

Step 7

Verify Work Completion with the Cleaning Verification Procedure or Clearance

When all the work is complete, and before interior space is reoccupied, you need to determine whether it is a safe environment to live in.

For Regulated Renovators and Maintenance Personnel:
If the work was performed by a contractor or landlord, either cleaning verification or clearance testing is required by the RRP Rule. (If the housing receives federal assistance, clearance testing is required.) If the cleaning verification procedure is chosen, an EPA certified renovator must perform the cleaning verification procedure. If clearance is chosen, a certified lead inspector, certified lead risk assessor, or certified lead sampling technician must conduct clearance testing.

For Do-it-Yourselfers:
After visual inspection in homes not receiving federal assistance, where the homeowner has completed the work, the homeowner is not required to conduct a cleaning verification procedure or clearance, but EPA strongly recommends that you choose one or the other to ensure that a complete cleaning was accomplished.

Cleaning Verification Procedure

After completion of cleaning, the cleaning verification procedure is performed by wiping all dust collection surfaces in the work area with a wet, disposable cleaning cloth and comparing that cloth visually to a cleaning verification card. Dust collection surfaces include window sills, countertops and other large horizontal surfaces such as fireplace mantles and built-in shelving, and floors. Cleaning verification cards are available from EPA by calling the **National Lead Information Center** at **1-800-424-LEAD (5323)**. Cleaning verification may only be performed by an EPA Certified Renovator if renovations covered by the Renovation, Repair and Painting rule were performed.

Note: For exterior work, only a visual inspection for dust, paint chips or debris is required.

The cleaning verification procedure for window sills is described below:

- Each window sill in the work area is wiped using a single, wet, disposable cleaning cloth.

- Once the entire window sill surface is wiped, the wipe is compared to the cleaning verification card. (See "Interpreting the Cleaning Verification Procedure" on page 27).

The cleaning verification procedure for countertops and floors is described below:

- Each countertop is wiped by the Certified Renovator using a wet disposable cleaning cloth:

  - For smaller countertops and other horizontal surfaces such as fireplace mantles and built-in shelving with a total surface area less than 40 square feet—wipe the entire surface with a single wipe and compare to the cleaning verification card.

  - Large area surfaces, such as large countertops and floors, have surface areas larger than 40 square feet—each of these large countertops and floors must be divided into roughly equal sections that are 40 square feet or less. Wipe each section separately using a new wet disposable cleaning cloth for each separate section. When conducting cleaning verification on floors, the wipe will be attached to the handle of a wet mopping system. The use of the wet mopping system handle allows the Certified Renovator to apply uniform pressure on the cleaning cloth. Each wipe is then compared to the cleaning verification card.

Interpreting the Cleaning Verification Procedure

- Compare each wipe representing a specific surface section to the cleaning verification card. If the cloth used to wipe a surface section within the work area is cleaner than the example wipes on the cleaning verification card, then that surface section has been adequately cleaned.

- If the cloth is not cleaner than the cleaning verification card, re-clean that surface section. Then use a new wet disposable cleaning cloth to wipe the surface section again. If the second cloth is cleaner than the cleaning verification card, that surface section has been adequately cleaned.

- If the second cloth is not cleaner than the cleaning verification card, re-clean the surface, wait for 1 hour or until the surface section has dried completely, whichever is longer.

- Wipe the surface section with a dry electrostatic cleaning cloth. The cleaning verification procedure is now complete and the surface is considered clean.

- When all of the surfaces in the work area have passed comparison with the cleaning verification card, or have completed the post-renovation cleaning verification, the project is complete and the area can be turned over to occupants unless the housing is receiving federal assistance, or state or local laws require dust clearance testing, in which case the project must pass dust clearance testing before the area can be turned over to occupants.

Dust Clearance Testing

Clearance testing is conducted by certified lead-based paint inspectors, certified lead risk assessors, or certified lead dust sampling technicians. For homes receiving federal assistance, the clearance testing must be done by a person independent of the renovation firm.

- Although optional under the Renovation, Repair and Painting Rule, some states and localities may require clearance. Also, a homeowner may specifically request that a clearance test be performed in their contract. In this case, clean up the work area and check your work, then contact a certified lead-based paint inspector, risk assessor or lead dust sampling technician to arrange for clearance testing.

- HUD requires clearance testing after renovation or repair work in pre-78 homes receiving federal assistance, which are regulated under the Lead Safe Housing Rule. Contractors must determine whether the home is federally-assisted. Federal assistance may be channeled through a state or local government, community development corporation or other similiar entity.

- Clearance sampling for interior jobs will consist of a floor sample taken in each room where work was performed (to a maximum of four samples) and an additional sample on the floor outside the entry to the work area. Where window sills and window troughs were present in the work area, a window sill or window trough sample will be collected in each room where work was performed (to a maximum of four samples).

- All clearance samples must be sent to an EPA-recognized dust-lead laboratory for analysis. You can view the list of laboratories at **www.epa.gov/lead/pubs/nllap.htm**.

- For exterior jobs, EPA, like HUD, requires only a visual assessment of the work area to pass clearance.

Interpret the Clearance Sampling Results

The laboratory will report the amount of lead in the dust. A dust sample at or above the following limits for lead is considered hazardous:

- Floors: 40 micrograms per square foot

- Window sills: 250 micrograms per square foot

- Window troughs: 400 micrograms per square foot

If the laboratory report shows lead levels at or above these thresholds, the home fails the dust wipe test. The home must be cleaned and retested until compliance with these clearance limits is achieved. Re-cleaning must be done by the contractor.

It is a good idea for homeowners to specify in the initial contract that a dust clearance test will be done at the end of the job and that the contractor will be responsible for re-cleaning if the home fails this test. No one besides the contractor and the clearance examiner should enter the work area until the area has been cleaned.

Learn More About Lead Safety

To learn more about lead safe work practices, contact the National Lead Information Center at **1-800-424-LEAD (5323)** and see the following link **http://www.epa.gov/lead/nlic.htm**. The Center is the federal government's leading source of quality information on lead poisoning prevention and lead hazards.

Take a Course.
Get trained in lead safety. Professional trainers and community colleges in your area may offer training. For information on courses, contact the National Lead Information Center. One relevant course is:

- **Lead Safety For Renovation, Repair and Painting** (EPA-740-R-09-001, February 2009). EPA and HUD developed this 8 hour training course to instruct renovators, painters and maintenance personnel how to work safely in homes with lead-based paint. The course is interactive and includes hands-on activities for practicing the skills workers need to avoid creating lead hazards in the homes where they work. More information can be found at: **http://www.epa.gov/lead/pubs/epahudrrmodel.htm.**

Find Out About Local Rules and Resources.
The National Lead Information Center can provide information on how to contact your state, local and/or tribal programs to get general information about lead poisoning prevention.

- Local health departments can provide information about local programs, including assistance for poisoned children.

- State and tribal lead poisoning prevention or environmental protection programs can provide information about the lead regulations that apply in your community and can tell you about possible sources of financial aid for reducing lead hazards. They also may be able to tell you about the costs and availability of individuals certified to test lead paint and/or lead dust.

- Building code officials can tell you the regulations that apply to the renovation and remodeling work that you are planning.

Access Additional Resource Materials.

The National Lead Information Center can also provide copies of the following general reference and how-to guidance materials:

- Renovate Right: Important Lead Hazard Information for Families, Child Care Providers and Schools (EPA-740-F-08-002, March 2008).
  http://www.epa.gov/lead/pubs/renovaterightbrochure.pdf

- Small Entity Compliance Guide to Renovate Right: A Handbook for Contractors, Property Managers and Maintenance Personnel Working in Homes, Child Care Facilities and Schools Built Before 1978. (EPA-740-F-08-003, December 2008).
  http://www.epa.gov/lead/pubs/sbcomplianceguide.pdf

- Contractors: Lead Safely During Renovation (EPA 740-F-08-001, March 2008). This short pamphlet provides a quick summary of general information on lead safe work practices to contain, minimize and clean up dust.
  http://www.epa.gov/lead/pubs/contractor_brochure.pdf

- Protect Your Family from Lead in Your Home (EPA 747-K-99-001, June 2003). This is a general information pamphlet on lead-based paint, lead hazards, the effects of lead poisoning and steps you can take to protect your family.
  http://www.epa.gov/lead/pubs/leadpdfe.pdf

- Lead Paint Safety: A Field Guide for Painting, Home Maintenance, and Renovation Work (HUD-1779-LHC, March 2001). This guide gives step-by-step instruction on lead safe work practices for different jobs in the home.
  http://www.hud.gov/offices/lead/training/LBPguide.pdf

Other Resources

For other resources on lead, visit the following Web sites:

http://www.epa.gov/lead/ — EPA is playing a major role in addressing residential lead hazards, including deteriorating lead-based paint, lead contaminated dust and lead contaminated residential soil. This Web site provides information about lead and lead hazards and provides some simple steps to protect your family. It contains links to basic information, as well as more detailed information and documents on lead in the news, rules and regulations, education and outreach materials, training, and other lead links.

http://www.hud.gov/offices/lead/ — The U.S. Department of Housing and Urban Development's Office of Healthy Homes and Lead Hazard Control (OHHLHC) is unique among federal agencies dealing with lead-hazards, as it is staffed to bring lead health science to bear directly upon America's housing. The site will direct you to resources on lead paint regulations, training, guidance/technical guidelines and compliance and enforcement.

http://www.osha.gov/SLTC/lead/index.html — The mission of the U.S. Department of Labor's Occupational Safety and Health Administration (OSHA) is to assure the safety and health of America's workers by: setting and enforcing standards; providing training, outreach, and education; establishing partnerships; and encouraging continual improvements in workplace safety and health. OSHA has established the reduction of lead exposure as a high strategic priority. This site contains links to lead recognition, evaluation, compliance, and training resources.

http://www.cdc.gov/lead — The U.S. Department of Health and Human Services Centers for Disease Control and Prevention (CDC) are committed to achieving improvements in people's health. This site provides CDC's compiled information on lead and includes materials and links for parents, health professionals, researchers, students and others interested in the topic of lead. The key resources include fact sheets, guidelines and recommendations and questions and answers.

Pre-Renovation Education Requirements

The pre-renovation education requirements of the Renovation, Repair and Painting Rule ensure that owners and occupants of pre-1978 homes and child-occupied facilities are provided information about potential hazards of lead-based paint exposure before renovations are begun.

Who is affected? The requirements apply to any person paid to do work that disturbs paint in residential housing or child-occupied facilities built before 1978. This includes residential rental property owners and managers, general contractors and special trade contractors such as painters, plumbers, carpenters and electricians.

What properties are affected? All residential properties and child-occupied facilities built before 1978 are affected unless they meet one of the exceptions listed below.

Are there any exceptions? The requirements do not apply to housing designated for elderly or disabled persons (unless children under age 6 live there), zero-bedroom dwellings (studio apartments, dormitories, etc.), housing determined to be free of lead-based paint by a lead-based paint inspection, emergency renovations and repairs, and minor repairs that disturb less than 6 square feet of paint on interior surfaces or less than 20 square feet of paint on exterior surfaces.

What are the requirements? The Renovation, Repair and Painting Rule requires the distribution of the lead pamphlet *Renovate Right: Important Lead Hazard Information for Families, Child Care Providers and Schools* before the work starts.

- In residential housing, the pamphlet must be provided to both the owner and occupants, and the contractor is required to document the receipt or mailing of the brochure.
- In multi-family residential housing, the pamphlet must be distributed to each affected unit.
- When common areas of multi-family residential housing are affected by work, the pamphlet may be delivered to each unit or a notice can be sent to each unit notifying them of the location and duration of the work and the location of information postings about lead hazards and the work to be performed.
- In child-occupied facilities, the pamphlet must be provided to the owner, to the responsible party and to parents.

How do I get the pamphlet? The pamphlet is available from the **National Lead Information Center** at **1-800-424-LEAD (5323)**. Ask for the *Renovate Right: Important Lead Hazard Information for Families, Child Care Providers, and Schools* pamphlet, or download it at: **http://www.epa.gov/lead/pubs/renovaterightbrochure.pdf**.

Note: In federally-assisted housing, HUD requires notification to be distributed to occupants within 15 days after lead-based paint or lead-based paint hazards are identified in their unit (or common areas, if applicable), and within 15 days after completion of hazard control work in their unit or common areas.

Shopping List

Set It Up Safely

- ❑ Signs
- ❑ Barrier tape or rope
- ❑ Cones
- ❑ Heavy duty plastic sheeting
- ❑ Masking tape, duct tape, or painters' tape
- ❑ Stapler
- ❑ Utility knife or scissors

Minimize the Dust

- ❑ Wet-dry sandpaper, sanding sponge
- ❑ Misting bottle or pump sprayer
- ❑ Chemical strippers without methylene chloride
- ❑ High Efficiency Particulate Air (HEPA) vacuum cleaner (a special vacuum cleaner that can remove very small particles from floors, window sills, and carpets)
- ❑ Heavy-duty plastic bags
- ❑ Tack pads (large, sticky pads that help remove dust), paper towels, or disposable wipes
- ❑ Low-temperature heat gun (under 1,100 degrees Fahrenheit)
- ❑ Chemical strippers without methylene chloride
- ❑ Power tools with HEPA filter vacuum attachments

Protect Yourself

- ❑ Protective eyewear
- ❑ Painter's hat
- ❑ Disposable coveralls
- ❑ Disposable N-100 rated respirator
- ❑ Disposable latex/rubber gloves
- ❑ Disposable shoe covers

Clean the Work Area

- ❑ Heavy-duty plastic bags
- ❑ HEPA vacuum cleaner
- ❑ Masking tape, duct tape, or painters' tape
- ❑ Misting bottle or pump sprayer
- ❑ Disposable wet-cleaning wipes or hand towels
- ❑ Detergent or general-purpose cleaner

Prevent Lead Exposure During Renovation, Repair, and Painting

Understand that Renovation, Repair and Painting Jobs Can Create Hazards. People, especially children, may swallow the lead dust or paint chips created during the job and get poisoned. Lead poisoning has serious health effects.

Read *Renovate Right*, EPA and HUD's Lead Hazard Information Pamphlet. Contractors are required by law to give clients in pre-1978 homes and child-occupied facilities a copy of *Renovate Right*. *Renovate Right* explains the danger of lead-based paint and its associated hazards. You can get copies of *Renovate Right* by calling **1-800-424-LEAD (5323)** or you can download it at **http://www.epa.gov/lead/pubs/renovaterightbrochure.pdf**.

Use Lead-Safe Work Practices. Follow practices that will protect you and residents from exposure to lead. These practices may take a small amount of additional time and money, but they are necessary to protect children, residents, workers and workers' families from exposure to lead dust.

Conduct Lead Testing Before and/or After the Work is Performed. Pre-job testing can identify any lead paint in the home and allow workers to target lead safe work practices to the areas where there is lead paint. Using the cleaning verification procedure or clearance testing at the end of the job ensures that no dust has been left behind.

Learn More About Lead. To learn more about working safely with lead, contact the National Lead Information Center at **1-800-424-LEAD (5323)** or visit EPA's Web site at **www.epa.gov/lead** or HUD's Web site at **www.hud.gov/offices/lead**.

March 2009, EPA-740-K-09-003
U.S. Environmental Protection Agency, Office of Pollution Prevention and Toxics
U.S. Dept. of Housing and Urban Development, Office of Healthy Homes and Lead Hazard Control
Printed with Vegetable Oil-Based Inks, Recycled Paper

Appendix 6:

Hands-on Exercises

LEADSAFETY for Remodeling, Repair and Painting

Appendix 6: Hands-on Exercises

The following exercises can be used in place of the hands-on exercises or as supplemental activities. Exercise worksheets and answers are provided.

- Skill Set #1: Using EPA-Recognized Test Kits
- Skill Set #2: Setting up Barriers, Signs, and Flapped Entry Doors
- Skill Set #3: Cover or Remove Furniture
- Skill Set #4: Establish Interior Containment
- Skill Set #5: Establish Exterior Containment
- Skill Set #6: Personal Protective Equipment
- Skill Set #7: Interior Final Cleaning
- Skill Set #8: Exterior Final Cleaning
- Skill Set #9: Bagging Waste
- Skill Set #10: Visual Inspection
- Skill Set #11: Cleaning Verification Procedure

Recommended Supplies for Hands-on Activities
Test Kits Supplies List
<ul><li>Disposable plastic drop cloth 2' by 2'</li><li>Disposable shoe covers</li><li>Disposable wet cleaning wipes</li><li>Disposable, non-latex gloves</li><li>HEPA vacuum with attachments (for cleanup after sampling)</li><li>EPA-recognized test kit(s) w/ manufacturer's instructions</li><li>Heavy duty garbage bags</li><li>Kit-specific supplies as required in the manufacturer's instructions</li><li>Manufacturer provided test verification card with lead-based paint layer</li><li>Painted wood surface with no lead-based paint layer</li><li>*Participant Progress Log*</li><li>Pen or pencil</li><li>Tape (duct, painters, and masking)</li><li>*Test Kit Documentation Form*</li><li>Digital camera (*Optional*)</li><li>Numbered index cards (*Optional*)</li></ul>
Setup Supplies List
<ul><li>Barrier tape</li><li>Broom handle, or dowels, or 1" x 1" x 30" wood or metal stock</li><li>Cutting tool (e.g., razor knife, box cutter or scissors)</li><li>Disposable tack pad</li><li>Doorway to use for work area entry setup</li><li>Fencing stakes</li><li>Heavy duty plastic sheeting</li><li>Magnetic covers</li><li>Orange cones</li><li>Rope and/or barrier tape (bright color preferable)</li><li>Stapler and Staples</li><li>Tape (duct, painters, and masking)</li></ul>

Recommended Supplies for Hands-on Activities - Continued

Setup Supplies List - Continued
- Tape measure
- Warning signs
- Pre-engineered containment systems (*Optional for Skill Set 2*)

Personal Protective Equipment (PPE) Supplies List
- Disposable coveralls
- Disposable non-latex gloves
- Disposable foot covers
- Eye protection
- Leather or canvas work gloves
- N-100 respirators
- Disposable waste bags
- Duct tape
- Hand washing facilities and hand soap

Cleanup Supplies List
- Baby powder or corn starch
- Cleaning verification card, one per student to take away and retain
- Cutting tool (e.g., razor knife, box cutter or scissors)
- Disposable foot covers
- Disposable non-latex gloves
- Disposable wet cleaning wipes
- Electrostatically charged, white, disposable cleaning cloths designed for cleaning hard surfaces
- Flashlight
- Garden sprayer
- Heavy duty plastic bags
- Heavy duty plastic sheeting
- HEPA vacuum with attachments and a powered beater bar
- Long-handled mop designed for wet cleaning wipes
- Tape (duct, painters, and masking)
- Tape measure
- Two-sided mop bucket with wringer (or equivalent), disposable mop heads, long handled mop to which disposable cleaning cloths can be attached; or, a wet mopping system.
- Watch or clock

Participant Progress Log

Name of Trainee	Module 3 (15 Min) Skill Set 1: Using EPA-Recognized Test Kits	Skill Set 2: Setting up Barriers, Signs, and Flapped Entry Doors	Module 4 (45 Min) Skill Set 3: Cover or Remove Furniture	Skill Set 4: Establish Interior Containment	Skill Set 5: Establish Exterior Containment	Module 5 (10 Min) Skill Set 6: Personal Protective Equipment	Skill Set 7: Interior Final Cleaning	Skill Set 8: Exterior Final Cleaning	Module 6 (50 Min) Skill Set 9: Bagging Waste	Skill Set 10: Visual Inspection	Skill Set 11: Cleaning Verification Procedure

Date of Training: _____

Certified Renovator Name: _____

LEADSAFETY for Remodeling, Repair and Painting

Participant Progress Log

Name of Trainee	Module 3 (15 Min)		Module 4 (45 Min)		Module 5 (10 Min)			Module 6 (50 Min)			
	Skill Set 1: Using EPA-Recognized Test Kits	Skill Set 2: Setting up Barriers, Signs, and Flapped Entry Doors	Skill Set 3: Cover or Remove Furniture	Skill Set 4: Establish Interior Containment	Skill Set 5: Establish Exterior Containment	Skill Set 6: Personal Protective Equipment	Skill Set 7: Interior Final Cleaning	Skill Set 8: Exterior Final Cleaning	Skill Set 9: Bagging Waste	Skill Set 10: Visual Inspection	Skill Set 11: Cleaning Verification Procedure

Date of Training: _____

Certified Renovator Name: _____

Certified Renovator Training Hands-On Skills Assessment

Date: _____ Address: _____ City & State _____
Student Name: _____ Student Signature: _____

Skill Set	Skill Description	Student has demonstrated proficiency at the following skills consistent with the requirements of the EPA RRP Rule.	Trainer's Initials
#1	Using EPA-Recognized Test Kits	Using test kit to properly test for lead-based paint and document results.	
#2	Setting up Barriers, Signs, and Flapped Entry Doors	Placing critical barriers and posting signs to isolate work area from access by unauthorized individuals.	
#3	Cover or Remove Furniture	Identifying the proper steps in determining when and how to cover or remove furniture and belongings from the work area.	
#4	Establish Interior Containment	Using the proper steps to cover floors and close and seal doors and windows in the work area.	
#5	Establish Exterior Containment	Taking proper steps to restrict entry to the exterior work area and to protect the ground under and around the work area from becoming contaminated.	
#6	Personal Protective Equipment	Using dust reduction techniques while performing common renovation, repair, and painting work activities.	
#7	Interior Final Cleaning	Cleaning the interior work area after the completion of work and prior to the visual inspection and cleaning verification procedure or dust clearance examination.	
#8	Exterior Final Cleaning	Cleaning the exterior work area after the completion of the work and prior to visual inspection and (if required) cleaning verification or dust clearance examination.	
#9	Bagging Waste	Taking steps to bag and gooseneck waste, wrap large pieces of debris, and to carry them out of the work area.	
#10	Visual Inspection	Conducting a visual inspection of the work area prior to the cleaning verification procedure.	
#11	Cleaning Verification Procedure	Conducting cleaning verification procedure.	

I am the trainer for the Certified Renovator course offered on the date and location described above. I verify that the student has demonstrated the skills as described above.

Trainer Name: _____ Trainer Signature: _____
Trainer Phone: _____ Organization: _____ Date: _____

LEADSAFETY for Remodeling, Repair and Painting

Skill Set #1: Using EPA-Recognized Test Kits
<u>Time</u>: **15 minutes**
Feb 09

Supplies needed:

- EPA-recognized test kit(s) w/ manufacturer's instructions
- Kit-specific supplies as required in the manufacturer's instructions
- Disposable plastic drop cloth 2' by 2'
- Tape (duct, painters, and masking)
- Disposable, non-latex gloves
- Disposable shoe covers
- Manufacturer provided test verification card with lead-based paint layer
- Disposable wet cleaning wipes
- Heavy duty garbage bags
- Painted wood surface with no lead-based paint layer
- *Test Kit Documentation Form*
- *Participant Progress Log*
- Pen or pencil
- Digital camera (*Optional*)
- Numbered index cards (*Optional*)
- EPA vacuum with attachments (for cleanup after sampling)

Note to Instructor: *It is strongly suggested that instructors prepare plastic bags containing all materials needed for the hands-on exercises, prior to the exercise, in order to meet the time limits allocated to Skill Set #1.*

Purpose: The purpose of this hands-on exercise is to teach students how to correctly use EPA-recognized test kits to determine if lead-based paint is present on components and surfaces affected by renovation work.

Note to Instructor: *Read the purpose of this activity to students and remind them to document all areas where the paint color or substrate reactions may cause an incorrect result. These surfaces should not be tested with a test kit, but should either be tested by Certified Inspectors or Certified Risk Assessors; or must be assumed to contain lead-based paint.*

Demonstration: The course instructor must show and explain all of the steps involved in the use of EPA-recognized test kits. The demonstration should not take longer than 5 minutes including the time needed to hand out materials.

Evaluating the Students: Allow students to practice the eight steps on the following page. Watch each student follow the steps. Make corrections and suggestions as the exercise proceeds and determine if additional practice is necessary. This should take no longer than 10 minutes. Students must complete all required steps to be "Proficient". Evaluate the work of each student and once the student can use a test kit correctly, the instructor should write the word "Proficient" in the field on the Participant Progress Log that corresponds to Skills Set #1 and that particular student's name.

LEADSAFETY for Remodeling, Repair and Painting

Skill Set #1: Using EPA-Recognized Test Kits - Continued

Skills Practice:

Step 1: Read the manufacturer's instructions

Step 2: Write required information and observations about the test location on the *Test Kit Documentation Form*.*

Step 3: (Optional) Secure a small disposable plastic drop cloth (2ft x 2 ft) on the floor beneath the test location with masking tape.

Step 4: Put on disposable non-latex gloves and shoe covers.

Step 5: Follow the manufacturer's instructions for use of the test kit to conduct the test.* Perform one test on the test card provided by the manufacturer, to observe a positive test result; conduct one test of a painted wood surface with no lead-based paint layer to observe a negative test result.*

Step 6: Use one wet cleaning wipe to remove residual chemicals left on the surface tested. Use a second cleaning wipe to remove any visible debris or dust on the floor beneath the sample collection area and place the used cleaning wipe in the trash bag.*

Step 7: Check documentation for completeness and note the result of the testing on the *Test Kit Documentation Form*.*

Step 8: (Optional) Number the test location in sequence on the *Test Kit Documentation Form*, then select the corresponding numbered index card and tape it next to the test location with masking tape and take a picture of the numbered test location to photo-document conduct and possibly the result of the test.

*Indicates required skills that must be accomplished for a "Proficient" rating.

Interpreting the Results of Test Kit Sampling:

The manufacturer's instructions will indicate the targeted indicator color change for lead in paint. Once the test is conducted, note the result and refer to the manufacturer's guidelines for interpreting the result. All painted surfaces that show the manufacturer's listed color change for lead in paint (a positive test result) must be treated as lead-based paint until additional testing performed by a Certified Lead Inspector or Risk Assessor proves it is not.

Documenting Test Kit Results:

A report of the findings from use of the test kit must be submitted to the person contracting the work within 30 days following the completion of the renovation work. The completed *Test Kit Documentation Form* should be kept by the Certified Firm for 3 years after the work is completed.

LEADSAFETY for Remodeling, Repair and Painting

Test Kit Documentation Form

Owner Information

Name of Owner/Occupant: _____

Address: _____

City: _____ State: _____ Zip code: _____ Contact #: (____) ____-_____

Email: _____

Renovation Information

Fill out all of the following information that is available about the Renovation Site, Firm, and Certified Renovator.

Renovation Address: _____ Unit# _____

City: _____ State: _____ Zip code: _____

Certified Firm Name: _____

Address: _____

City: _____ State: _____ Zip code: _____ Contact #: (____) ____-_____

Email: _____

Certified Renovator Name: _____ Date Certified: ___ / ___ / ___

Test Kit Information

Use the following blanks to identify the test kit or test kits used in testing components.

Test Kit #1

Manufacturer: _____ Manufacture Date: _____/_____/_____

Model: _____ Serial #: _____

Expiration Date: _____

Test Kit #2

Manufacturer: _____ Manufacture Date: _____/_____/_____

Model: _____ Serial #: _____

Expiration Date: _____

Test Kit #3

Manufacturer: _____ Manufacture Date: _____/_____/_____

Model: _____ Serial #: _____

Expiration Date: _____

LEADSAFETY for Remodeling, Repair and Painting

Test Kit Documentation Form

Renovation Address: _____ Unit# _____

City: _____ State: _____ Zip code: _____

Test Location # ____ Test Kit Used: (Circle only one) Test Kit # 1 Test Kit # 2 Test Kit # 3

Description of test location: _____

_____

Result: Is lead present? (Circle only one) YES NO Presumed

Test Location # ____ Test Kit Used: (Circle only one) Test Kit # 1 Test Kit # 2 Test Kit # 3

Description of test location: _____

_____

Result: Is lead present? (Circle only one) YES NO Presumed

Test Location # ____ Test Kit Used: (Circle only one) Test Kit # 1 Test Kit # 2 Test Kit # 3

Description of test location: _____

_____

Result: Is lead present? (Circle only one) YES NO Presumed

Test Location # ____ Test Kit Used: (Circle only one) Test Kit # 1 Test Kit # 2 Test Kit # 3

Description of test location: _____

_____

Result: Is lead present? (Circle only one) YES NO Presumed

Test Location # ____ Test Kit Used: (Circle only one) Test Kit # 1 Test Kit # 2 Test Kit # 3

Description of test location: _____

_____

Result: Is lead present? (Circle only one) YES NO Presumed

Test Location # ____ Test Kit Used: (Circle only one) Test Kit # 1 Test Kit # 2 Test Kit # 3

Description of test location: _____

_____

Result: Is lead present? (Circle only one) YES NO Presumed

Test Location # ____ Test Kit Used: (Circle only one) Test Kit # 1 Test Kit # 2 Test Kit # 3

Description of test location: _____

_____

Result: Is lead present? (Circle only one) YES NO Presumed

Skill Set #2: Setting Up Barriers, Signs and Flapped Entry Doors
Time: 10 minutes
Feb 09

Supplies needed:
- Barrier tape
- Warning signs
- Doorway to use for work area entry setup
- Cutting tool (e.g., razor knife, box cutter or scissors)
- Heavy duty plastic sheeting
- Tape (duct, painters, and masking)
- Stapler and staples
- Broom handle, or dowels, or 1" x 1" x 30" wood or metal stock
- Optional: Pre-engineered containment systems may also be used for this exercise.

Note to Instructor: It is strongly suggested that instructors prepare plastic bags containing all materials needed for the skills practice prior to the exercise in order to meet the time limits allocated to Skill Set #2.

Purpose: The purpose of this hands-on exercise is to show students the proper steps in determining where to place critical barriers, and to give them practice in erecting barriers and posting signs to isolate the work area from access by unauthorized personnel.

Note to Instructor: Read the purpose of this activity to students. Remind them that these setup steps must be completed before the disturbance of more than 6 ft^2 per room of lead-based paint, or, whenever window replacement or demolition is to be accomplished.

Demonstration: The course instructor must show and explain all of the steps involved in establishing a critical barrier and in placement of signage. Critical barriers are plastic sheeting barriers secured over openings, doors, and windows that must remain in place until cleaning verification or clearance is achieved in order to keep dust inside of the work area. While they are not always required, they can assist with controlling the spread of dust to other areas of the home. Use students to assist in the erection of the demonstration critical barriers. Note: In the interest of time, use precut barriers for installation in the doorway. Velcro attached barriers may be used for demonstration and practice. Velcro sign attachments may also be used.

Evaluating the Students: The instructor should allow students to practice the steps on the following page while watching each student follow the steps. Make corrections and suggestions as the exercise proceeds and determine if additional practice is necessary. *Option: Have students say the steps as they work.* Students must complete all required Steps to be "Proficient". Evaluate the work of each student and once the student has completed all required elements of the exercise correctly record the performance as "Proficient" in the field on the Participant Progress Log that corresponds to Skill Set #2 and that particular student's name.

Skill Set #2: Setting up Barriers, Signs, and Flapped Entry Doors - Continued

Skills Practice:

Step 1:   Ask occupants to leave and remain out of the room where work will be done.

Step 2:   Have them stay out until the cleaning verification procedure is complete or until clearance is passed. Install barrier tape to establish a controlled perimeter.

Step 3:   Post a "Do Not Enter" sign at the doorway to the work area.* Also post a sign that states that no eating, drinking, or smoking is allowed the doorway to the work area.*

Step 4:   Cover the work area entry doorway with 2 layers of plastic sheeting, by doing the following:*

Step 5:   Cut first plastic sheeting layer slightly wider and longer than (about 3 inches longer) than the door frame.*

Step 6:   Make a small "S" fold at the top of plastic sheeting and tape so that all layers are secured to the top of the door frame.* Make a similar "S" fold at the bottom of the plastic sheeting and tape so that all layers are secured to the floor.* This will ensure that the plastic sheeting is not tight and allows it to give instead of tearing when people move through it. Secure both sides of the plastic sheeting to the door frame with tape.

Step 7:   Staple top corners to the door frame for reinforcement.*

Step 8:   For exiting and entering the room, use duct tape to create a vertical line about the size of a man from floor to header in the middle of the plastic sheeting on both sides.* Cut a long vertical slit through the duct tape; leave about 6 inches at the top and the bottom uncut.* Reinforce the top and bottom of the slit with horizontal duct tape to prevent the plastic sheeting from tearing.*

Step 9:   Tape a second layer of plastic sheeting to the top of the door frame.* This layer is cut slightly shorter than the door frame so that it will hang down flat against the first sheet of plastic sheeting.

Step 10:   Weight the bottom of the second layer of plastic sheeting by taping a dowel rod to the bottom of the second layer of plastic sheeting with duct tape. This creates a self-sealing flap over the doorway and seals the opening that was cut in the plastic sheeting during step 8.

*Indicates required skills that must be accomplished for a "Proficient" rating.

Skill Set #3: Cover or Remove Furniture

<u>Time</u>: 10 minutes
<u>Feb 09</u>

Supplies needed:

- Heavy duty plastic sheeting
- Cutting tool (e.g., razor knife, box cutter or scissors)
- Tape (duct, painters, and masking)

Purpose: The purpose of this hands-on exercise is to show students the proper steps for determining when and how to cover or remove furniture and belongings from a work area.

> ***Note to Instructor:*** *Read the purpose of this activity to students. Remind them that these setup steps must be completed before the disturbance of more than 6 ft^2 per room of lead-based paint, or, whenever window replacement or demolition is to be accomplished. Also remind them that the best solution to the problem of moving furniture and belongings is to notify residents to remove them prior to the work. Remind them also that it is better to remove personal property than to cover it. Provide students with the opportunity to observe/practice both methods (covering and removal).*

Demonstration: The course instructor should explain all of the steps involved in covering and/or removing furniture and belongings from the work area. Use students to demonstrate moving chairs out of the work area. Then cover a table with plastic sheeting and secure the plastic sheeting with tape so that no part of the table is exposed. Discuss placing other items under the table for maximized efficiency in preparing the work area. The demonstration should not take longer than 3 minutes including the time needed to hand out materials.

Evaluating the Students: The instructor should allow students to practice the steps on the following page while watching each student follow the steps. Make corrections and suggestions as the exercise proceeds and determine if additional practice is necessary. *Option: Have students say the steps as they work.* Students must complete all required Steps to be "Proficient". Evaluate the work of each student and once the student has completed all required elements of the exercise correctly record the performance as "Proficient" in the field on the Participant Progress Log that corresponds to Skill Set #3 and that particular student's name.

Skill Set #3: Cover or Remove Furniture – Continued

Skills Practice:

Step 1:   Move all the furniture out of the work area.

Note: If the training area is small, designate an area against one wall that is "out of the work area", where furniture removed from the work area can be placed. In a classroom setting, move the chairs and most of the tables to the designated area, and cover the tables.

Step 2:   Have the students team into groups of 2 to 6 per group. Cover several of the tables where students were sitting. This is done as follows:

Step 3:   Cut a piece of plastic sheeting large enough to cover the table and to overlap the floor by 3-6 inches.*

Step 4:   Secure the plastic sheeting to the table and/or the floor with tape.*

Step 5:   If the table will not need to be moved during the work, the plastic sheeting can be secured to the floor using duct tape or masking tape as is appropriate to the surface.*

Step 6:   If the table will need to be moved during the work, wrap the table with plastic sheeting including the legs and secure the plastic sheeting to the table with tape. Take care when applying tape so that there is no damage to the finished surfaces of the furniture.*

Note: Students should understand that they are to remove or cover all window treatments, furniture and rugs within 6 feet of surfaces that will be renovated, repaired or painted. Removal of furniture is recommended whenever possible.

*Indicates required skills that must be accomplished for a "Proficient" rating.

Skill Set #4: Establish Interior Containment

Time: 10 minutes
Feb 09

Supplies needed:

- Orange cones
- Rope and/or barrier tape (bright color preferable)
- Warning signs
- Tape measure
- Tape (duct, painters, and masking)
- Heavy duty plastic sheeting
- Cutting tool (e.g., razor knife, box cutter or scissors)
- Magnetic covers
- Disposable tack pad

Purpose: The purpose of this hands-on exercise is to show students the proper steps in covering floors, and closing and sealing the doors, windows and HVAC in the work area.

Note to Instructor: Read the purpose of this activity to students. Remind them that these setup steps must be completed before the disturbance of more than 6 ft^2 per room of lead-based paint, or, whenever window replacement or demolition is to be accomplished.

Demonstration: The course instructor should explain all of the steps involved in covering and sealing floors and other horizontal surfaces in the work area, and in closing and sealing doors and windows between the work area and non-work areas. Use students to demonstrate closing and taping the windows and doors with masking tape. Remind them that they are trying to keep dust from escaping the work area.

Evaluating the Students: Allow students to practice the steps for covering the floors, closing and sealing windows, and closing and sealing doors. Watch each student follow the steps on the following page. Make corrections and suggestions as the exercise proceeds and determine if additional practice is necessary. *Option: Have students say the steps as they work.* Students must complete all required Steps to be "Proficient". Evaluate the work of each student and once the student has completed all required elements of the exercise correctly, record the performance as "Proficient" in the field on the Participant Progress Log that corresponds to Skill Set #4 and that particular student's name.

Skill Set #4: Establish Interior Containment - Continued

Skills Practice:

Step 1:   At each non-entry doorway leading from the work area, place an orange cone, barrier tape, and a "Do Not Enter" sign.*

Step 2:   Close all doors and windows leading to/from the work area.*

Step 3:   Tape the seams around each door and window casing with painter's tape, masking tape, or duct tape.*

Step 4:   Cut plastic sheeting so that it covers all exposed surfaces within 6 feet of the component(s) that are to be affected by the work.*

Step 5:   Secure the plastic sheeting to the floor and walls as appropriate with tape.*

Step 6:   Use plastic sheeting floor runners to avoid stepping on the carpet or floors when walking out of the work area. Secure them to the floor with tape.*

Step 7:   Close and cover all air and heat diffusers and intakes with magnetic covers, tape, or plastic sheeting and tape.* Also, if possible, turn off the HVAC system while working.* HVAC units may be turned on after cleaning verification or clearance has been achieved.

Step 8:   Stage all of the tools, supplies and equipment you will need to conduct the renovation, repair or painting work on the plastic sheeting in the work area to avoid contaminating the work area.*

Step 9:   Place a disposable tack pad at the corner of the plastic sheeting nearest the entry door to control tracking dust off of the plastic sheeting.*

*Indicates required skills that must be accomplished for a "Proficient" rating.

Skill Set #5: Establish Exterior Containment

<u>Time</u>: **15 minutes**
Feb 09

<u>Supplies needed:</u>

- Orange cones
- Rope and/or barrier tape (bright color preferable) and fencing stakes
- Warning signs
- Heavy duty plastic sheeting
- Tape (duct, painters, and masking)
- Cutting tool (e.g., razor knife, box cutter or scissors)
- Tape measure
- Disposable tack pad

<u>Purpose:</u> The purpose of this hands-on exercise is to show students the proper steps for restricting entry to the exterior work area, and to protect the ground under and around the work area from becoming contaminated.

> ***Note to Instructor:*** *Read the purpose of this activity to students. Remind them that these setup steps must be completed before the disturbance of more than 20 ft^2 of paint on components that have been determined to be lead-based paint, or, whenever window replacement or demolition is to be accomplished.*

<u>Demonstration:</u> The course instructor should explain all of the steps involved in restricting access to and containing dust within the work area. Emphasize to students that proper setup will restrict access, and will keep dust and debris from escaping the work area.

<u>Evaluating the Students:</u> Allow students to cover the ground and establish barriers to prevent unauthorized access to the work area. Watch each student follow the steps on the following page. Make corrections and suggestions as the exercise proceeds and determine if additional practice is necessary. *Option: Have students say the steps as they work.* Students must complete all required Steps to be "Proficient". Evaluate the work of each student and once the student has completed all required elements of the exercise correctly, record the performance as "Proficient" in the field on the Participant Progress Log that corresponds to Skill Set #5 and that particular student's name.

Skill Set #5: Establish Exterior Containment - Continued

Skills Practice:

Step 1: At each non-entry doorway leading into the work area, place an orange cone, barrier tape, and a "Do Not Enter"sign.*

Step 2: Close all doors and windows within 20 feet of the work area.*

Step 3: Place plastic sheeting as ground cover a minimum of 10 feet in all directions from the actual location of a paint disturbance.*

Step 4: Weigh down the edges of the plastic sheeting with 2x4s or bricks or stake down the edges of the plastic sheeting.*

Step 5: Secure the plastic sheeting to the floor and walls with tape or furring strips and tacks.*

Step 6: Place barrier fencing or a rope around the perimeter of the work area 20 feet from the work area and on all exposed sides.*

Step 7: Establish an entry point to the work area and place a "Do Not Enter, No Food or Drinks or Smoking Allowed"sign.*.

Step 8: Curb the edges of the plastic sheeting to prevent dust from blowing off.* Curbs can be made by running a low rope near the ground and draping the plastic sheeting over the top of the rope. The rope should be only a few inches above the ground. A staked 2x4 may also be used to raise the edges of the plastic sheeting instead of the rope method.

Step 9: Stage all of the tools, supplies, and equipment you will need to conduct the renovation, repair, or painting work on the plastic sheeting in the work area to avoid contaminating the work area.*

Step 10: Place a disposable tack pad at the corner of the plastic sheeting nearest the entry door to control tracking dust off of the plastic sheeting.*

*Indicates required skills that must be accomplished for a "Proficient" rating.

Skill Set #6: Personal Protective Equipment
Time: 10 minutes
Feb 09

Supplies needed:
- Disposable coveralls
- Disposable non-latex gloves
- Disposable foot covers
- Eye protection
- Leather or canvas work gloves
- N-100 respirators
- Disposable waste bags
- Duct tape
- Hand washing facilities and hand soap

Purpose: The purpose of this hands-on exercise is to show students the proper steps for putting on (donning) and taking off (doffing) personal protective equipment, and the steps for decontaminating and disposing of used equipment.

Note to Instructor: Read the purpose of this activity to students.

Demonstration: The course instructor should explain all of the steps involved in putting on personal protective equipment while actually dressing a volunteer student in personal protective equipment. Emphasize to students that this equipment prevents their exposure to lead as well as prevents the contamination of areas outside of the work area.

Evaluating the Students: Watch each student as they follow the steps on the next page. Make corrections and suggestions as the exercise proceeds and determine if additional practice is necessary. *Option: Have students say the steps as they work.* Students must complete all required Steps to be "Proficient". Evaluate the work of each student and once the student has completed all required elements of the exercise correctly record the performance as "Proficient" in the field on the Participant Progress Log that corresponds to Skills Set #6 and that particular student's name.

Skill Set #6: Personal Protective Equipment – Continued

Skills Practice:

Step 1:   Put on (don) a set of protective coveralls.*

Step 2:   Put on disposable gloves.*

Step 3:   Put on boot covers over shoes.*

Step 4:   Put on safety glasses.*

Step 5:   Put on work gloves.*

Step 6:   When dressed in this Personal Protective Equipment, discuss the use of respirators and show the proper method for putting on and securing the respirator in place.
Note: Students should not wear a respirator if they are not currently enrolled in the training firm's respiratory protection program. Watch the demonstration but do not try on a respirator if this note applies you.

Step 7:   Remove the work gloves and place them in a marked waste bag.*

Step 8:   Remove the boot covers by pulling them off from the heel and rolling the cover inside out as it is rolled toward the toes. Once removed, place them in a marked waste bag.*

Step 9:   Remove your suit by unzipping it and rolling it dirty side in to prevent releasing dust. Once removed, place the suit in a marked waste bag.*

Step 10:   Remove your disposable non-latex gloves by grasping the cuff of one glove and peeling the glove inside out off of the hand. Hold the glove that was removed in the palm of the gloved hand. Place one finger under the cuff of the gloved hand and remove this glove by peeling it off of the gloved hand inside out and over the balled up glove you had already removed. Once removed, you should have one glove inside the other, with the dirty side contained. Dispose of the gloves in the marked waste bag.*

Step 11:   Wash your hands, face and shoes with soap and water. Dry your hands and face with a disposable towel.*

*Indicates required skills that must be accomplished for a "Proficient" rating.

Skill Set #7: Interior Final Cleaning
Time: 10 minutes
Feb 09

Supplies needed:
- Heavy duty plastic sheeting
- Duct tape
- HEPA vacuum with attachments and a powered beater bar
- Garden sprayer
- Cutting tool (e.g., razor knife, box cutter or scissors)
- Disposable wet cleaning wipes
- Heavy duty plastic bags
- Two-sided mop bucket with wringer (or equivalent), disposable mop heads, long handled mop to which disposable cleaning cloths can be attached; or, a wet mopping system.

Purpose: The purpose of this hands-on exercise is to show students the proper steps for cleaning the interior work area after the completion of the work and prior to the visual inspection and cleaning verification procedure, or a clearance examination.

Note to Instructor: Read the purpose of this activity to students. Remind them that they are trying to completely clean all visible dust and debris in the work area, and that their work will be checked. Remind them that this level of cleanliness is achievable, but does require attention and careful execution.

- The course instructor should explain all of the steps involved in cleaning the work area. Emphasize to students that there are no short cuts to passing the visual inspection.

- Recommended personal protective equipment during final cleaning activities is a set of disposable coveralls, disposable gloves, and shoe covers.

- If plastic sheeting is not already in place from previous exercises, have plastic sheeting for the floor or carpets put down.

Evaluating the Students: Watch each student follow the steps on the following page. Make corrections and suggestions as the exercise proceeds and determine if additional practice is necessary. Students must complete all required Steps to be "Proficient". Evaluate the work of each student and once the student has completed all required elements of the exercise correctly, record the performance as "Proficient" in the field on the Participant Progress Log that corresponds to Skills Set #7 and that particular student's name.

Skill Set #7: Interior Final Cleaning - Continued

Skills Practice:

Step 1: Wrap and seal, or bag all components and other large materials and then remove them from the work area.*

Step 2: Clean off the plastic sheeting using a HEPA vacuum (this procedure is not required, but it is faster than wiping up dust and debris by hand). Mist the plastic sheeting and fold dirty side inward. Either seal the edges of the folded plastic sheeting with tape or place it in a heavy-duty plastic bag. Dispose of the protective sheeting.*

Step 3: Remove all waste from the work area and place in appropriate waste containers.*

Step 4: Clean all surfaces within the work area and in the area 2 feet beyond the work area until no dust or debris remains. Start cleaning at the top of the walls and work down toward the floor, HEPA vacuum or wet wipe all wall surfaces in the work area. HEPA vacuum all remaining surfaces in the work area, including furniture and fixtures. Use the upholstery attachment for the window surfaces and the crevice tool along the edge of the walls. Use the HEPA vacuum with a beater bar for carpeting. Work from the end farthest from the work area entrance back to the entrance, making sure never to step back into areas that have already been cleaned.*

Step 5: Next, wipe all remaining surfaces and objects in the work area except for carpeted and upholstered surfaces, with a disposable wet cleaning wipes. Also mop uncarpeted floors using a two-bucket method or wet mopping system. Work from the end farthest from the work area entrance back to the entrance, making sure never to step back into areas that have already been cleaned. For carpeted areas, conduct a second pass with the HEPA vacuum using the beater bar attachment instead of wiping with a wet cleaning cloth.*

Step 6: If the property is HUD-regulated, repeat Step 4 for walls, countertops and floors, and then continue to Step 7. Otherwise, continue to Step 7.

Step 7: After completion of cleaning procedures, check your work. Conduct a careful visual inspection of the work area for visible dust and debris. If visible dust or debris is found, repeat Steps 4 and 5 as needed to make sure no visible dust or debris is present, and then re-check your work with a thorough visual inspection of the work area. When there is no visible dust or debris present, proceed to step 8.*

Step 8: Notify the Certified Renovator in charge of the project that the work area is ready for visual inspection.*

*Indicates required skills that must be accomplished for a "Proficient" rating.

Skill Set #8: Exterior Final Cleaning

<u>Time</u>: **10 minutes**

Feb 09

<u>Supplies needed:</u>
- Heavy duty plastic sheeting
- Heavy duty plastic bags
- Tape (duct, painters, and masking)
- Cutting tool (e.g., razor knife, box cutter or scissors)
- Flashlight.
- Disposable wet cleaning wipes
- HEPA vacuum with attachments
- Two-sided mop bucket with wringer (or equivalent), disposable mop heads, long handled mop to which disposable cleaning cloths can be attached, <u>or</u>, a wet mopping system.

Purpose: The purpose of this hands-on exercise is to show students the proper steps for cleaning an exterior work area after the completion of the work and prior to the visual inspection and (if required) the cleaning verification procedure or a clearance examination.

> ***Note to Instructor:*** *Read the purpose of this activity to students. Remind them that they are trying to clean all visible dust and debris within the work area, and that their work will be checked. Remind them that this level of cleanliness is achievable, but does require attention and careful execution.*

- The course instructor should explain all of the steps involved in cleaning the work area. Emphasize to students that there are no short cuts to passing the visual inspection.

- Recommended personal protective equipment during cleaning activities is a set of disposable coveralls, disposable gloves, and shoe covers.

- If plastic sheeting is not already in place from previous exercises, have plastic sheeting for the floor or carpets put down.

Evaluating the Students: Watch each student follow the steps on the following page. Make corrections and suggestions as the exercise proceeds and determine if additional practice is necessary. *Option: Have students say the steps as they work.* Students must complete all required Steps to be "Proficient". Evaluate the work of each student and once the student has completed all required elements of the exercise correctly, record the performance as "Proficient" in the field on the Participant Progress Log that corresponds to Skills Set #8 and that particular student's name.

Skill Set #8: Exterior Final Cleaning - Continued

Skills Practice:

Step 1:   Wrap and seal, or bag all components and other large materials and then remove them from the work area.*

Step 2:   Clean off the plastic sheeting using a HEPA vacuum (this procedure is not required, but it sure is faster than wiping up dust and debris by hand). Mist the plastic sheeting and fold dirty side inward. Either seal the edges of the plastic sheeting with tape or place it in a heavy-duty plastic bag. Dispose of plastic sheeting.*

Step 3:   Remove all waste from the work area and place in appropriate waste containers.*

Step 4:   Clean all surfaces in the work area and areas within 2 feet beyond the work area until no visible dust, debris, or paint chips remain.*

Suggested Cleaning Procedure For Exterior Cleanable Surfaces: Start cleaning at the top of the walls and work down to the floor, HEPA vacuum or wet wipe all cleanable surfaces in the work area, including furniture and fixtures. Use the HEPA vacuum with the upholstery attachment for windows and use the crevice tool along the walls. Work from the end farthest from the work area entrance back to the entrance, making sure never to step back into areas that have already been cleaned.

Step 5:   After completion of cleaning, check your work. This is done by conducting a careful visual inspection of the work area for visible dust, debris, or paint chips on hard surfaces, and for visible dust, debris, or paint chips in the soil areas under the work area protective sheeting. If dust or debris is found, re-clean, and then re-check your work with a thorough visual inspection of the work area. Once there is no visible dust, debris, or paint chips present, proceed to step 6.*

Step 6:   Notify the Certified Renovator in charge of the project that the work area is ready for visual inspection.*

*Indicates required skills that must be accomplished for a "Proficient" rating.

Skill Set #9: Bagging Waste

<u>Time</u>: **10 minutes**
Feb 09

<u>Supplies needed:</u>
- Used plastic sheeting and used personal protective equipment (from previous exercises)
- Dust and debris (from previous exercises)
- Heavy duty plastic sheeting
- Heavy duty plastic bags
- Cutting tool (e.g., razor knife, box cutter or scissors)
- HEPA vacuum with attachments
- Duct tape

<u>Purpose:</u> The purpose of this hands-on exercise is to show the students the proper steps to bag and gooseneck waste, wrap large pieces of debris, and remove waste from the work area.

<u>Note to Instructor:</u> Read the purpose of this activity to students.

- **Demonstration:** The course instructor should demonstrate the proper gooseneck technique for sealing waste bags.

- **Optional Bagging Relay Race:** This exercise can be conducted as a relay race. Divide students into teams and have each team member select a waste bag, load it with simulated waste material, make a gooseneck in the waste bag, vacuum the bag and submit it as complete in the simulated waste storage area. This will allow the instructors to observe proficiency in the method of closing the bags and making goosenecks and provides a fun way to learn for the students.

<u>Evaluating the Students:</u> Watch each student make a gooseneck closure on a waste bag. Students must complete all required Steps to be "Proficient". Once the student has completed all required elements of the exercise correctly, record the performance as "Proficient" in the field on the Participant Progress Log that corresponds to Skills Set #9 and that particular student's name.

Skill Set #9: Bagging Waste - Continued

Skills Practice:

Note: This exercise requires that the waste materials generated throughout the exercises be stored in unsealed bags or in sheets of plastic.

Gooseneck Procedure for Waste Bags:

Step 1:   Each student should get a waste bag and place some material in it that will be discarded as simulate waste. Do not overfill bags.

Step 2:   Gather the open end of the bag just below the opening into one hand.*

Step 3:   Twist the bag so that the neck of the bag twists in the same direction and forms an 8"-10" column.*

Step 4:   Fold the twisted column over on itself, in a similar manner to how you would fold a hose over onto itself to cut off the flow of water.*

Step 5:   Grasp the folded neck of the bag in one hand and wrap tape around the folded neck to secure the fold in place.*

Step 6:   Now wrap the tape about 2 or 3 inches from the top of the fold, several times so that the bag cannot come open. The resulting bags neck looks like the neck of a goose folded back on itself (a goose neck seal).*

Step 7:   Use the HEPA vacuum to remove any dust from the exterior of the bags. Carry the bags out of the work area to the appropriate waste container.*

Wrapping large pieces of debris:

Step 1:   Cut a piece of plastic so that it can be wrapped around the debris to be disposed of.*

Step 2:   Once wrapped in plastic, tape the seams of the package.*

Step 3:   Wrap tape around the width of the package in three spots to keep the package from unraveling.*

Step 4:   Use the HEPA vacuum to remove any dust from the exterior of the package and carry the wrapped debris out of the work area to the appropriate waste container.*

*Indicates required skills that must be accomplished for a "Proficient" rating.

Skill Set #10: Visual Inspection
Time: 5 minutes
Feb 09

Supplies needed:
- Disposable foot covers
- Flashlight

Purpose: The purpose of this hands-on exercise is to show the students the proper steps for conducting a visual inspection of the work area prior to conduct of the cleaning verification procedure.

> ***Note to Instructor:*** *Read the purpose of this activity to students. Remind them that they are trying to verify that all visible dust and debris has been cleaned from the work area. Remind them that this level of cleanliness is achievable, but does require attention and careful execution. Also read the note to the students below.*

> ***Note to Students:*** *If a clearance examination is to be performed, the Certified Renovator should still conduct a visual inspection before submitting to the two-part clearance examination. A clearance examination consists of a separate visual inspection and dust wipe testing. The two-part clearance examination is conducted by a Certified Lead Inspector, Certified Lead Risk Assessor, or Certified Sampling Technician.*

Demonstration: The course instructor should explain all of the steps involved in performing a visual clearance in the work area. Emphasize to students that there are no short cuts to passing the visual inspection.

Evaluating the Students: Watch each student conduct a visual inspection and listen as they point out problems that must be fixed. Students must complete all required Steps to be "Proficient". Evaluate the work of each student and once the student has completed all required elements of the exercise correctly, record the performance as "Proficient" in the field on the Participant Progress Log that corresponds to Skills Set #10 and that particular student's name.

Skill Set #10: Visual Inspection - Continued

Skills Practice:

Step 1:   Put on disposable foot covers so that you do not track dust and debris into the work area, then enter the work area.*

Step 2:   Turn on all of the lights that are available in the work area. Bring a bright, white-light flashlight to make sure there is adequate lighting.*

Step 3:   Systematically look at every horizontal surface in the work area, working from the farthest area from the entry to the entry without recovering your tracks. Get close to the surfaces you are inspecting.*

Note: Remember this is a visual inspection, but the cleaning verification is going to wipe dust up to compare with the cleaning verification card. If you suspect a surface to be dirty, have it re-cleaned with a wet cleaning cloth.

Step 4:   If you find visible dust or debris, re-clean the work area and repeat step 3.*

Step 5:   Once you have carefully inspected all of the surfaces and have found no dust or debris, proceed to the cleaning verification procedure in Skill Set #11.*

*Indicates required skills that must be accomplished for a "Proficient" rating.

Skill Set #11: Cleaning Verification Procedure

<u>Time</u>: **15 minutes**

Feb 09

Supplies needed:

- Baby powder or corn starch
- Disposable foot covers
- Flashlight
- Disposable non-latex gloves
- Disposable wet cleaning wipes
- Cleaning verification card, one per student to take away and retain
- Electrostatically charged, white, disposable cleaning cloths designed for cleaning hard surfaces
- Long-handled mop designed for wet cleaning wipes
- Tape measure
- Watch or clock

Purpose: The purpose of this hands-on exercise is to show the students the proper steps for conducting the cleaning verification procedure.

- The course instructor should explain all of the steps involved in performing the cleaning verification procedure.

Evaluating the Students: Watch each student conduct the cleaning verification procedure and listen as they point out problems that must be fixed. Students must complete all required steps to be "Proficient". Evaluate the work of each student and once the student has completed all required elements of the exercise correctly, record the performance as "Proficient" in the field on the Participant Progress Log that corresponds to Skills Set #11 and that particular student's name.

Skill Set #11: Cleaning Verification Procedure - Continued
Skills Practice:

Step 1: As you enter the work area put on disposable foot covers so that you do not track dust and debris into the work area.*

Step 2: Turn on all of the lights that are available in the work area. Make sure there is adequate lighting.*

For window sills:
Step 3: While wearing gloves, wipe each window sill in the work area with a clean, white, damp cleaning wipe.*

Step 4: Compare the cleaning wipe to the cleaning verification card. If the first wipe is the same as or whiter (lighter) than the cleaning verification card, the window sill is clean; continue to Step 6. If the first cleaning wipe is not the same as or whiter (lighter) than the cleaning verification card, re-clean the window sill, and, repeat Step 3 and then proceed to Step 5 (skip this step).*

Step 5: Compare the second cleaning wipe to the cleaning verification card. If the second wipe is the same as or whiter (lighter) than the cleaning verification card, the window sill is clean; continue to Step 6. If the second cleaning wipe is not the same as and not whiter (not lighter) than the cleaning verification card, wait one hour or until the wet surface is dry (for the purposes of this exercise you do not wait). Then re-clean the surface with a dry, electrostatically charged, white, disposable cleaning cloth designed for use on hard surfaces. The window sill is now clean and has completed the cleaning verification procedure.*

For Floors and Countertops:
Step 6: While wearing gloves, wipe each floor or countertop in the work area with a clean, white, damp cleaning wipe. For floors, use a long handled mop designed to hold a wet cleaning wipe. For floors, wipe no more than 40 square feet per wipe. For countertops wipe the whole surface of the countertop up to 40 square feet per wipe.*

Step 7: Compare each floor and countertop cleaning wipe to the cleaning verification card. If the first wipe is the same as or whiter (lighter) than the cleaning verification card, the floor or countertop is clean. If the first cleaning wipe is not the same as and not whiter (not lighter) than the cleaning verification card, re-clean the floor section or countertop section, wipe the floor or countertop section with a wet cleaning wipe, and repeat Step 6 for that section and proceed to Step 8 (skip this step).*

Step 8: Compare the second floor or countertop cleaning wipe to the cleaning verification card. If the second wipe is the same as or whiter (lighter) than the cleaning verification card, the floor or countertop section has been adequately cleaned. If the second cleaning wipe is not the same as and not whiter (not lighter) than the cleaning verification card, wait one hour or until the wet surface is dry (for the purposes of this exercise you do not wait). Then re-clean the surface with a dry, electrostatically charged, white, disposable cleaning cloth designed for use on hard surfaces. The floor or countertop section is now clean and has completed the cleaning verification procedure.*

Step 9:   Once the cleaning verification shows that all areas have been adequately cleaned, remove the signs and critical barriers around the work area.*

   *Indicates required skills that must be accomplished for a "Proficient" rating

Appendix 7:

State and Local Regulations

(Note: This Appendix is intentionally blank to allow training providers to add applicable state and local regulations.)

Appendix 7

State and Local Regulations

Appendix 7 is reserved for state and local regulations that apply to the Certified Renovator and the Certified Firm. Instructors must determine what additional state and local regulations apply to renovation work and include that information in Appendix 7. Provide copies or summaries of applicable state and local regulations, web links and/or copies of important pages, contact lists, training materials such as slides, brochures and pamphlets, etc.

Appendix 8:

Regulatory Status of Waste Generated by Contractors and Residents from Lead-Based Paint Activities Conducted in Housing

From: Elizabeth A. Cotsworth, Director
                  Office of Solid Waste

To: RCRA Senior Policy Advisors
                  EPA Regions 1 - 10

Subject: Regulatory Status of Waste Generated by Contractors and Residents from Lead-Based Paint Activities Conducted in Households

What is the purpose of this interpretation?

This memorandum clarifies the regulatory status of waste generated as a result of lead-based paint (LBP) activities (including abatement, renovation and remodeling) in homes and other residences. Since 1980, EPA has excluded "household waste" from the universe of RCRA hazardous wastes under 40 CFR 261.4(b)(1). In the 1998 temporary toxicity characteristic (TC) suspension proposal, we clarified that the household waste exclusion applies to "all LBP waste generated as a result of actions by residents of households (hereinafter referred to as "residents") to renovate, remodel or abate their homes on their own." 63 FR 70233, 70241 (Dec. 18, 1998). In this memorandum, EPA is explaining that we believe lead paint debris generated by contractors in households is also "household waste" and thus excluded from the RCRA Subtitle C hazardous waste regulations. Thus, the household exclusion applies to waste generated by either residents or contractors conducting LBP activities in residences.

What is the practical significance of classifying LBP waste as a household waste?

As a result of this clarification, contractors may dispose of hazardous-LBP wastes from residential lead paint abatements as household garbage subject to applicable State regulations. This practice will simplify many lead abatement activities and reduce their costs. In this way, the clarification in today's memorandum will facilitate additional residential abatement, renovation and remodeling, and rehabilitation activities, thus protecting children from continued exposure to lead paint in homes and making residential dwellings lead safe for children and adults.

LBP debris (such as architectural building components -- doors, window frames, painted wood work) that do not exhibit the TC for lead need not be managed as hazardous waste. However, LBP waste such as debris, paint chips, dust, and sludges generated from abatement and deleading activities that exhibit the TC for lead (that is, exceed the TC regulatory limit of 5 mg/L lead in the waste leachate), are hazardous wastes and must be managed and disposed of in accordance with the applicable RCRA subtitle C requirements (including land disposal restrictions) except when it is "household waste." Under 40 CFR 261.4(b)(1), household wastes are excluded from the hazardous waste management requirements. Today, EPA is clarifying that waste generated as part of LBP activities conducted at residences (which include single family homes, apartment buildings, public housing, and military barracks) is also household waste, that such wastes are no longer hazardous wastes and that such wastes thus are excluded from RCRA's hazardous waste management and disposal regulations. Generators of residential LBP waste do not have to make a RCRA hazardous waste determination. This interpretation holds regardless of whether the waste exhibits the toxicity characteristic or whether the LBP activities were performed by the residents themselves or by a contractor.

Where can I dispose of my household LBP waste?

LBP waste from residences can be discarded in a municipal solid waste landfill (MSWLF) or a municipal solid waste combustor. Dumping and open burning of residential LBP waste is not allowed. Certain LBP waste (such as large quantities of concentrated lead paint waste -- paint chips, dust, or sludges) from residential deleading activities may be subject to more stringent requirements of State, local, and/or tribal authorities.

What is the basis for this interpretation?

The household waste exclusion implements Congress's intent that the hazardous waste regulations are "not to be used either to control the disposal of substances used in households or to extend control over general municipal wastes based on the presence of such substances." S. Rep. No. 94-988, 94th Cong., 2nd Sess., at 16. EPA regulations define "household waste" to include "any waste material (including garbage, trash, and sanitary wastes in septic tanks) derived from households (including single and multiple residences, hotels and motels, bunkhouses, ranger stations, crew quarters, campgrounds, picnic grounds and day-use recreation areas)." 40 CFR 261.4(b)(1). The Agency has applied two criteria to define the scope of the exclusion: (1) the waste must be generated by individuals on the premises of a household, and (2) the waste must be composed primarily of materials found in the wastes generated by consumers in their homes (49 FR 44978 and 63 FR 70241).

In 1998, EPA concluded that LBP waste resulting from renovation and remodeling efforts by residents of households met these criteria. (63 FR 70241-42, Dec. 18, 1998). In short, the Agency found that more and more residents are engaged in these activities and thus the waste can be considered to be generated by individuals in a household and of the type that consumers generate routinely in their homes. Wastes from LBP abatements performed by residents were also considered household wastes.

EPA clarifies that this interpretation also applies to contractor-generated LBP waste from renovations, remodeling and abatements in residences. Both the definition of household waste in section 261.4(b)(1) and the Agency's criteria for determining the scope of the exclusion focus on the type of waste generated and the place of generation rather than who generated the waste (e.g., a resident or a contractor). This approach is consistent with prior Agency policy.[1] Since contractor-generated LBP waste from residential renovations, remodeling, rehabilitation, and abatements are of the type generated by consumers in their homes, it is appropriate to conclude that such waste, whether generated by a resident or contractor, falls within the household waste exclusion. This clarification will facilitate lead abatements and deleading activities in target housing by reducing the costs of managing and disposing of LBP waste from residences.

What is the relationship of this interpretation to the on-going LBP debris rulemaking?

On December 18, 1998, EPA proposed new TSCA standards for management and disposal of LBP debris (63 FR 70190) and simultaneously proposed to suspend temporarily the applicability of the RCRA hazardous waste regulations that currently apply to LBP debris (63 FR 70233). This memorandum responds to stakeholders requests that EPA clarify whether the existing household waste exclusion applies to both homeowners and contractors conducting LBP activities in residences. While the Agency still intends to finalize aspects of the two proposals, we are making this clarification in advance of the final rule to facilitate LBP abatement in residences without unnecessary delay.

How does this interpretation affect EPA's enforcement authorities?

Under this clarification, LBP wastes generated by residents or contractors from the renovation, remodeling, rehabilitation, and/or abatement of residences are household wastes that are excluded from EPA's hazardous waste requirements in 40 CFR Parts 124, and 262 through 271. The household waste provision of 40 CFR 261.4(b)(1) only excludes such wastes from the RCRA regulatory requirements. However, it does not affect EPA's ability to reach those wastes under its statutory authorities, such as RCRA §3007 (inspection) and §7003 (imminent hazard). See 40 CFR §261.1(b).

What are the "best management practices" for handling residential LBP waste?

---

[1] In the final rule establishing standards for the tracking and management of medical waste, EPA concluded that waste generated by health care providers (e.g., contractors) in private homes would be covered by the household waste exclusion. 54 FR 12326, 12339 (March 24, 1989). In the specific context of LBP, the Agency stated in a March 1990 "EPA Hotline Report" (RCRA Question 6) that lead paint chips and dust resulting from stripping and re-painting of residential walls by homeowner or contractors (as part of routine household maintenance) would be part of the household waste stream and not subject to RCRA Subtitle C regulations. Similarly, in a March 1995 memorandum on the "Applicability of the Household Waste Exclusion to Lead-Contaminated Soils," we found that if the source of the lead contamination was as a result of either routine residential maintenance or the weathering or chalking of lead-based paint from the residence, the hazardous waste regulations do not apply so long as the lead-contaminated soil is managed onsite or disposed offsite according to applicable solid waste regulations and/or State law mandated by RCRA.

Although excluded from the hazardous waste regulations, EPA encourages residents and contractors managing LBP waste from households to take common sense measures to minimize the generation of lead dust, limit access to stored LBP wastes including debris, and maintain the integrity of waste packaging material during transfer of LBP waste. In particular, we continue to endorse the basic steps outlined in the 1998 proposals for the proper handling and disposal of LBP waste (63 FR 70242) as the best management practices (BMPs) including:

- Collect paint chips and dust, and dirt and rubble in plastic trash bags for disposal.
- Store larger LBP architectural debris pieces in containers until ready for disposal.
- Consider using a covered mobile dumpster (such as a roll-off container) for storage of LBP debris until the job is done.
- Contact local municipalities or county solid waste offices to determine where and how LBP debris can be disposed.

In addition, contractors working in residential dwellings are subject to either one or both of the following:

- The HUD Guidance for contractors doing publically-funded rehabilitation/renovation projects in public housing. (See Guidelines for the Evaluation and Control of Lead-Based Paint Hazards in Housing. U.S. Department of Housing and Urban Development, June 1995) The HUD guidelines can be accessed via the Internet at: http://www.hud.gov/lea/learules.html

- TSCA 402/404 training and certification requirements. (See 40 CFR Part 745; 61 FR 45778, August 29, 1996) and the proposed TSCA onsite management standards (See 40 CFR Part 745, Subpart P; 63 FR 70227 - 70230, Dec. 18, 1998). [EPA expects to issue the final rule next year.]

The above-mentioned BMPs for households are similar to those included in the HUD Guidelines for individuals controlling LBP hazards in housing. HUD requires that contractors using HUD funding adhere to LBP hazard control guidelines. Non-adherence to these guidelines can potentially result in the loss of funding.

Does this interpretation apply in my State and/or locality?

We encourage contractors and residents to contact their state, local and/or tribal government to determine whether any restrictions apply to the disposal of residential LBP waste. This verification is necessary since, under RCRA, States, local and tribal governments can enforce regulations that are more stringent or broader in scope than the federal requirements. Thus, under such circumstances, LBP waste from households may still be regulated as a hazardous waste as a matter of State regulations.

We are distributing this memorandum to all 56 States and Territories, and Tribal Programs and various trade associations. We encourage States to arrange for implementation of the interpretation discussed in this memo in their States to facilitate residential LBP abatements making residential dwellings lead-safe. We encourage trade associations to inform their memberships about this memo and instruct them about ways to manage residential LBP waste.

Whom should I contact for more information?

If you have additional questions concerning the regulatory status of waste generated from lead-based paint activities in residences, please contact Ms. Rajani D. Joglekar of my staff at 703/308-8806 or Mr. Malcolm Woolf of the EPA General Counsel's Office at 202/564-5526.

cc: Key RCRA Contacts, Regions 1 - 10
       RCRA Regional Council Contacts, Regions 1 - 10
       RCRA Enforcement Council Contacts, Regions 1 - 10
       Association of State and Territorial Solid Waste Management Officials (ASTSWMO)

Appendix 9:

For More Information

APPENDIX 9: For More Information

If you are a hearing- or speech-impaired person, you may reach the telephone numbers below via TTY by calling the Federal Information Relay Service at 1-800-877-8339.

Where can I get copies of the *Renovate Right: Important Lead Hazard Information for Families, Child Care Providers and Schools* pamphlet in English or Spanish?

- ✓ Download electronic copies at: http://www.epa.gov/lead/pubs/renovation.htm.
- ✓ Use camera-ready copies from the National Lead Information Center to reproduce the pamphlet, providing that you reproduce the text and graphics in full: 1-800-424-LEAD (5323).
- ✓ Order bulk copies from the Government Printing Office (GPO) which cost $53.00 for a package of 50 pamphlets: 202-512-1800; refer to the pamphlet by name or order online at http://bookstore.gpo.gov.

Where can I get copies of *Small Entity Compliance Guide to Renovate Right* handbook?

- ✓ Download electronic copies in PDF format at http://www.epa.gov/lead/pubs/renovation.htm.
- ✓ Contact the National Lead Information Center at: 1-800-424-LEAD (5323)

Where can I find additional information and resources related to lead-based paint?

- ✓ National Lead Information Center: 1-800-424-LEAD (5323)
- ✓ EPA's Office of Pollution Prevention and Toxics (OPPT): www.epa.gov/lead
- ✓ HUD's Office of Healthy Homes and Lead Hazard Control: www.hud.gov/offices/lead or by email to lead.regulations@hud.gov.